Nebraska
Symposium on
Motivation
1974

*Nebraska Symposium on
Motivation, 1974*, is Volume 22
in the series on
CURRENT THEORY AND
RESEARCH IN MOTIVATION

University of Nebraska Press
Lincoln 1975

# Nebraska Symposium on Motivation 1974

James K. Cole and
Theo B. Sonderegger
Editors

**Elliott M. Blass**
*Associate Professor of Psychology*
*Johns Hopkins University*

**Bartley G. Hoebel**
*Professor of Psychology*
*Princeton University*

**Larry Stein**
*Manager, Department of Psycho-*
*pharmacology, Wyeth Laboratories,*
*and Adjunct Professor of*
*Psychiatry, University of*
*Pennsylvania Medical School*

**Aryeh Routtenberg**
*Professor of Psychiatry and*
*Biological Sciences,*
*Northwestern University*

**C. R. Gallistel**
*Associate Professor of Psychology*
*University of Pennsylvania*

**Elliot S. Valenstein**
*Professor of Psychology*
*University of Michigan*

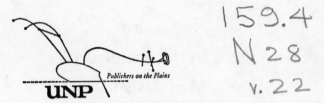

Copyright © 1975 by the University of Nebraska Press
International Standard Book Number 0–8032–0617–8 (Clothbound)
International Standard Book Number 0–8032–5622–1 (Paperbound)
Library of Congress Catalog Card Number 53–11655
Manufactured in the United States of America

This volume of the *Nebraska Symposium on Motivation* is dedicated to the memory of a former staff member of the Department of Psychology of the University of Nebraska–Lincoln, Professor Katherine E. Baker, who died recently after a short illness. Although her area of specialization was sensation and perception, she taught courses in motivation at both undergraduate and graduate levels. Her incisive questioning in the formal sessions of the symposia and her warm humor in the informal discussions which followed are well remembered by all who attended during the 17 years in which she participated in these meetings. All who knew her are acutely aware of her dedication, service, and contributions to teaching and to psychology. We in the Department of Psychology of the University of Nebraska–Lincoln feel a keen personal and professional loss. It is altogether fitting that we dedicate this, the twenty-second volume in the series, to our former colleague.

Katherine E. Baker
1921-1973
Teacher, Scholar, and Friend

# Contents

# Introduction

$T$he topics discussed in the *Nebraska Symposium on Motivation* during the past 21 years parallel the history of major theoretical concerns in the area of motivation. The symposium presentations of 1974, all of which deal with the central nervous system and motivation-related behaviors, continue the trend. In the present volume, we are exposed to new theories based upon recent brain research, current concerns with the use of physiological techniques for brain control, and a lively controversy over the role of norepinephrine in neural reward systems. The papers in this volume, moreover, show how "rewarding electrical brain stimulation" has been used since James Olds, in the 1955 *Nebraska Symposium on Motivation*, discussed his pioneering work only a year after the discovery of the phenomenon.

As in previous years, the papers presented in this volume were read in two separate three-paper sessions. In the fall session of the symposium, two papers were oriented primarily toward a re-examination of physiological factors in feeding, drinking, and sexual behavior, whereas the third paper of this session as well as the three of the spring session were focused on electrical brain stimulation — applied through chronically implanted electrodes in the brain — and related theoretical, applied, and ethical issues.

In the initial paper of this symposium, Professor Elliott Blass organizes his presentation in the framework suggested by the new *double-depletion hypothesis of thirst*. This hypothesis is based upon the fact that body water is stored in two separate compartments and that thirst may be stimulated by depletion of either of these, that is, the cellular or the extracellular phase. The author examines "thirst and its expression as the motivated behavior of drinking" to maintain a positive fluid balance in mammals following either cellular or extracellular body fluid depletion or both.

Professor Blass's paper deals exclusively with "primary drinking," the type of fluid-seeking which occurs when there is a negative fluid balance in one of the water compartments. After reviewing past and present theories of thirst, he describes a series of experiments which demonstrate that cellular dehydration alone is an adequate and sufficient stimulus in thirst. He proposes a model of a mechanism, sensitive to this stimulus, in which drinking may be mobilized by a 1-2% increase in osmotic pressure. The osmotic change is detected by receptors in the lateral forebrain which, in turn, mediate the release of antidiuretic hormone. This model is applicable as well to a mechanism for the inhibition of feeding.

Review of a similar but different set of studies discloses evidence for an extracellular control of drinking. In this work renal blood changes as well as intravascular changes without osmotic pressure alterations are manipulated to produce changes in the drinking behavior of the subjects. Interestingly enough, an appetite for sodium also develops. The renin-angiotensin system appears in these studies to be one mediator of extracellular thirst but it does not explain all aspects of this phenomenon, for example the sodium appetite.

If we are to understand drinking behavior, Professor Blass believes we must deal with simultaneous cellular or extracellular depletions by experimentally manipulating cellular water or by depriving the subjects of water. Factors which terminate drinking initiated by such dual depletion include the temporal contiguity or ingestion with respect to postingestional consequences, the modulatory effects of oral and gastric variables, cellular overhydration, and the context of the ingested fluid as determined by its taste and odor. Professor Blass suggests a possible way in which dual depletion functions to maintain a normal fluid balance as a consequence of the "cellular overhydration that develops in close temporal contiguity with the ingestive act."

Although the *double-depletion hypothesis of thirst* has been used effectively in research, Professor Blass cautions that it is still just a hypothesis and has limitations, for example, in dealing with spontaneous drinking. He concludes with the hope that a future speaker in the symposium may be able to discuss the neurophysiology of thirst "rather than confine his remarks to drinking behavior" as he was forced to do because of the current state of knowledge.

Professor Bartley Hoebel discusses electrical self-stimulation of the brain and escape from such stimulation in his paper entitled "Brain reward and aversion systems in the control of feeding and sexual behavior." Data are presented from a series of studies designed to investigate physiological and pharmacological factors related to feeding or sexual behavior produced by various brain stimulation techniques.

Professor Hoebel reviews work in which hyperphagia or overeating to the point of obesity was produced by lesioning of the ventromedial nucleus of the hypothalamus of rats (so-called VMH animals); damage to one of the major noradrenergic pathways of the brain, the ventral bundle, with the neurotoxin 6-hydroxydopamine (VNAB animals); and intraventricular injections of a drug which depletes serotonin, parachlorophenylalanine (PCPA animals).

Feeding in VMH rats is characterized by a preference for only palatable foods ("finickiness"), a higher body weight level or set-point for cessation, independence from pituitary function, an increase rather than decrease in feeding from amphetamines, and a lipogenic metabolic disorder whereby fats are produced by day rather than only at night.

The PCPA and VNAB animals displayed some of these responses but neither of these groups had exactly the same syndrome as the VMH animals. The VNAB animals, for example, did not exhibit "finickiness," and were less responsive to amphetamines. The differences in these hyperphagic syndromes are seen by Professor Hoebel as ways to understand eventually the neural organization of satiety.

Professor Hoebel and others also used brain-stimulation-induced eating and self-stimulation procedures to study feeding and related factors. Appropriate use of any of these methodologies produces predictable, recurrent patterns of behavior which suggest involvement of the same feeding function. For example, it was reasoned that if lateral hypothalamic self-stimulation functions in a fashion analogous to food, then the stimulation should become aversive after a large meal. This prediction was confirmed experimentally, in general, although with some unexpected results when taste factors were manipulated. Other experiments, using brain-stimulation-induced sexual behavior, produced data which parallel those of the reward-aversion studies of feeding.

These findings have led Professor Hoebel to formulate a general theory of brain control of appetitive behavior which incorporates the new evidence that escape from self-stimulation increases after excessive feeding or ejaculation. Self-stimulation and escape from self-stimulation are viewed as manifestations of neural mechanisms which regulate approach or avoidance of stimuli associated with food or sex. The animal's homeostatic condition determines whether it is manifested in approach or avoidance behaviors. Professor Hoebel suggests, as have other symposium speakers, that the self-stimulation technique may be used to study underlying neural mechanisms, in this case mechanisms for approach and withdrawal, and that it "can also demonstrate for us how these mechanisms are controlled by internal and external stimuli."

The relationship of norepinephrine (NE)-containing neurons to the reward systems of the brain has been a major research concern of Dr. Larry Stein and his colleagues for more than a decade. His paper, "Norepinephrine reward pathways: Role in self-stimulation, memory consolidation, and schizophrenia," reviews much of the work which leads to a proposed relationship between malfunctioning NE-systems and schizophrenia.

If self-stimulation of the brain through chronically implanted electrodes directly activates the brain's normal reward systems, then identification of the neural pathways that support self-stimulation should reveal those that subserve reward. Evidence from anatomical mapping and pharmacological studies of self-stimulation lead the writer to conclude that the catecholamine, NE, and NE-containing neurons play a critical role in self-stimulation. Results from pharmacological studies are given to show that drugs which affect the synthesis, release, depletion, or receptor-binding activity of the catecholamines also affect self-stimulation. Dr. Stein also presents data to show that self-stimulation may be obtained from major ascending NE-fiber systems in the rat brainstem, although there is some question concerning self-stimulation effects in the ventral bundle, the same structure lesioned by Professor Hoebel to produce hyperphagic rats.

The synthesis of NE in the brain requires the formation of dopamine (DA) and its alteration by means of an enzyme, dopamine beta-hydroxylase (DBH), into NE. The role of DA in self-stimulation is the subject of some controversy at present. If it can be shown that DA-neurons support self-stimulation, then DA as well as NE could function in reward systems and the former would not require the presence of DBH to function. Dr. Stein describes a series of carefully conducted studies from his own and other laboratories designed to elucidate the role of DA. A major methodological problem is to destroy or stimulate DA-neurons without affecting NE-neurons. As yet the DA-NE problem has not been resolved.

Two other types of studies are described which investigate feeding behavior and retention of passive avoidance responses. Norepinephrine appears to be involved in both, although with long-term (memory-consolidation) rather than with short-term memory in the case of the avoidance responses. Dr. Stein states: "If reward and memory-consolidation functions are actually subserved by NE, as this work suggests, then the involvement in associative thinking and goal-directed behavior should be obvious." He argues that malfunction of the NE-systems would also drastically affect normal behavior and logical thought, functional deficits similar to those found in schizophrenia.

Postmortem studies of the brains of schizophrenics do, indeed, show a deficiency in the amount of DBH enzyme in the NE metabolic chain. Malfunction of the NE-systems would be produced by such a DBH deficiency. Other studies designed to examine factors which could produce a DBH deficiency are discussed and lead to the conclusion that possibly the disorder itself rather than other variables produce the deficit of DBH.

Dr. Stein cautions: "In view of the many false hopes and disappointments that the biochemical studies of schizophrenia have produced, our findings must be viewed with skepticism until other researchers provide confirmation." He does feel, however, that there are therapeutic implications from the NE work. For example, one might try to elevate NE levels in the brains of schizophrenics through use of appropriate pharmacological precursors in the manner that DA levels are altered in the brains of people suffering from Parkinson's disease.

The anatomy of self-stimulation has been a major research interest of Professor Aryeh Routtenberg and is the work he has chosen to present in his paper, "Intracranial self-stimulation pathways as substrate for memory consolidation." He uses data obtained from this approach to formulate a model relating intracranial self-stimulation (ICSS) to memory consolidation.

Professor Routtenberg reviews ICSS studies from his own and other laboratories and argues, contrary to Dr. Stein's view, that ICSS actually may be supported by other than NE-systems. The NE-ICSS relationship in this interpretation may be simply correlational.

He points out that in the light of our current knowledge of the complexities of the fiber pathways and the neuropharmacological synaptic events surrounding the tips of stimulation electrodes implanted in the brain, some of the initial attitudes toward positive identification of the sites of brain stimulation effects were far too optimistic. To elaborate upon some of the problems associated with interpreting brain-stimulation effects, data from his laboratory are presented describing ICSS in the brachium conjunctivum (BC), a cerebellar pathway. The BC contains fibers from the dorsal adrenergic bundle which originate in a brainstem nucleus known as the locus coeruleus. Professor Routtenberg and his co-workers obtained ICSS in the BC even after the locus coeruleus had been destroyed. Work with the ventral noradrenergic bundle, moreover, leads him to caution that definitive evidence is yet needed to demonstrate unequivocally the role of ICSS in this structure. He suggests that there are several unknown pathways in the BC, not necessarily containing NE, which are involved in ICSS. These findings lead him to suggest that "the two major norepinephrine systems which have been implicated in ICSS, the dorsal bundle–locus coeruleus system and the ventral bundle, are suspect as candidates for supporting ICSS" and that norepinephrine may not be involved in ICSS.

What has been learned about the specific brain areas associated with ICSS, however, leads Professor Routtenberg to conclude that there is an association between these sites and the brain areas where stimulation during or after learning causes memory disruption. He offers interpretations of some of the work of other speakers in this symposium to support his view of the relationship between ICSS and memory disruption.

In his concluding remarks he suggests that perhaps an unnecessary distinction has been made between emotional and cognitive states and that it would be better to envisage "a neural mechanism which when active in one state engages memory consolidation mechanisms and when active at another state forms a substrate of an emotional condition." He proposes that the subsequent interaction of the two states would result in an optimal level of activity compatible with both memory consolidation and appropriate affect.

Professor C. R. Gallistel, whose paper is entitled "Motivation as central organizing process: The psychophysical approach to its functional and neurophysical analysis," views electrical brain stimulation in the light of Deutsch's theory, that is, as a means of manipulating both motivation and reinforcement processes. He proposes that the psychophysical methods as used in neurophysiology be applied in brain stimulation work to permit quantitative and qualitative characterizations of the underlying substrates.

Empirical data are presented which trace the recovery from refractoriness produced in neural pathways by electrical brain stimulation. Two types of recovery curves occur which are used to demonstrate the existence of both a motivational and a reinforcement effect as a consequence of brain stimulation.

The writer reviews studies in which psychophysical methods are used to study the refractory periods in nerves and muscles as a means of analyzing the substrate. He labels and describes two classical psychophysical paradigms as follows: (a) *output-vs.-input* paradigm — "the output is plotted as a function of some experimentally varied parameter of the input (the stimulus)"; (b) *equivalent-stimuli* or *trade-off* paradigm — "one determines which combinations of values for the various parameters of the stimulus are equivalent from the standpoint of the output." He has used these paradigms in brain-stimulation studies to obtain strength-duration and temporal summation curves. Results of this work lead him to the conclusion that a neural pathway such as the medial forebrain bundle, which supports self-stimulation, has different neural substrates that mediate the functionally distinct processes of reinforcement and motivation. In this context, motivation is viewed as a time-dependent and reinforcement as an event-dependent process.

Professor Gallistel's conclusion regarding the specificity of a neural substrate for motivation is interesting in a general, epistemological sense as well. Past volumes of the symposium have included papers which questioned or supported the concept of motivation as a meaningful, valid, or useful organizing principle in psychology (see, for example, Lazarus, 1968, vol. XVI, or Bindra, 1969, vol. XVII).

Finally, Professor Gallistel has applied psychophysical methodology to the stimulation-elicited consummatory behaviors of eating and drinking as well as to such behavioral consequences of brain stimulation as analgesia and grooming and has analyzed the results with respect to the possible substrates or systems involved. The psychophysical approach may ultimately provide a "linkage" between neurophysiological and behavioral systems, in his view, and the use of this strategy in an electrophysiological analysis of self-stimulation makes it possible to study the neurophysiological bases of reinforcement and motivation.

Professor Elliot Valenstein, in the concluding paper, "Brain stimulation and behavior control," and in his recent book, *Brain control: A critical evaluation of brain stimulation and psychosurgery*, discusses electrical brain stimulation studies and the controversial topic of "brain control."

He traces two major trends in brain stimulation research during the past 24 years: (a) the pressure to obtain evidence demonstrating that electrical stimulation of specific brain sites "evokes natural drive states," and (b) the preoccupation, principally of American researchers, to use brain stimulation for behavior control. The first trend, according to Valenstein, developed from the need in the early 1950s of drive reduction proponents for new theoretical input and the general realization that the use of electrical brain stimulation to manipulate and measure drives would provide such information. Not only did subsequent experimental work result in a series of papers documenting brain stimulation–evoked behaviors but, as well, "the impression that a large number of motivational states could be reliably controlled by 'tapping into' discrete brain sites."

Reports of these experiments and their ensuing distortions in the media as the "new brain technology" instigated the second trend, a concern for brain control. Valenstein argues that the evidence does not support many interpretations which have been made of brain-stimulation experimental data and cites, for example, the explanation often given when Delgado stopped a charging bull through electrical stimulation applied to the caudate nucleus. Rather than accepting the widely held belief that the stimulation altered the bull's aggressive tendencies, a more plausible statement according to Professor Valenstein, is that stimulation of the caudate nucleus produces a motor response incompatible with charging.

Professor Valenstein describes work from his own laboratory which shows that behaviors evoked by brain stimulation are different from those produced by natural drive states and reviews the factors that must be considered to understand correctly brain stimulation–evoked behaviors, for example, sensory, motor, and visceral changes as well as motivational, environmental, species-specific, and pre-potent response variables. He feels that since "every area of the brain is involved in many different functions and all but the simplest functions have multiple representation in the brain," a need to eliminate variability or to control phenomena in brain research work may "distort reality by concealing the very plasticity that is an essential aspect of adaptive behavior."

The final section of his paper describes "facts and fantasies of controlling human behavior" using either brain stimulation or psychosurgery. A critical examination of the experimental evidence, particularly with respect to amygdala-violence relationships, leads Professor Valenstein to conclude this section of his paper with an admonition to researchers not to let "frustration from an inability to stem the accelerating rate of violence" lead to the waste of creative effort in seeking brain controls. Rather than considering violence to be the product of a diseased brain, drug factors excluded, he feels violence should be considered as the product of a diseased society and treated accordingly.

A substantial portion of the cost for the symposium was provided by the Clinical Psychology Training Grant provided by the National Institute of Mental Health. Additional support has come from the University of Nebraska–Lincoln. The faculty and students associated with the symposium wish to express their gratitude for this support.

JAMES K. COLE
*Professor of Psychology*

THEO B. SONDEREGGER
*Associate Professor of Psychology*

# The Physiological, Neurological, and Behavioral Bases of Thirst[1]

## Elliott M. Blass
*Johns Hopkins University*

### I. INTRODUCTION

*T*his article is concerned with the contribution of thirst, and its expression as the motivated behavior of drinking, to the maintenance of positive body fluid balance in mammals. At the outset it should be recognized that drinking is but one of a variety of effector mechanisms that are mobilized to defend the fluid economy. Renal and hemodynamic effectors have been extensively investigated and the importance of their synergistic interaction with behavior has recently been stressed (Blass, 1973; Fitzsimons, 1972; Stricker, 1973).

Research in thirst has lagged behind that concerned with the kidney; indeed, a major control was discovered by Fitzsimons in 1961 (b). The past decade, however, has been marked by exciting and important new advances in analyzing the behavioral contribution. For one, there has been a significant change in the modus operandi — from dealing with the intervening varible of thirst to analyzing the neurological and physiological mechanisms that control drinking. Also, a new and powerful tool, the *double-depletion hypothesis of thirst*, has provided a context for many recent findings and is helping direct current analyses.

The double-depletion hypothesis provides the basic framework of this communication, in which the characteristics of drinking and motivated behavior following cellular or extracellular body fluid

1. Research in the author's laboratory has been supported by Grant NS 09305 from the Institute of Neurological Diseases and Stroke. The author is very much indebted to Alan Epstein, Warren Hall, Jeffrey Peck, Curt Richter, Edward Stricker, and especially William Stark for their very helpful comments on an earlier draft of this manuscript.

depletion will be analyzed. A synthesis based on this theory will be used to fulfill the major aim of this article, namely, to elucidate some of the features of drinking subsequent to water deprivation, a natural and common event that causes absolute loss of both cellular and extracellular fluid.

## II. THIRST AND DRINKING

Various definitions of thirst have been provided over the years and a distinction has been drawn between homeostatic and nonhomeostatic thirst. In this writer's view the presence of a thirst sensation may be inferred only when drinking or fluid-seeking behavior occurs during any of the following circumstances:
1. Reduction in cellular volume
2. Reduction in intravascular volume
3. Elevation in the circulating levels of the hormone angiotensin (see section VI)
The intake of water or sapid solutions under these circumstances will be referred to as *primary drinking*. Primary drinking is precipitated by an absolute or relative lack of body water in one or the other major fluid compartment. Also, except for unusual circumstances (e.g., delivering shock during drinking or severely adulterating the drinking fluid) primary drinking is terminated in large part by its hydrational consequences.

*Secondary drinking* does not appear to share either of these characteristics. It refers to drinking that occurs when animals are in positive fluid balance, that is not dehydrated. The situations when secondary drinking occurs are diverse and range from drinking to avoid shock (Williams & Teitelbaum, 1956) to the excessive drinking of certain sapid solutions (Ernits & Corbit, 1973). In short, the events controlling secondary drinking cannot be presently categorized in terms of either drinking onset or termination, and it is this writer's opinion that these forms of drinking will be better understood when the bases of avoidance and escape behaviors and of pleasure and pain have been established. Because of their diverse etiologies, the bases of secondary drinking will not be better understood by proposing a blanket intervening variable of nonhomeostatic thirst.
Secondary drinking is not discussed below, in part for the reasons

just stated, but mainly because of the excellence and completeness of recent reviews by Falk (1971), Kissileff (1973), and Oately (1973). The exclusion of secondary drinking from this discussion does not minimize its importance. Drinking seen under nonhydrational circumstances does occur naturally, is motivated, and is subject to rigorous experimental analysis.

III. HISTORICAL CONSIDERATIONS OF THE
PHYSIOLOGICAL BASES OF THIRST

The sensation of thirst and the characteristics of drinking have been investigated since at least the 18th century. Dupuytren (cited by Rullier, 1821) demonstrated that intravenous infusion of water assuaged the thirst of dogs dehydrated by running in the sun. Latta (1832) confirmed this in man during the cholera epidemic of 1832 by infusing large volumes of isotonic solutions intravenously to relieve the intense thirst caused by the vomiting and diarrhea which accompany cholera. Both were important observations, for they showed that the mouth could be bypassed to relieve thirst. Claude Bernard (1856) studied a horse with an esophageal fistula and a dog with a gastric fistula to show the converse, namely, that irrigating the mouth with enormous volumes of fluid did not relieve thirst, provided the water was allowed to escape through the fistulous openings. However, when fluid was placed directly into the stomach, drinking quickly terminated.

Yet attention focused on the mouth as the seat of thirst. Walter Cannon (1918), whose name is most widely associated with this work, argued that while the origins of thirst may be of a general need, the sensation is not general and is specifically referred to the dry oropharynx. Cannon's view was that although the general need could be relieved by introducing fluids through unusual routes, as shown by Latta, bypassing the mouth does not speak to the thirst receptors or to the nature of the sensation.

From these considerations there arose three theories of thirst. Cannon's was one, namely, that thirst was a sensation of local origin in the oropharynx. The second, stated by Bernard and even more explicitly by Wettendorf in 1901, was that because all tissues of the body share in dehydration, thirst must also be a sensation of a general nature. All agreed that dryness of the oropharynx is a vivid feature of thirst, but few felt that it was a necessary component, and none believed that drinking occurs simply to relieve a dry mouth. The third early theory was that a thirst center existed in the central nervous system. The evidence, based on tumors, circulatory infarcts, and injuries to the brain, was exclusively of a clinical origin. For example, Nothnagal (1881) described the case of a man who had been thrown and kicked in the stomach by a horse and fell and hit the back of his head on a rock. The patient became immensely thirsty and during the next three hours drank three liters of a mixture of water and warm beer. Because drinking preceded diuresis, Nothnagel argued for the presence of a central thirst center.

The current status of these theories will be briefly stated, with greater detail being provided later, when appropriate. The dry-mouth theory of Cannon has fallen into disfavor. Desalivate animals do not over-drink, and drink normally to specific hydrational challenges (Epstein, Spector, Samman & Goldblum, 1964; Vance 1965). Desalivate rats do drink more water than normal rats when only dry food is available, but this is thought to be another case of secondary drinking. Such rats take a very small aliquot of water after each bite of food, and it is believed that this form of ingestion is an operant to lubricate the mouth and thereby facilitate the passage of a dry bolus of food through a dry oropharynx (Kissileff, 1969, 1973).

The evidence is overwhelmingly against the idea that thirst is a sensation of general origin. More detail will be given directly, but it suffices to say that there are specific receptors within the brain that are sensitive to hydrational challenges and that if these receptors are hydrated, drinking does not occur despite gross systemic dehydration.

No one currently questions the existence of central receptors, and consideration of their anatomical location and mode of operation will constitute a major portion of this presentation.

## IV. THE DISTRIBUTION OF BODY WATER

Sixty-seven percent of the body weight of the mature human is water which is distributed into two unequal phases. The major portion, the cellular phase, contains approximately twice the volume of water as does the extracellular phase. However, it is through the latter phase, which includes the vascular water, that the daily exchange of fluids with the environment occurs. Water moves freely across the two phases, following osmotic and hydrostatic pressure gradients, and can therefore be shifted between cellular and extracellular space experimentally simply by changing the concentration of the major extracellular cation, sodium. For example, introducing hypertonic sodium chloride, which does not permeate cells, into the extracellular space will give rise to the withdrawal of cellular fluid. (Actually, any substance excluded from the cells will achieve the same end.) On the other hand, removing extracellular sodium causes the concentration of cellular cations, especially potassium, to exceed that of extracellular cations, which shifts water accordingly from the extracellular space into the cells (see Falk, 1961). Another means of producing a pure extracellular depletion is through hemorrhage. Water abstinence, of course, depletes both cellular and extracellular compartments.

## V. CELLULAR DEHYDRATION AS A STIMULUS OF DRINKING

Because the characteristics of drinking to cellular dehydration have been recently reviewed in detail (Blass, 1973) only the most salient aspects are presented below.

### A. The Physiological Stimulus

Cellular dehydration, which is caused by the net loss of cellular fluid, is a sufficient stimulus for thirst. Its most common natural occurrence is during water abstinence where hypotonic fluid is lost from lungs and skin. Relative cellular dehydration occurs after eating, especially of foods rich in salt. Here water is osmotically withdrawn from the cells and sequestered in the extracellular space.

The fact that elevated osmotic pressure acts as a stimulus for drinking has been recognized at least since 1901 when Mayer and Wettendorf, working independently, observed a rise in blood osmolality of water-deprived dogs. Mayer concluded that increased osmotic pressure was a stimulus of thirst. Wettendorf was more cautious, however, and suggested that it was not the increase in osmotic pressure per se but rather the loss of tissue water that gave rise to a general sensation of thirst. That is, all tissues contributed to the net water loss and therefore also contributed to the sensation.

These early important observations were largely ignored for more than three decades. Research in thirst labored under the vast and well-deserved influence of Cannon. In 1937, however, Alfred Gilman did the critical study that positively identified the cellular control of thirst. Gilman discovered that dogs drank twice as much water following intravenous infusions of hypertonic saline, which dehydrates cells, as they did following equiosmotic infusions of urea, which does not.

Gilman's classical finding was later confirmed and clarified after World War II by Holmes and Gregersen (1950a, 1950b), who pointed out that one could not discern whether drinking elicited by hypertonic saline reflected the activation of a cellular control or whether it was specifically in response to hypernatremia (increased sodium levels). They showed that dogs drank copiously only after the intravenous infusion of substances, nonelectrolyte as well as electrolyte, excluded from cells. Moreover, drinking was not determined by either the serum sodium or serum chloride level, since these titers were quite low following infusions of hypertonic sucrose or sorbitol, both potent dipsogens. Taken together, these findings reinforced Gilman's notion of cellular dehydration as an adequate drinking stimulus.

In an important series of studies, Fitzsimons (1961a, 1963) demonstrated that nephrectomized rats (i.e., rats with both kidneys surgically removed), whose osmoregulation is entirely behavioral, drank precisely the amount of water necessary to dilute the body fluids to isotonicity when the tonicity of the fluids was raised by intravenous infusion of hypertonic solutes. Hypertonic NaCl, $Na_2SO_4$, and the nonelectrolyte sucrose, all of which are excluded from the cells, were equally effective dipsogens, and drinking elicited by them persisted until isotonicity was attained. Restoration to isotonicity was incidental, however, because hyperosmotic glucose, methyl glucose, and fructose, all of which readily penetrate cells and do not cause the withdrawal of cellular water, did not cause drinking, despite the elevated osmotic pressure. Urea caused intermediate amounts of drinking. Although urea enters cells, it does not readily

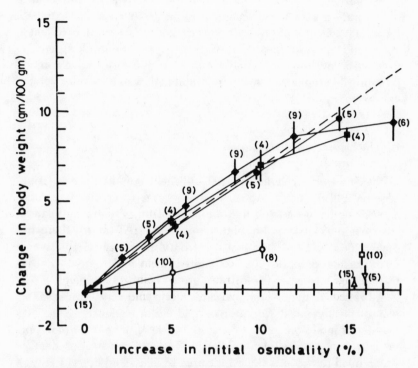

FIG. 1. Relationship between water intake (expressed as an increase in body weight) and increases in effective osmotic pressure in the rat. Symbols: ($\bullet$) = NaCl; ($\blacklozenge$) = $Na_2SO_4$; ($\blacksquare$) = sucrose; ($\bigcirc$) = urea; ($\triangle$) = glucose; ($\triangledown$) = methyl glucose; ($\square$) = fructose. (Data from Fitzsimons, 1971.)

cross the blood-brain barrier, and causes an effective osmotic gradient across the brain (Reed & Woodbury, 1962).

Fitzsimons then went on to show that the system does not adapt. That is, when water was withheld for 24 hours from cellular-dehydrated nephrectomized rats, the amount drunk in the ensuing 6 hours was equal to that drunk by similarly treated nephrectomized rats with immediate access to water.

Finally, Fitzsimons demonstrated that drinking elicited by cellular dehydration is not reduced by expanding the extracellular volume. Drinking to a given challenge was constant across different degrees of extracellular expansion with isotonic saline infused intravenously.

In short, cellular dehydration can be considered a consequence of natural stresses which cause drinking in every animal studied, including man (Wolf, 1950), rat (Fitzsimons, 1961), dog (Gilman, 1937) and pigeon (Hawkins & Corbit, 1973). The drinking is activated at a low threshold, about 1.5% increase in effective osmotic pressure, does not adapt, and is not inhibited by extracellular volume expansion.

## B. The Neurological Mediation

In their now classic series of studies, Teitelbaum and Epstein (1962; Epstein & Teitelbaum, 1964; Epstein, 1971, for review) reported a permanent adipsia to all hydrational challenges following bilateral destruction of the lateral hypothalamic area (LHA). Shortly thereafter Blass (1968) showed that massive frontal pole area lesions, which included the preoptic area, separated the cellular from the extracellular controls of drinking. Figure 2 illustrates the point.

All rats were nephrectomized and injected with hypertonic saline. Neurologically intact rats drank rapidly and copiously. Rats with massive frontal pole lesions did not. Yet these same rats drank normally to an extracellular challenge. The critical area of damage was refined to the lateral preoptic area by Blass and Epstein (1971), who found that destruction of the anterior medial aspect of the lateral preoptic area (LPO) replicated the effect seen in Blass's earlier work. Blass and Epstein (1971), using rats, and Peck and Novin (1971), using rabbits, demonstrated that LPO was osmosensitive for thirst and that the deficit in drinking to cellular dehydration was not simply caused by interruption of fibers of passage to the LHA. Specifically, drinking was activated selectively by intracranial injections of solutions excluded from cells. Intracranial hypertonic sucrose and saline were effective dipsogens, but hyperosmotic urea was not, even at 1.5 times the concentration of the hypertonic solutions.

Blass and Epstein showed that rehydrating the LPO bilaterally with distilled water arrested the drinking of rats made thirsty by systemic cellular dehydration. Distilled water in LHA was ineffective. This is important because it suggests that the sensation of cellular thirst is central in origin, for drinking was elicited by dehydrating a select group of cells in rats that were in positive fluid balance. Moreover, the counterexperiment of restoring water to those select

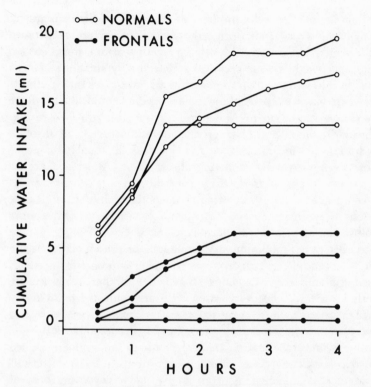

FIG. 2. Water intake by nephrectomized rats with extensive frontal brain damage (○) and by nephrectomized neurologically intact rats (●). (Data are of individual rats.) (From Blass, 1968.)

cells attentuated drinking in rats whose cells in the rest of the body, including the brain, were presumably dehydrated.

Peck and Novin showed that hypertonic saline injected into LPO caused rabbits to choose water over the normally preferred isotonic saline. Hypertonic saline placed in the LHA caused rabbits to drink saline, presumably reflecting the nonspecific activation of other efferent systems for thirst. This finding raises the possibility that this choice behavior seen to systemic cellular dehydration may be mediated by central receptors rather than peripheral mechanisms.

Taken together, the Blass and Epstein (1971) and Peck and Novin (1971) studies support the view that at least one form of thirst is central in origin and that the receptors are in, or in the vicinity of, the lateral preoptic area.

Before summarizing the mechanism of cellular thirst, it is necessary to discuss an alternative detection model put forth by Andersson
(1971). Andersson contends that there are no central osmoreceptors.
Rather, increased osmotic pressure is detected by sodium receptors
located in the third ventricle. Andersson acknowledges that solutions
other than NaCl elicit drinking when injected peripherally. They
are effective according to Andersson, because they do not readily
permeate the blood-brain barrier. Consequently there is an absolute
dehydration of the brain, causing an increase in brain Na concentration. Based upon the following observations, Andersson argues
that sodium receptors are in the third ventricle. First, drinking was
elicited in goats by intraventricular injection of hypertonic saline
solutions. Second, other solutions, including hypertonic sucrose, were
nondipsogenic when injected intraventricularly.

It is this writer's opinion that the evidence presented argues in
favor of central osmoreceptors as the receptors for cellular
dehydration thirst. First, sucrose *is* effective in the brain. Second,
restoring water to the dehydrated LPO area arrested drinking in
dehydrated rats whose ventricular space presumably remained
dehydrated. Third, hypertonic saline in LPO caused rabbits to shift
to the less preferred water. Yet hypertonic saline in the LHA led
to increased saline intake. This suggests that the latter injections
nonspecifically activated systems mediating some other form of
thirst, whereas the LPO injections triggered osmoreceptors. Finally,
some of this writer's unpublished observations (1973) have shown
that, of seven rats which drank when their intracranial injectors
terminated in LPO, only two drank when the injectors terminated
in the ventricles, and that in both cases, the threshold for eliciting
drinking was higher in the ventricles.

A model is proposed in figure 3 to account for the mechanisms
sensitive to cellular dehydration. A 1–2% increase in effective
osmotic pressure is detected by lateral preoptic and supraoptic
receptors in the basal forebrain, which mobilize drinking and cause
the release of antidiuretic hormone (ADH), respectively. ADH in
turn acts directly on the distal tubules of the kidney to conserve
water, thereby causing the excretion of hypertonic urine. It is
assumed that activation of the lateral preoptic thirst osmoreceptors
is the necessary and sufficient stimulus for cellular dehydration
thirst, although there is a preliminary but unconfirmed report of
portal osmoreceptors (Haberich, 1968). The connection is presented

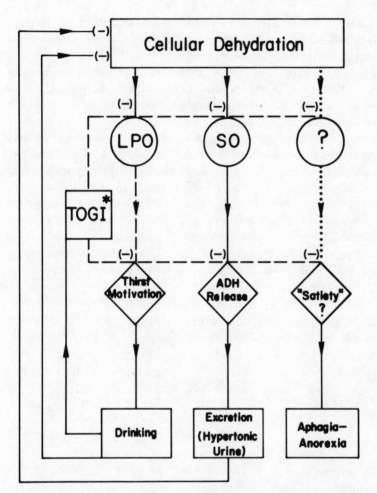

FIG. 3. Schematic of events underlying cellular dehydration thirst. (From Blass, 1973.)

\* TOGI: Temporary Oropharyngeal-Gastric Inhibition

as a dashed line in the model because the neurology-mediating signals arising from the LPO is unknown, save for the fact that the lateral hypothalamic area is involved.

The intervening variable of thirst remains necessary because the relationships among cellular dehydration, the willingness to work for water, and the nature and intensity of the thirst sensation have yet to be established.

Because the rate of ingestion exceeds that of absorption there appears to be a mechanism by which peripheral information from mouth and stomach summate to terminate drinking in advance of cellular rehydration (presented as TOGI in fig. 3). Peripheral information has been presumed to be realized at an integrative level (e.g., LHA). However, Nicolaïdis (1969) has recently reported changes in the firing rate of single units located in the supraoptic-anterior hypothalamic receptive zone in response to irrigating an anesthetized cat's tongue with water or saline.

Cellular dehydration also effectively inhibits feeding. Because the neurology underlying dehydration-anorexia is unknown, the connections in the third vertical column of the model are dotted rather than dashed. Rats with LPO lesions, which do not drink to cellular dehydration, and rats with diabetes insipidus, caused by supraoptic-anterior hypothalamic lesions, which cannot concentrate their urine to cellular dehydration, reduce food intake to cellular dehydration (E. M. Blass & J. W. Peck, unpublished data, 1973). That is, destruction of the known central osmoreceptive areas does not relieve the inhibition of feeding exerted by cellular dehydration. Moreover, Kissileff (1969) reported that overhydrating rats with LHA lesions increased feeding, suggesting that the neurology of the feeding-inhibition mechanism may not directly involve the LHA.

VI. THE EXTRACELLULAR CONTROLS

Because of the excellence of Stricker's (1973) and Fitzsimons's (1970, 1971, 1972) recent reviews, attention will focus mainly on the most recent developments in the neurology of extracellular controls of drinking.

A. The Physiological Stimuli

The extracellular phase serves as the interface between the animal and its environment. It is the primary avenue through which water losses and gains are made. It is therefore quite labile, and its most mobile phase, the circulating blood, is vital and must be defended against perturbations by efficient and rapidly acting mechanisms. It is therefore not surprising that the vasculature is well endowed with elaborate mechanisms for ensuring the constancy of the pressure and volume of the intravascular fluid (see Stricker, 1973).

The existence of a separate extracellular control of drinking, however, remained a subject of vigorous debate for several decades. There was considerable clinical evidence in favor of an extracellular control, starting with Latta's (1832) observations on cholera patients. Also, there were numerous clinical reports that drinking occurs following burns where isosmotic plasma is sequestered in the form of a local edema at the wound site.

Yet the experimental evidence for an extracellular control was not entirely convincing. Darrow and Yannet (1935) reported that dogs did not drink following glucose dialysis which caused water to move from the vasculature into the cells. The same negative finding was obtained in rats by Schneiden (1962), using hemorrhage, and by Gregersen and Bullock (1933) in humans. On the other hand, in his classical study, McCance (1936) described intense thirst elicited by salt depletion in man, and Cizek, Semple, Huang, and Gregersen (1951) observed that salt-depleted hyponatremic dogs, which lost extracellular fluid, drank copiously for the duration of the hyponatremia. When salt was restored to the diet, drawing water from the cells back into the vasculature, drinking returned to normal levels. Also in his important address to the 1961 Nebraska Symposium, Falk presented evidence that glucose dialysis caused drinking in rats. Overall the evidence was not altogether compelling, however. There were the negative reports. Also severe hyponatremia caused confusion in man so that drinking under this circumstance was perhaps pathological and not under physiological control. The major stumbling block for the acceptance of an independent extracellular control, however, was that the cellular control was believed to be able to account for all drinking despite Adolph's admonition that the amount drunk following overnight water deprivation could only occur to a cellular stimulus that was well outside the physiological range (Adolph, Barker, & Hoy, 1954).

The most articulate champion of the exclusiveness of the cellular control was Wolf (1950), who wrote that change in cellular balance in either direction (i.e., overhydration as well as dehydration) was a sufficient cause of drinking. This was consistent with the hyponatremia data of McCance but is not entirely logical. Drinking in response to cellular overhydration would place the animal in positive feedback. That is, during hyponatremia water moves along an osmotic gradient into the cells. If drinking occurs, the new water also invades the cells, which, according to the cellular-overhydration theory, should lead to more drinking, and so on. In 1961, the dispute was laid to rest when Fitzsimons reported that drinking could be reliably elicited in rats by depleting the vasculature without any change in osmotic pressure. In short, an extracellular control was unequivocally established. Stricker, in 1966, confirmed Fitzsimons and also showed that loading rats with water, causing hyponatremia and cellular overhydration in the absence of any cellular deficit, did not cause drinking

The evidence for an extracellular control of drinking is now substantial and its existence is no longer seriously questioned. Stricker (1968) found, as shown in figure 4, that water intake is linearly related to the severity of the intravascular deficit. Here intravascular depletion was caused by the subcutaneous administration of polyethylene glycol (PG), a hyperoncotic colloid that sequesters a protein-free, isosmotic filtrate from the vasculature to the injection site. Yet despite extensive water intake, rats do not make good their intravascular deficit. This is because water is distributed between the cellular and extracellular phases according to their volume. Therefore less than 10% of the water ingested during hypovolemia remains in the vasculature, but about 67% of the water gains access to and ultimately overhydrates the cellular phase. Stricker has presented substantial evidence in support of the notion that cellular overhydration terminates drinking to a variety of extracellular stimuli in advance of making good the extracellular deficit. Specifically, Stricker (1969) found that preloading rats with 15–30 ml. of water arrested drinking to polyethylene glycol. Preloading isotonic saline did not.

However, given only isotonic saline to drink, rats drink the amount necessary to precisely restore the deficit. Also, when .45 molar

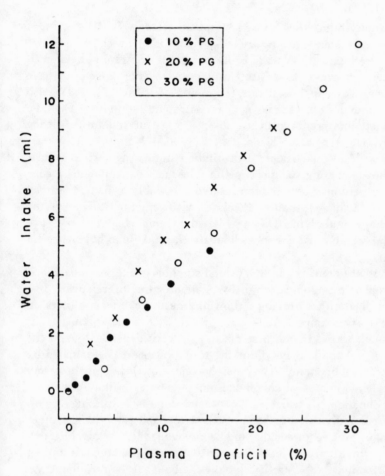

FIG. 4. Water intake of rats following 5 ml. subcutaneous injections of various concentrations of polyethylene glycol. (Data from Stricker, 1968.)

(3 times isotonic) saline is offered, rats mix an isotonic cocktail (Stricker & Jalowiec, 1970). That is, significant quantities of the otherwise shunned saline solution are drunk to restore intravascular space to normal. Thus intravascular depletion is a complex stimulus that gives rise to specific appetites for both salt and water. The mechanisms leading to increased drinking are understood only in part and will be discussed directly.

No single mechanism underlying Na appetite of hyponatremic states has been positively identified. Although aldosterone can, in sufficiently high doses, cause salt appetite (Fregly & Waters, 1966) the adrenal glands are not necessary for either its short- or long-term development (Wolf & Stricker, 1967). The renin-angiotensin mechanism, which is critical in thirst, does not appear to have a role in Na appetite in rats (Fitzsimons & Stricker, 1971). Also hyponatremia per se is not an adequate stimulus. That is, hyponatremia produced in the absense of a true sodium deficiency by intragastric water loads does not elicit Na appetite in rats (Stricker & Wolf, 1966). This finding argues against a cellular detector mediating sodium appetite. The most parsimonious theory is that there may be a sodium reservoir, possibly in bone, that may monitor available sodium (Wolf & Stricker, 1967). Finally, the neurology underlying Na appetite also remains a mystery save for the fact that LHA lesions eliminate Na appetite to hyponatremia (Wolf, 1971).

Another potent extracellular thirst stimulus is altering renal blood flow either by hypotension or by ligation of the inferior vena cava (caval ligation). Drinking following these treatments differs in at least two important regards from that seen following intravascular loss. In the first place, it is very dependent upon the integrity of the kidneys. Drinking to hypotension is eliminated by bilateral nephrectomy (Houpt & Epstein, 1972) and nephrectomy severely attenuates, although does not eliminate, drinking following caval ligation (Fitzsimons, 1969). In contrast, drinking to intravascular depletion is very resistant to nephrectomy. The other distinguishing feature is that unlike hypovolia, neither caval ligation nor hypotension produces an immediate salt appetite. According to Fitzsimons, rats start seeking salt about 24 hours after caval ligation. In the case of intravascular depletion, sodium appetite appears within 5 hours.

B. The Role of the Renin-Angiotensin Mechanism
   in Extracellular Thirst

To date only one mediator of extracellular thirst, the renin-angiotensin system, has been positively identified. Under conditions of hypovolia, hyponatremia, and hypotension, renin, a proteolytic enzyme, is released from the juxtaglomerular cells of the kidney. Renin in turn acts with angiotensinogen, a fraction of the blood plasma, to form the decapeptide angiotensin I. Angiotensin I is hydrolyzed by a converting enzyme to form the octapeptide angiotensin II, which will be referred to as angiotensin. Angiotensin is a potent vasoconstrictor of vascular smooth muscle and therefore defends against hypotension. It also causes release of aldosterone from the adrenal cortex and thereby defends against hyponatremia; and in the rat, monkey, dog, and Barbary dove, it is a potent stimulus of thirst (cf. Fitzsimons, 1972).

Fitzsimons and Simons (1969) reported that intravenous infusions of renin or angiotensin produced copious drinking in rats. The effects were dose related. Moreover, angiotensin in doses as low as 5 nanograms injected into the limbic system or preoptic area caused drinking (Epstein, Fitzsimons, & Simons, 1971). This is within the physiological range of circulating angiotensin and is compelling evidence for the contribution of this hormone to thirst.

A paradox developed, however, because those brain sites that were considered to be angiotensin sensitive on the basis of the Epstein et al. report do not bind radioactively labeled angiotensin (Osborne, Pooters, Anglès d'Anriac, Epstein, Worcel, & Meyer, 1971). In fact, the only region that showed radioactivity after the infusion of labeled angiotensin was the ventricular area (Volcier & Loew, 1971). Johnson (1972) used this information to help resolve the paradox of why, on the one hand, drinking could be elicited following stimulation of a large number of limbic and hypothalamic loci and, on the other hand, why angiotensin was taken up only in the ventricular space. He showed that an angiotensin-sensitive locus remained sensitive only when the guide cannula passed through the lateral ventricles. When cannulae were angled into the brain so that their paths missed the ventricles, then injections of angiotensin were ineffective, despite the fact that the cannulae opened into "sensitive" loci. On the other hand, loci which, on the basis of the Epstein et al. report, were considered to be insensitive became "sensitive" when the cannula path tranversed the ventricles. It seemed that the intracranial injections were effective by virtue of the fluid escaping up the guide cannula shaft into the ventricular space.

Recently Simpson and Routtenberg (1973) discovered that the subfornical organ (SFO), an ependymal structure that is in generous contact with the lateral ventricles, was an angiotensin thirst receptor. Using very fine 27-gauge cannulae, they elicited drinking

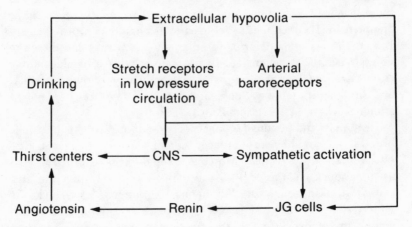

FIG. 5. Schematic of a possible mechanism underlying extracellular thirst. (From Fitzsimons, 1972.)

when angiotensin was injected into the SFO. Destruction of this organ eliminated or significantly reduced drinking in response to intracranial angiotensin. Johnson (1973) then reported a significant and highly positive correlation between the onset of drinking following intravenous infusion of radioactive angiotensin and the appearance of radioactivity in the cerebrospinal fluid, and logically concluded that under normal circumstances, angiotensin is effective as a thirst stimulus by gaining access to the SFO through the cerebrospinal fluid and not by crossing the blood-brain barrier.

A plan for the dynamics of the possible mechanism restoring normal extracellular volume, provided by Fitzsimons, is presented in figure 5. Intravascular depletion, with its concomitant hyponatremia, activates at least four effector mechanisms to restore normal fluid and sodium levels. The decrease of venous return to the heart causes the release of antidiuretic hormone, thereby retaining water. Elevated renin and angiotensin causes aldosterone to be released, which in turn acts on the kidneys to retain salt. Thirst is provoked by the renin-angiotensin system and also presumably by the putative baroreceptive mechanism. The bases of the salt appetite are not known at present. Sodium appetite survives adrenalectomy (Wolf & Stricker, 1967) and is not elicited by infusions of renin (Fitzsimons & Stricker, 1972). It is of course possible that aldosterone has a potentiating effect under these circumstances, but this must await experimental confirmation.

As previously indicated, the renin-angiotensin mechanism alone cannot account for all extracellular thirst, and a number of paradoxical findings suggest a complex interaction between angiotensin and the putative baroreceptor controls. Nephrectomy has variable effects. It abolishes drinking to hypotension, markedly attenuates that to caval ligation, but has only a marginal effect on drinking to intravascular depletion. Yet under all three circumstances, the levels of circulating renin are very much elevated (Stricker, 1973). Another puzzling phenomenon has been reported by Blair-West (1972), who observed that angiotensin levels in sheep were slightly elevated following 48 hours of deprivation, but became considerably heightened after the absorption of water. Yet drinking stopped despite the elevated levels and despite the fact that a marked intravascular depletion persisted.

Recent work in my laboratory concerning drinking in rats following lesions to the septal area may shed light on the problem of why, under certain circumstances, the otherwise potent angiotensin stimulus is relatively ineffective. Following bilateral lesions to the septal area, there is an immediate and sustained increase in daily water intake, at times exceeding the preoperative levels by threefold. Blass and Hanson (1970) reported that such rats overdrank selectively to intravascular depletion produced by intraperitoneal (i.p.) injection of hyperoncotic colloid. They did not drink more than normal rats to cellular dehydration and the increased daily intake was not secondary to a primary urine loss or to prandial drinking.

Unfortunately, the phenomenon could not be replicated with subcutaneous (s.c.) injections. In fact, a number of other laboratories have also obtained the same negative results. Yet each group of rats that was tested in our laboratory using the i.p. route of injection overdrank. Finally, Blass, Nussbaum, and Hanson (1974) used a within-subjects design to show, as seen in figure 6, that rats that drank more than normal to the i.p. treatment did not do so when the colloid was delivered subcutaneously. Figure 6 also shows that the s.c. route was much more effective than the i.p. route in eliciting drinking in normal rats, and it is of considerable interest that at the time that water was made available, the intravascular deficit was considerably greater in the s.c. condition.

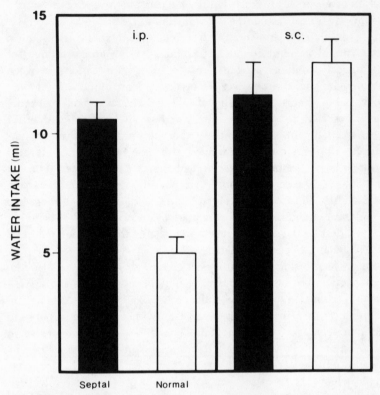

FIG. 6. Water intake of septal hyperdipsic and normal rats in response to polyethylene glycol delivered i.p. (left-hand panel) or s.c. (From Blass, Nussbaum & Hanson, 1974.)

Blass, Nussbaum, and Hanson (1974) then went on to find that septal hyperdipsic rats were specifically overresponsive to drinking stimuli known or thought to be mediated by angiotensin. They drank more to suprarenal ligation of the inferior vena cava, hypotension, intraperitoneal injections of renin, and intravenous infusions of angiotensin. Figure 7 plots the regression of septal intake against the intake of neurologically intact rats to these diverse challenges, whose only communality is that all produce elevated circulating levels of angiotensin. A linear relationship is seen. For every milliliter drunk by normal rats, hyperdipsic animals drank about 1.3 ml. Clearly, septal hyperdipsic rats selectively overdrank to angiotensin.

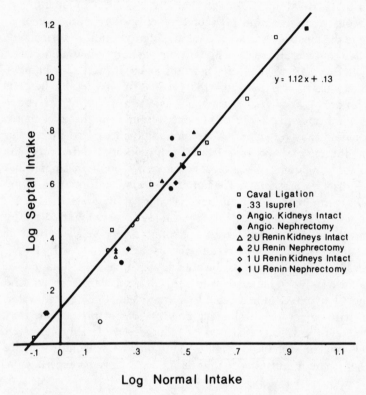

FIG. 7. Logarithmic relationship between water intake of septal hyperdipsic and neurologically intact rats to various stimuli thought to be mediated wholly or in part by the renin-angiotensin mechanism. (From Blass, Nussbaum & Hanson, 1974.)

The following summary provides perspective for these findings and their implications for understanding extracellular thirst: (1) Angiotensin is a remarkably potent dipsogen. (2) Following severe deprivation, water intake terminates despite very high levels of circulating angiotensin. (3) Nephrectomy eliminates or reduces drinking to hypotension or caval ligation but not to colloid-induced hypovolia, despite the fact that all three treatments substantially elevate circulating levels of renin. (4) Septal hyperdipsic rats drink more water than normal rats when hyperoncotic colloid is delivered intraperitoneally but not following subcutaneous delivery. (5) At the time of drinking onset, the intravascular deficit following intraperitoneal treatment was substantially less than following subcutaneous treatment; and (6) septal hyperdipsic rats are more sensitive to the dipsogenic properties of angiotensin than are normal rats.

Taken together, these data support the possibility that angiotensin may be a particularly effective dipsogen when the putative baroreceptor system indicates that venous return to the heart is either normal or slightly below normal. When the baroreceptive system indicates a markedly deficient return, then the angiotensin information may be "ignored" or the inhibition exerted by cellular overhydration may be especially effective. Stated differently, the efficacy of angiotensin as a dipsogen may be conditional upon that of the atrial baroreceptors. The notion of "losing" information during more severe instances of hypovolia may at first seem counterintuitive but is very logical when the fate of water ingested during hypovolia is considered. Recall that only a very small portion of the ingested fluid goes to restore the vascular loss, and that 67% reaches the cellular phase. If the animal which has no cellular deficit drinks excessively because of the heightened baroreceptive and hormonal activity and because it is anuric retains the ingested water, then actual or subclinical symptoms of water intoxication may become manifest. This risk may be reduced considerably, however, if hormonal information is ignored. Again, the speculative nature of this account must be emphasized, for it awaits experimental corroboration.

VII. DRINKING IN RESPONSE TO SIMULTANEOUS
CELLULAR AND EXTRACELLULAR DEPLETIONS

Only drinking elicited by deficits in either the cellular or extracellular compartment has been discussed to this point. Under normal circumstances, however, water is forfeited by both compartments. That is, it is only very occasionally that either a pure cellular or extracellular stimulus occurs. A number of investigators have inquired into the interaction between cellular and extracellular thirst stimuli. It has been found to be additive (Blass & Fitzsimons, 1970; Corbit, 1968; Fitzsimons & Oately, 1970; Stricker, 1969). This is clearly seen in figure 8. The amount drunk to the cellular and

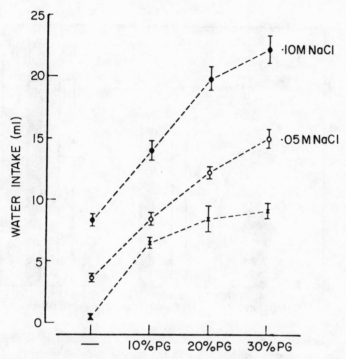

FIG. 8. Additivity of drinking produced by combining a cellular and an extracellular stimulus of thirst. (From Stricker, 1969.)

extracellular stimuli when presented in combination is equal to the algebraic sum of the amount drunk to each stimulus alone.

This important finding is amenable to at least two interpretations. It may reflect an addition of inputs into a hypothetical thirst system which then gives rise to a more intense thirst, or it may represent the delay of the cellular overhydration mechanism, described by Stricker (1969), that is known to arrest hypovolic thirst. This issue is not easily resolved in normal animals that drink to both cellular and extracellular depletions. However, animals with preoptic lesions that do not drink to cellular dehydration are perfectly suited for experiments that distinguish between these alternatives.

Such an analysis has been undertaken in my laboratory in collaboration with Marie Wallick and Martin Teicher. Drinking in response to water privation and to the combined treatments of water privation and cellular dehydration has been studied in normal rats and in rats with bilateral LPO lesions. Figure 9 shows that rats

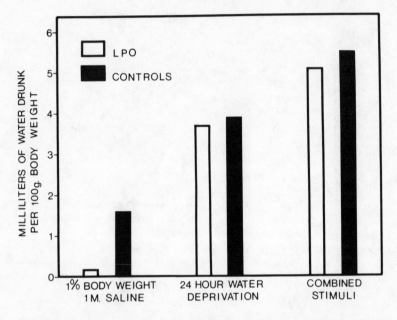

FIG. 9. Drinking of rats with LPO lesions and normal rats to cellular dehydration, water deprivation, and the combination of the two. (Note that the ordinate is expressed as percentage of body weight.)

with preoptic lesions that did not drink to cellular dehydration (left-hand column) drank normally to water privation (middle column). This replicates the findings of Andersson and Larsson (1956), using dogs, and Peck and Novin (1971), using rabbits. Moreover, LPO rats also drank as much as normal rats to the combined stimulus of water deprivation and cellular dehydration. That is, the amount drunk by the preoptic rats to the combined stimulus very closely approximates the amount drunk by these rats following deprivation alone plus the amount drunk by normal rats to cellular dehydration alone. This finding does not conform to the interpretation of additivity of individual afferents, which predicts that adding a cellular stimulus to the already existing thirst caused by water deprivation should not increase drinking in rats with LPO lesions. These data are in concert, however, with the view that increased intake seen following the combination of cellular and extracellular stimuli reflects delaying the onset of cellular overhydration. They also support the conclusion that cellular overhydration is detected by

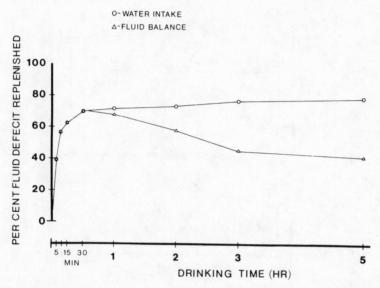

FIG. 10. Water intake (○) and retention (△) of 24-hour water-deprived rats expressed as a percentage of water loss.

receptors other than those signaling cellular dehydration (Blass, 1968; Blass & Epstein, 1971; Peck & Novin, 1971).

## VIII. DRINKING FOLLOWING WATER DEPRIVATION

### A. Hydrational Controls

This last finding and its interpretation serve as points of departure for analyzing the common and natural occurrence of drinking following water privation. The incomplete rehydration of water-deprived rats is described in the present section and a possible model based on body fluid alterations is provided to account for the phenomenon. Succeeding sections will stress the importance of the temporal relationship between drinking and rehydration, the contribution of the upper gastrointestinal tract as a modulator of drinking, and the role of context as a determinant of intake. In short, the contributions of the individual controls will be synthesized to

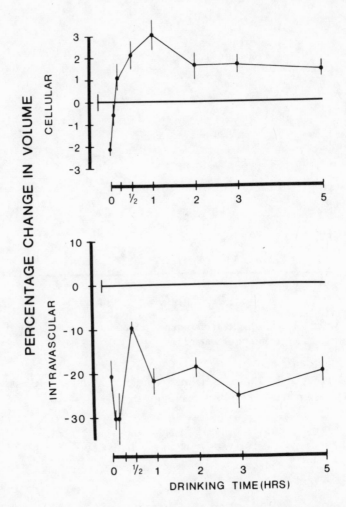

FIG. 11. Estimated changes in cellular and intravascular volume of 24-hour water-deprived rats allowed to drink water for various intervals.

provide a possible basis for drinking as it may occur spontaneously.

In the basic experimental paradigm, rats are deprived of water but not food for 22 hours, at which time food is also removed. Water is restored 2 hours later, and water intake and urine output are monitored for the next 5 hours. Then the rat is returned to ad libitum condition until the following test.

The percentage of the 24-hour fluid deficit restored through drinking is presented in figure 10, and because water is lost insensibly and in urine, the net repair is also shown. Only 80% of the water deficit was made good via drinking. This confirms Adolph's finding of voluntary dehydration. Drinking was at first sustained, almost all of it occurring during the first 15 minutes, and it was the very occasional rat that drank after 1 hour. An unexpected and counterintuitive finding was that less than 50% of what was drunk was retained. Owing to insensible water loss (primarily pulmonary) and to a brisk water diuresis, the net repair was only 43% of the deficit.

Warren G. Hall and I then sought a physiological basis for this phenomenon. Did both compartments remain dehydrated or was only one differentially depleted? We determined the blood profiles of rats sacrificed at various stages of rehydration. The fullness of the different spaces was estimated by plasma Na and osmolality for the cellular phase, and by hematocrit and plasma protein for the extracellular. The lower portion of figure 11 shows that the intravascular deficit was not repaired, and in fact remained quite substantial. On the other hand, cellular overhydration developed quickly and reached statistical significance by 15 minutes after the onset of drinking. This was of interest because it extended Stricker's findings to water deprivation; it provided a basis for the phenomenon of voluntary dehydration; and more important it was a step toward indentifying the factors that may govern intake as it occurs normally.

## B. The Importance of Contiguity

Blass and Hall (1974) then determined whether overhydration per se was the necessary and sufficient condition to terminate drinking. Deprived rats were intubated the amount retained on a previous test, and, unexpectedly, they drank an additional 5 ml. They were then preloaded, by gavage, the *total* amount drunk on a previous test, and 1 hour later, when cellular overhydration was at its zenith, were provided with water. An additional 3 ml. were drunk. This suggested an additional element. Perhaps some drinking had to occur to relieve mouth dryness or to reduce drive stimuli. Or perhaps the mouth helped meter intake. Another alternative was that perhaps intake and its postingestive consequences had to occur in *close temporal contiguity* to eliminate drinking.

Table 1 presents the experimental paradigm employed by Blass & Hall (1974) to assess these alternatives. Rats were water deprived for 23 hours, at which time they received the first half of their preload. The total preload equaled 55% of the water loss. The preloads were delivered either orally or intragastrically, and consisted of either distilled water or isotonic saline. The second half of the preload was delivered 1 hour later and the animals were allowed to drink at the 25-hour mark for 5 hours. The various combinations were presented to the 10 rats in a semirandom order. The results are shown in figure 12.

**Table 1**
*Outline of Deprivation, Preloading, and Drinking Schedule Followed in This Study*

| 0 hour | 23 hours | 24 hours | 25 hours |
|---|---|---|---|
| Water deprive (Purina lab pellets available) | Preload Intubate or drink water or .153M NaCl[a] | Preload Intubate or drink water or .153M NaCl[a] | Preload Drink water or .153M NaCl for 5 hours |

[a] The amount given was 27.5% of the water loss.

Total intake, that is preload plus amount drunk, is expressed as a percentage of the fluid deficit restored. The horizontal line is drinking following sham tubing where no fluid was injected, and therefore represents the baseline of voluntary dehydration. Open columns indicate that water was drunk during the test; the shaded column represents isotonic saline. The only conditions that further exaggerated incomplete rehydration were those in which cellular overhydration closely followed drinking the second preload: in the first column, where drinking followed intubation, and in the second column when water was drunk on both preload occasions. The crucial factor was not cellular overhydration per se. If it were, then the first four treatments where equal amounts of water were preloaded should have been equally effective in reducing drinking. They were not. Second, the crucial factor was not oral metering or drive stimulus reduction per se. If oral metering was the crucial variable, then the drink water–drink water preload condition should have depressed intake the most, followed by the intubate water–drink water, and

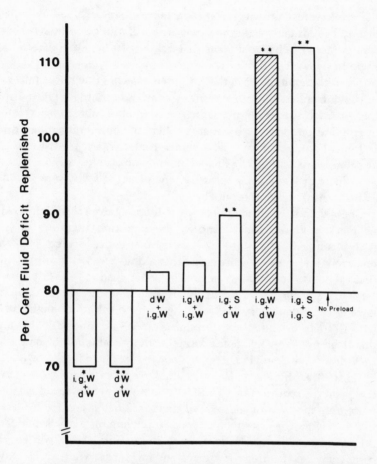

FIG. 12. Rehydration of deprived rats following various preloading schedules. Ordinate is the percentage of the incurred deficit restored. Horizontal line is drinking following sham tubing. The height of each column reflects the preload and amount drunk during test. Abbreviations: dw, drink water; i.g.w, intragastric water; ds, drink saline; i.g.s, intragastric saline. Open column, drink water during test. Shaded column, drink saline. First column of i.g.w + dw means that following 23 hours of water deprivation the first half of the preload was delivered intragastrically and after an hour's delay, the rats drank the second half of the preload. One hour later they were allowed to drink water for 5 hours. (From Blass & Hall, 1974.)

the drink water–intubate water conditions where equal amounts were drunk. The intubate water–intubate water condition should have been least effective. The prediction that follows from the oral-metering hypothesis was not borne out.

The fifth column shows that the effect was not due to the memory of having recently drunk water because here the first half of the preload was isotonic saline, which does not cause cellular overhydration. The sixth column, where isotonic saline was drunk following the water preloads, shows that thirst persisted: 12 ml. of saline were drunk. The final column demonstrates the importance of cellular overhydration, because when the preloads were isotonic saline, considerable water intake occurred.

These data suggest the importance of contiguity of ingestion with its postingestional consequences. The ingestion literature is rich with examples of how the absence of contiguity renders preloads relatively ineffective. In the case of drinking, Stricker (1969) found that almost three times as much water had to be given intragastrically as would normally be drunk, to arrest drinking to intravascular depletion. The same holds for drinking to angiotensin (Rolls & McFarland, 1973). Nachman and Valentino (1966) found that loading adrenalectomized rats with the amount of salt that they drank on a previous test did not reduce their intake of a .3M NaCl solution. Similarly, Janowitz and Grossman (1949) have shown that loading food intragastrically 20 minutes before feeding failed to depress intake in dogs, and Miller (1957) has presented evidence that rats work for more food or water following intragastric preloads than following oral preloads. Finally, Baile, Zinn, and Mayer (1971) have found that intragastric infusions of glucose were an effective suppressant in monkeys only when they were delivered at the inception of feeding. In light of the present evidence, these interpretations might be reevaluated and the influence of ingestion in contiguity with its postingestional consequences explored.


C. The Contribution of the Mouth and Stomach

Because drinking terminated while considerable fluid remained in the stomach, Hall and I felt it worthwhile to investigate the contribution of preabsorptive mechanisms. Although oral and gastric factors have generally been acknowledged as having a modulatory control in drinking, the empirical support is sparse and conflicting.

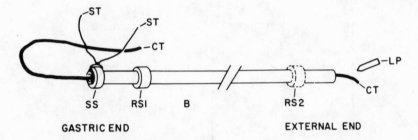

FIG. 13. Schematic of clamp used to prevent escape of fluid from the stomach. (From Hall, 1973.)

The older literature supports a modulatory influence. Fieder (1973), however, has correctly pointed out that fluid introduced into the stomach by intubation is quickly absorbed and therefore attenuation may be governed by postabsorptive factors. In support of a minimal contribution by the upper gastrointestinal tract, Fieder preloaded rats, via a nasopharyngeal tube that terminated in the stomach, with 15 ml. isotonic saline or tap water and allowed them to drink three minutes later. Intake was not depressed below sham intubation conditions or following saline infusions but was markedly suppressed following the water preloads. Fieder logically concluded that the diminution in drinking following water intubation was under the control of postabsorptive mechanisms and that the contribution of the upper gastrointestinal tract was minimal.

Hall and I believed, however, that the most informative way to assess the contribution of the stomach would be to allow the rat to fill it naturally by drinking, but not to allow the ingested fluid to escape into the intestine. In addition to providing the rat control over ingestion rate, this strategy has the virtue of assessing the consequences of drinking in contiguity with the postingestive event. To achieve this, Hall (1973) designed an ingenious stomach clamp, a blueprint of which is shown in figure 13. The clamp is essentially a hangman's noose, fashioned from nylon line, that articulates about the pyloric sphincter. When pulled taut, it prevents water from evacuating into the intestine. It can then be released and pushed to its regular position to allow absorption. Infection-free preparations have been studied for up to eight weeks in our laboratory.

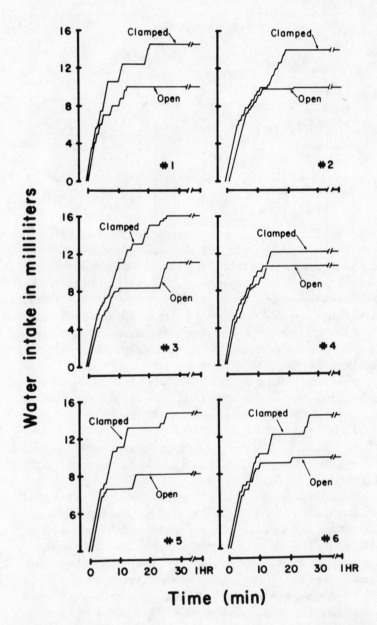

FIG. 14. Drinking patterns of individual rats with stomach clamped or open. (From Hall, 1973.)

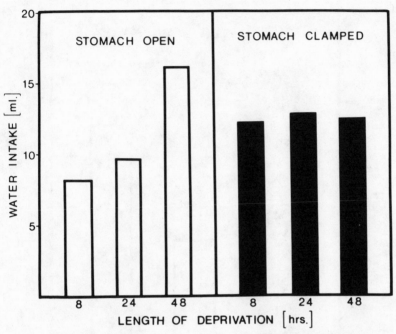

FIG. 15. One hour water intake of 8-, 24-, or 48-hour water-deprived rats with stomach clamped or open.

In order to assess the contribution of the stomach to drinking, 6 rats, equipped with pyloric clamps, were water deprived for 24 hours, at which time they were allowed to drink with the clamp open or closed. As shown in figure 14, more was drunk by all 6 rats when the clamp was closed. This of course points to the importance of the postingestive controls. However, closer inspection of figure 14 reveals a striking similarity in pattern between open and closed conditions, suggesting perhaps a subtle contribution. We have explored this further by clamping the stomachs of rats deprived of water but not food for 8, 24, or 48 hours to find, as shown in figure 15, that while intake when the stomach was open was related to deprivation, drinking with the stomach clamped was remarkably invariant. Termination under clamped circumstances presumably reflected the activation of an emergency mechanism, one that is probably never activated during the normal course of events. The important point is that the influence exerted by the mouth and stomach did

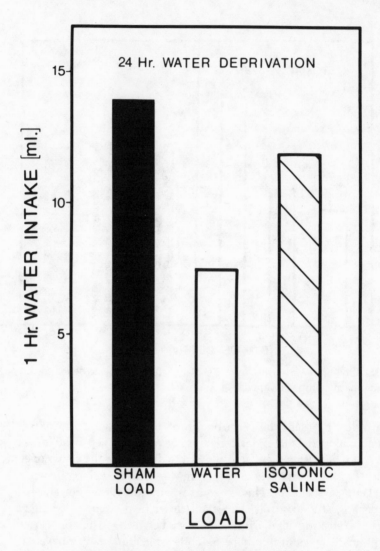

FIG. 16. One hour water intake of rats drinking with stomach clamped following 5 ml. absorbed preloads of water or isotonic saline.

not appear to be at all related to the level of deprivation. The contribution of the stomach at this point looked bleak indeed.

But these tests were artificial in a sense because absorption normally follows drinking and the clamp prevented absorption. Signals from the upper gastrointestinal tract do not occur in isolation but are orchestrated with those arising from subsequent changes in body fluid balances. Perhaps such signals become meaningful only following a shift in fluid balance. This idea was tested by preloading 24-hour water-deprived rats with 5 ml. of water or isotonic saline and 1 hour *later* clamping the stomach. The left-hand column of figure 16 is the amount drunk by rats, whose stomachs were clamped, with no preload. The middle column represents water intake following an absorbed water preload. The right-hand column is water intake following an absorbed saline preload. The saline preload was ineffective despite the fact that it eased the extracellular deficit. Water was remarkably effective, however, as drinking was reduced from almost 15 ml. to less than 7 ml., a reduction greater than the preload itself. This may be interpreted to mean that rehydrating the cellular phase permits information arising from the upper gastrointestinal tract, especially the stomach, to be utilized before the activation of the emergency mechanism. The stomach is sensitized by the correction in cellular balance and serves to brake drinking behavior, thereby preventing even more severe overhydration.

In light of the data presented above, the events preceding the modulation and termination of drinking may be viewed as follows. Water is yielded by both the cellular and extracellular phases during fluid deprivation. Rats do not drink enough water to make good their intravascular deficit. Water is quickly absorbed and gains access to the cells. This permits stomach influences to slow down drinking. Then the water remaining in the stomach is absorbed and cellular overhydration develops in close temporal contiguity with the ingestive act. It is this last event that appears to terminate drinking.

This scenario places considerable responsibility on the cellular mechanism and demands a reevaluation of its contribution to drinking. The cellular phase is the larger of the two fluid compartments, and a reduction in its volume has always been regarded as an adequate drinking stimulus. It may be more appropriate,

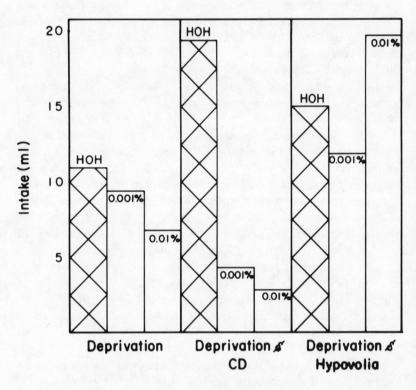

FIG. 17. Intake of water or quinine hydrochloride following deprivation alone (left-hand panel), deprivation and cellular dehydration (middle panel), or deprivation and hypovolia. (From Blass, 1973.)

however, to view the contribution of the cellular phase to the maintenance of normal fluid balance as varied and subtle. Under certain circumstances it can indeed provoke drinking. However, such circumstances are probably rare and unusual. In this writer's view, the major contribution of the cellular phase is modulatory, because in addition to exciting thirst, the cellular phase permits information arising from the stomach to be realized; it successfully opposes the signals arising from the extracellular space and also modulates food intake. The extracellular space functions in a less subtle way; it is basically excitatory.

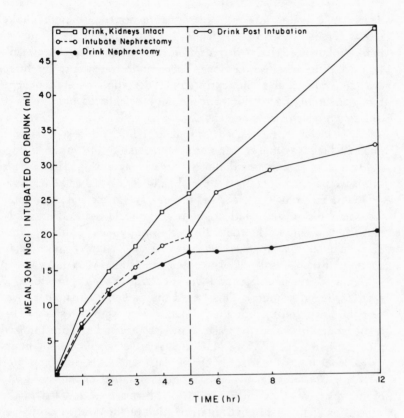

FIG. 18. Intake of .30M NaCl of deprived nephrectomized rats (see text for details).

## IX. CONTEXT AS A DETERMINANT OF INTAKE

We have dealt almost exclusively with the way rats utilize water in their defense against dehydration. However, under natural circumstances, water is not necessarily available and thirst must be slaked by a variety of liquids. In 1971, Burke, Mook, and Blass pursued this issue and allowed water-deprived rats to drink either water or quinine solutions of differing concentrations. On other tests either cellular dehydration or hypovolia was superimposed upon the water deprivation and the rats were allowed to rehydrate.

Figure 17 presents the outcome of the experiments. When either the cellular or extracellular stimulus was superimposed upon deprivation, water intake increased as expected. Quinine intake, like water intake, also increased with hypovolia. However, quinine intake following cellular dehydration was actually depressed below that drunk to dehydration alone. This demonstrated that the thirsts arising from cellular and extracellular depletion differed qualitatively, a finding consistent with the double-depletion hypothesis of different physiological and neurological controls.

This conclusion has raised a number of interesting speculations, one of which was that quinine was interpreted by the rat as belonging to a class of solutions that are cellular dehydrating. Therefore to drink would further embarass the already contracted cellular phase.

To test this, rats were deprived of fluid, and at the end of 24 hours were nephrectomized. Half of the rats were allowed to drink .30M NaCl for 12 hours. The remaining rats were yoked to the rats with immediate access, and received, by gavage, slightly more NaCl every hour than was drunk. The outcome was unexpected. As shown in figure 18, considerable fluid was ingested by the nephrectomized rats (15 ml. in 5 hours). This raised the possibility that there was an inhibitory control but that it had a very high threshold. This turned out not to be the case, however, because nephrectomized rats that had received .30M NaCl by gavage every hour for 5 hours drank a substantial amount of .30M NaCl when it became available after 5 hours. This again points to the importance of the contiguity of ingestion with its postingestional consequences and led to the conclusion that our original interpretation of the quinine phenomenon was not tenable. That is, cellular dehydration does not inhibit intake of hypertonic solutions per se, because a hypertonic saline solution was readily drunk by the cellularly dehydrated rats.

This finding leads directly to the importance of context. It presented the alternative that quinine was interpreted as belonging to a class of substances labeled food. It is well known that feeding of dry food is reduced during water deprivation, a phenomenon that can be readily understood as caused by the mechanical discomfort engendered by the passage of food through a dry oropharynx. Alternatively, it could be a characteristic of the system. That is, less is eaten of substances that are classified as food regardless of the ease of passage. This was evaluated by allowing 24-hour food- and water-deprived rats access to a solution of .60 osmolar sucrose, a concentration of the same strength as the .30M NaCl just discussed. As seen in figure 19, sucrose intake, unlike NaCl intake, was

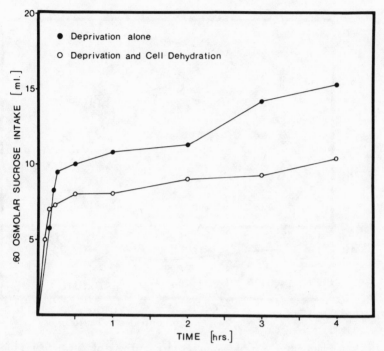

FIG. 19. Intake of .60 osmolar sucrose of 24-hour water- and food-deprived rats following 2 ml. injections of water or various concentrations of NaCl.

depressed by cellular dehydration. Water intake, of course, was increased, indicating the rats' behavioral competence.

This suggests that rats segregate fluids into at least two classes, water and food, and have sets of rules dealing with each class. This is consistent with the finding that fluids of equal concentration and tonicity were treated so very differently by the rat. The phenomenon cannot be explained in terms of the hedonic value of the fluids because the sugar is much more palatable to the rat than the salt. Nor can we dismiss it in terms of mechanical difficulty. And it shows that something does not have to be chewed and eaten to be treated as food. The phenomenon makes sense only when the context in which an act occurs is considered. In these experiments when the rat approaches the spout it is both hungry and thirsty. The context is set by the taste or odor of the ingested fluid. Certain sugar solutions and possibly quinine appear to be treated as food. Intake therefore is reduced below baseline by cellular dehydration. However,

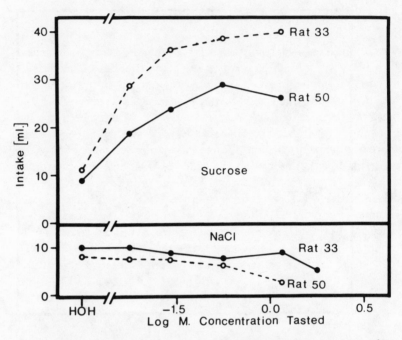

FIG. 20. Sham drinking of various concentrations of sucrose or saline by water- and food-deprived rats. Water equal to the amount of solution drunk was injected intragastrically in all cases. (Adapted from Mook, 1963.)

water or certain salt solutions are viewed as rehydrating and intake of these solutions is increased. It is increased with the salt because normally the rat can, by virtue of the capabilities of its renal mechanism, derive water from that solution.

The classic study of Mook (1963) also bears upon this interpretation. Mook prepared rats in such a way that allowed him to separate the oral from the postingestional consequences of intake. Specifically, he severed the rat's esophagus so that whatever was drunk spilled out of the body through the cut end of the esophagus. The stomach portion of the esophagus was cannulated, and with the appropriate relay and pumping devices fluids were introduced into the stomach. The beauty of the preparation is that rats could ingest one fluid and a second fluid differing in a variety of dimensions could be introduced into the stomach. Figure 20 demonstrates the effects of allowing rats to drink different concentrations of saline or sucrose. Under all circumstances water was delivered systemically at the rate at which drinking occurred. Look first at the saline portion of the figure. The normal preference aversion function for saline is shown to disappear with a flat intake function across many concentrations of saline. This may be interpreted to mean that rats responded to saline in the context of drinking. That is, they treat saline as if it were water and therefore the mechanisms of development of cellular overhydration in contiguity with drinking terminated intake. On the other hand, enormous quantities of sucrose were ingested, much more than would occur if sucrose was infused systemically. This may be interpreted to mean that the context here was feeding, and that the context was determined by the taste of the solution and, as the cellular space became overhydrated, the inhibition exerted upon feeding was relieved. Cellular overhydration therefore either facilitates or inhibits, depending upon the context; in this case context is set by the taste of the fluid, and this does not mean its intensity or hedonic value.

X. EPILOGUE

I have marked the progress realized in drinking research during the past decade, and have also indicated some potentially fruitful directions for the future. A few words of caution are appropriate. Understanding drinking as it occurs spontaneously remains distant. Although the double-depletion hypothesis has helped organize a substantial volume of data pertaining to the hydrational controls of drinking, its ultimate utility in the analysis of spontaneous drinking must, at this point, remain open to conjecture. Indeed, two of the leading investigators of drinking have recently suggested that the experience of true thirst is a rare event in mature mammals, and have raised the possibility that the more fruitful analysis may be of the nonphysiological determinants (Fitzsimons, 1973; Oately, 1973). The double-depletion hypothesis must be regarded as hypothesis only, and it is necessary to remain vigilant not to accept it as fact.

Finally, inasmuch as this is a symposium on motivation, it is appropriate to express the hope that the art will have developed sufficiently in the near future so that the next person who is invited to discuss the neuropsychology of thirst will be able to do so, rather than confine his remarks to drinking behavior.

References

Adolph, E. F. Thirst and its inhibition in the stomach. *American Journal of Physiology*, 1950, **161**, 374-386.

Adolph, E. F., Barker, J. P., & Hoy, P. A. Multiple factors in thirst. *American Journal of Physiology*, 1954, **178**, 538-562.

Andersson, B. Thirst and brain control of water balance. *American Scientist*, 1971, **59**, 408-415.

Andersson, B., & Larsson, S. Water and food intake and the inhibitory effect of amphetamine on drinking and eating before and after "prefrontal lobotomy" in dogs. *Acta Physiologica Scandinavica*, 1956, **38**, 22-30.

Baile, C. A., Zinn, W., & Mayer, J. Feeding behavior of monkeys: Glucose utilization rate and site of glucose entry. *Physiology and Behavior*, 1971, **6**, 537.

Bernard, C. *Leçons de physiologie expérimental appliquée à la médicine faites au Collège de France*. Paris: Baillière, 1856. Vol. 2, pp. 50-51.

Blair-West, J. R., Brook, A. H., & Simpson, P. A. Renin responses to water restriction and rehydration. *Journal of Physiology* (London), 1972, **226**, 1-13.

Blass, E. M. Separation of cellular from extracellular controls of drinking in rats by frontal brain damage. *Science*, 1968, **162**, 1501-1503.

Blass, E. M. Cellular-dehydration thirst. In A. N. Epstein, H. R. Kissileff & E. Stellar (Eds.), *The neuropsychology of thirst: New findings and advances in concepts*. Washington, D.C.: V. H. Winston & Sons, 1973. pp. 37-72.

Blass, E. M., & Epstein, A. N. A lateral preoptic osmosensitive zone for thirst in the rat. *Journal of Comparative and Physiological Psychology*, 1971, **76**, 378-394.

Blass, E. M., & Fitzsimons, J. T. Additivity of effect and interaction of a cellular and extracellular stimulus of drinking. *Journal of Comparative and Physiological Psychology*, 1970, **70**, 200-205.

Blass, E. M., & Hall, W. G. Behavioral and physiological bases of drinking inhibition in water deprived rats. *Nature*, 1974, **249**, 485–486.

Blass, E. M., & Hanson, D. G. Primary hyperdipsia in the rat following septal lesions. *Journal of Comparative and Physiological Psychology*, 1970, **70**, 87-93.

Blass, E. M., Nussbaum, A. I., & Hanson, D. G. Septal hyperdipsia: Specific enhancement of drinking to angiotensin in rats. *Journal of Comparative and Physiological Psychology*, 1974, **87**, 422-439.

Burke, G. H., Mook, D. G., & Blass, E. M. Hyperreactivity to quinine associated with osmotic thirst in the rat. *Journal of Comparative and Physiological Psychology*, 1972, **78**, 32-39.

Cannon, W. B. The physiological basis of thirst. *Proceedings of the Royal Society* (London), 1918, series b, **90**, 283-301.
Cizek, L. J., Semple, R. E., Huang, K. C., & Gregersen, M. I. Effect of extra-cellular electrolyte depletion on water intake in dogs. *American Journal of Physiology*, 1951, **164**, 415-422.
Corbit, J. D. Cellular dehydration and hypovolaemia are additive in producing thirst. *Nature*, 1968, **218**, 886-887.
Darrow, D. C., & Yannet, H. The changes in the distribution of body water accompanying increase and decrease in extracellular electrolyte. *Journal of Clinical Investigation*, 1935, **14**, 226-275.
Epstein, A. N. The lateral hypothalamic syndrome: Its implications for the physiological psychology of hunger and thirst. In E. Stellar & J. M. Sprague (Eds.), *Progress in physiological psychology.* New York: Academic Press, 1971. Vol. 4.
Epstein, A. N., Fitzsimons, J. T., & Simons, B. J. Drinking induced by injection of angiotensin into the brain of the rat. *Journal of Physiology* (London), 1971, **210**, 457-474.
Epstein, A. N., Spector, N. D., Samman, A., & Goldblum, C. Exaggerated prandial drinking in the rat without salivary glands. *Nature*, 1964, **201**, 1342.
Epstein, A. N., & Teitelbaum, P. Severe and persistent deficits in thirst produced by lateral hypothalamic damage. In M. J. Wayner (Ed.), *Thirst.* London: Pergamon, 1964. Pp. 395-406.
Ernits, T., & Corbit, J. D. Taste as a dipsogenic stimulus. *Journal of Comparative and Physiological Psychology*, 1973, **83**, 27-31.
Falk, J. L. The behavioral regulation of water-electrolyte balance. In M. R. Jones (Ed.), *Nebraska symposium on motivation, 1961.* Lincoln: University of Nebraska Press, 1961. Pp. 1-33.
Falk, J. L. The nature and determinants of adjunctive behavior. *Physiology and Behavior*, 1971, **6**, 577-588.
Fieder, A. Feedback control of thirst in rats. *Physiology and Behavior*, 1973, **8**, 1005-1011.
Fitzsimons, J. T. Drinking by nephrectomized rats injected with various substances. *Journal of Physiology* (London), 1961, **155**, 563-579. (a)
Fitzsimons, J. T. Drinking by rats depleted of body fluid without increase in osmotic pressure. *Journal of Physiology* (London), 1961, **159**, 297-309. (b)
Fitzsimons, J. T. The effect of slow infusions of hypertonic solutions on drinking and drinking thresholds in rats. *Journal of Physiology* (London), 1963, **167**, 344-354.
Fitzsimons, J. T. The role of renal thirst factor in drinking induced by extracellular stimuli. *Journal of Physiology* (London), 1969, **201**, 349-368.

Fitzsimons, J. T. Interactions of intracranially administered renin or angiotensin and other stimuli on drinking. *Journal of Physiology* (London), 1970, **210**, 152-153P.

Fitzsimons, J. T. The physiology of thirst: A review of the extraneural aspects of the mechanisms of drinking. In E. Stellar & J. M. Sprague (Eds.), *Progress in physiological psychology*. New York: Academic Press, 1971. Vol. 4, pp. 119-201.

Fitzsimons, J. T. Thirst. *Physiological Reviews*, 1972, **52**, 468-561.

Fitzsimons, J. T., & Oately, K. Additivity of stimuli for drinking in rats. *Journal of Comparative and Physiological Psychology*, 1968, **66**, 450-455.

Fitzsimons, J. T., & Simons, B. J. The effect on drinking in the rat of intravenous infusion of angiotensin, given alone or in combination with other stimuli of thirst. *Journal of Physiology* (London), 1969, **203**, 45-57.

Fitzsimons, J. T., & Stricker, E. M. Sodium appetite and the renin-angiotensin system. *Nature, 1972*, **231**, 58-60.

Fregly, M. J., & Waters, I. W. Effect of mineralocorticoids on spontaneous sodium chloride appetite of adrenalectomized rats. *Physiology and Behavior*, 1966, **1**, 65-74.

Gilman, A. The relation between blood osmotic pressure, fluid distribution, and voluntary water intake. *American Journal of Physiology*, 1937, **120**, 323-328.

Gregersen, M. I., & Bullock, L. T. Observations on thirst in man in relation to changes in salivary flow and plasma volume. *American Journal of Physiology*, 1933, **105**, 39-40.

Haberich, F. J. Osmoreception in the portal circulation. *Federation Proceedings*, 1968, **27**, 1137-1141.

Hall, W. G. A remote stomach clamp to evaluate oral and gastric controls of drinking in the rat. *Physiology and Behavior*, 1973, **11**, 897-901.

Hawkins, R. C., & Corbit, J. D. Drinking in response to cellular dehydration in the pigeon. *Journal of Comparative and Physiological Psychology*, 1973, **84**, 265-267.

Holmes, J. H., & Gregersen, M. I. Observations on drinking induced by hypertonic solutions. *American Journal of Physiology*, 1950, **162**, 326-337. (a)

Holmes, J. H., & Gregersen, M. I. Role of sodium and chloride in thirst. *American Journal of Physiology*, 1959, **162**, 338-347. (b)

Houpt, K. A., & Epstein, A. N. The complete dependence of beta-adrenergic drinking on the renal dipsogen. *Physiology and Behavior*, 1972, **7**, 897-902.

Janowitz, H. D., & Grossman, M. I. Some factors affecting the food intake of normal dogs and dogs with esophagostomy and gastric fistula. *American Journal of Physiology*, 1949, **159**, 143.

Johnson, A. K. Localization of angiotensin in sensitive areas for thirst within the rat brain. Paper presented at the Eastern Psychological Association Meeting, Boston, 1972.

Johnson, A. K. Ventricular involvement in intracranial angiotensin drinking. Paper presented at the Eastern Psychological Association Meeting, Washington, D.C., 1973.

Kissileff, H. R. Oropharyngeal control of prandial drinking. *Journal of Comparative and Physiological Psychology*, 1969, **67**, 309-319.

Kissileff, H. R. Nonhomeostatic controls of drinking. In A. N. Epstein, H. R. Kissileff, & E. Stellar (Eds.), *The neuropsychology of thirst: New findings and advances in concepts*, Washington, D.C.: V. H. Winston & Sons, 1973. Pp. 163-198.

Latta, T. Letter from Dr. Latta to the Secretary of the Central Board of Health, London, affording a view of the rationale and results of his practice in the treatment of cholera by aqueous and saline injections. *Lancet*, 1832, 274-277.

Mayer, A. Variations de la tension osmotique du sang chez les animaux privés des liquides. *Comptes Rendus des Séances de la Société de Biologie*, 1900, **52**, 153-155.

McCance, R. A. Experimental sodium chloride deficiency in man. *Proceedings of the Royal Society* (London), 1936, series B, **119**, 245-268.

Miller, N. E. Experiments on motivation: Studies combining psychological, physiological and pharmacological techniques. *Science*, 1957, **126**, 1271.

Mook, D. G. Oral and postingestional determinants of the intake of various solutions in rats with esophageal fistulas. *Journal of Comparative and Physiological Psychology*, 1963, **56**, 645-649.

Nachman, M., & Valentino, D. A. Roles of taste and postingestional factors in the satiation of sodium appetite in rats. *Journal of Comparative and Physiological Psychology*, 1966, **62**, 280.

Nicolaïdis, S. Early systemic responses to orogastric stimulation in the regulation of food and water balance: Functional and electrophysiological data. *Annals of New York Academy of Science*, 1969, **157**, 1176-1203.

Nothnagel, H. Durst and Polydipsie. *Virchow's Archiv für Pathologische Anatomie und Physiologie und Klinische Medizin*, 1881, **86**, 435-477.

Oately, K. Simulation and theory of thirst. In A. N. Epstein, H. R. Kissileff, and E. Stellar (Eds.), *The neuropsychology of thirst: New findings and advances in concepts*, Washington, D.C.: V. H. Winston & Sons. 1973. Pp. 199-224.

Osborne, M. J., Pooters, N., Anglès d'Anriac, G., Epstein, A. N., Worcel, M., & Meyer, P. Metabolism of tritiated angiotensin II in anesthetized rats. *Pfluger's Archives*, 1971, **326**, 101-114.

Peck, J. W., & Novin, D. Evidence that osmoreceptors mediating drinking in rabbits are in the lateral preoptic area. *Journal of Comparative and Physiological Psychology*, 1971, **74**, 134-147.

Reed, D. J., & Woodbury, D. M. Effect of hypertonic urea on cerebrospinal fluid pressure and brain volume. *Journal of Physiology* (London), 1962, **164**, 252-264.

Rolls, B. J., & McFarland, D. J. Hydration releases inhibition of feeding produced by intracranial angiotensin. *Physiology and Behavior*, 1973, **11**, 881-884.

Rullier. *Dictionnaire des sciences medicales par une société de medicins et de chirugiens*. Paris: Panckoucke, 1821. Vol. 51, pp. 448-490.

Schneiden, H. Solution drinking in rats after dehydration and after hemorrhage. *American Journal of Physiology*, 1962, **203**, 560-562.

Simpson, J. B., & Routtenberg, A. Subfornical organ: Dipsogenic site of action of angiotensin II. *Science*, 1973, **181**, 1172-1174.

Stricker, E. M. Extracellular fluid volume and thirst. *American Journal of Physiology*, 1966, **211**, 232-238.

Stricker, E. M. Some physiological and motivational properties of the hypovolemic stimulus for thirst. *Physiology and Behavior*, 1968, **3**, 379-385.

Stricker, E. M. Osmoregulation and volume regulation in rats: Inhibition of hypovolemic thirst by water. *American Journal of Physiology*, 1969, **217**, 98-105.

Stricker, E. M. Thirst, sodium appetite and complementary physiological contributions to the regulation of intravascular volume. In A. N. Epstein, H. R. Kissileff, & E. Stellar (Eds.), *The neuropsychology of thirst: New findings and advances in concepts*. Washington, D.C.: V. H. Winston & Sons, 1973. Pp. 73-98.

Stricker, E. M., & Jalowiec, J. E. Restoration of intravascular fluid volume following acute hypovolemia in rats. *American Journal of Physiology*, 1970, **218**, 191-196.

Stricker, E. M., & Wolf, G. Blood volume and toxicity in relation to sodium appetite. *Journal of Comparative and Physiological Psychology*, 1966, **62**, 275-279.

Stricker, E. M., & Wolf, G. The effects of hypovolemia on drinking in rats with lateral hypothalamic damage. *Procceedings of the Society of Experimental Biology and Medicine*, 1967, **124**, 816-820.

Teitelbaum, P., & Epstein, A. N. The lateral hypothalamic syndrome: Recovery of feeding and drinking after lateral hypothalamic lesions. *Psychological Review*, 1962, **69**, 74-90.

Vance, W. B. Observations on the role of salivary excretion in the regulation of food and fluid intakes in the white rat. *Psychological Monographs*, 1965, **79**, (5, whole no. 598).

Volcier, L., & Loew, C. G. Penetration of angiotensin II into the brain. *Neuropharmacology,* 1971, **10,** 631, 676.

Wettendorf, H. Modifications du sang sous l'influence de la privation d'eau: Contribution a l'etude de la soif. *Travaux du Laboratoire de Physiologie, Instituts Solvay,* 1901, **4,** 353-484.

Williams, D. R., & Teitelbaum, P. Control of drinking behavior by means of an operant-conditioning technique. *Science,* 1956, **124,** 1294-1296.

Wolf, A. V. Osmometric analysis of thirst in man and dog. *American Journal of Physiology,* 1959, **161,** 75-86.

Wolf, G. Neural mechanisms for sodium appetite: Hypothalamus positive-hypothalamofugal pathways negative. *Physiology and Behavior,* 1971, **6,** 381-390 .

Wolf, G., & Stricker, E. M. Sodium appetite elicited by hypovolemia in adrenalectomized rats. *Journal of Comparative and Physiological Psychology,* 1967, **63,** 252-257.

# Brain Reward and Aversion Systems in the Control of Feeding and Sexual Behavior[1]

Bartley G. Hoebel

*Princeton University*

## INTRODUCTION AND OVERVIEW

*I*n the *Nebraska Symposium* of 1955, P. T. Young summarized his theory that hedonism steers behavior. He postulated that hedonic processes could be measured as approach or avoidance responses. It was in the same symposium that James Olds described how a rat's behavior could be steered by brain stimulation. To outward appearances it was as if the brain stimulation generated a hedonic process that caused approach to the stimulus. Approach is a mild word for it; the animals would press a lever for self-stimulation three thousand times an hour. This complemented the discovery by Delgado, Roberts, and Miller (1954) that animals will also learn to escape from brain stimulation. The revelation was the existence of brain reward and aversion systems that could be studied experimentally using implanted electrodes. Olds proposed that the reward measured as self-stimulation interacts with other neural functions in a cell assembly to provide the affect, or "pleasure," experienced by the animal. This fit Young's ideas beautifully, but looking cautiously into the future, Young commented, "Whether or not Dr. Olds has put his finger upon the physiological basis of affectivity remains to be seen."

Now, nineteen years later, I will try to convince you that they were indeed on a path leading to new understanding of brain control of complex behavior. The evidence strongly suggests that self-stimulation and stimulation-escape can reflect the reward and aversion of feeding. This follows from the fact that physiological factors which control feeding exert a corresponding control over

1. Current research from the author's laboratory reported or referred to in this paper was supported by USPHS Grant MH 08493, NSF Grants GB 8431 and GB 43407, grants from Allegheny Pharmaceutical Company, Hofmann-LaRoche Pharmaceutical Company, and a training grant from the Spencer Foundation.

lateral hypothalamic self-stimulation and stimulation-escape. It will be suggested that this reward-aversion system is an important element in the neural control of food intake. We also find evidence for a reward-aversion system controlling sexual behavior. These findings suggest a broader theory that such reward-aversion systems in the brain translate physiological stimuli into behavioral action by rewarding appropriate behavior and punishing the inappropriate.

The self-stimulation side of the story was foretold in 1957 when Olds found that male rats increased their self-stimulation rate at some brain sites when food-deprived and at other brain sites when injected with androgen. Then Margules and Olds (1962) reported that the deprivation-induced increase in self-stimulation was obtained reliably in the lateral hypothalamus. Hoebel and Teitelbaum (1962) reported that food intake decreased lateral hypothalamic self-stimulation, and we suggested that the reward of self-stimulation is similar to the rewards of eating. Additional evidence for a feeding-reward system was collected (Hoebel, 1969), and a "copulation-reward" area was localized where self-stimulation varied with castration and androgen replacement (Caggiula & Hoebel, 1966).

What is new is the evidence that stimulation-escape increases after excessive feeding or ejaculation. The possible importance of these aversion mechanisms in the control of behavior will be discussed.

The fact that parallel observations have been made for both feeding and mating has broader implications for a general theory of brain function which will be proposed. Simply put, the idea is that self-stimulation and stimulation-escape are manifestations of brain mechanisms that facilitate approach to food or sex stimuli when physiological conditions call for it and facilitate withdrawal responses when the animal is physiologically satiated. Thus, these neural mechanisms control appetitive behavior by linking homeostasis to approach and withdrawal.

HYPOTHALAMIC CONTROL OF FEEDING:
ANALYSIS OF THREE PHENOMENA

In order to understand the relation between hypothalamic self-stimulation and feeding, it is first necessary to discover what physiological and pharmacological factors control feeding by an action in the hypothalamus. Once this is known, then these factors are logical candidates for tests with self-stimulation. In an effort to find the factors involved in hypothalamic control of feeding, three phenomena have been analyzed: (1) hyperphagia following hypothalamic damage, (b) feeding induced by hypothalamic stimulation, and (c) self-stimulation itself. Study of hyperphagia following ventromedial hypothalamic lesions demonstrated that the hypothalamus responds to some correlate of body weight. Then discovery of a new hyperphagia syndrome resulting from noradrenergic depletion allowed us to compare and contrast the new hyperphagia phenomenon with classical hypothalamic hyperphagia, and thereby bring into focus factors involved in one, or the other, or both syndromes. In particular, we have focused on the role of noradrenergic agonists that produce satiety. Simultaneously, the study of electrically elicited feeding showed us that the same postingestional factors and noradrenergic agonists which control natural food intake have a predictable influence on electrically induced feeding. Thus factors influencing electrically induced behavior have become guideposts in the study of self-stimulation at the same electrodes. Hypothalamic self-stimulation proved to be related to appetite by the same considerations of physiology and pharmacology explored earlier. This led us to look at the factors controlling stimulation-escape, and again the results fit a pattern. From there it was logical to predict comparable findings in the realm of sexual approach and withdrawal. What follows is a review of this analysis, pointing out the various factors that influence hypothalamic feeding mechanisms as seen from our particular vantage point and leading to our current theoretical formulation.

## 1. Hypothalamic Hyperphagia

In the 1961 Nebraska Symposium, Teitelbaum described two syndromes of disturbance in feeding which follow hypothalamic lesions. These have become classic examples of the analysis of brain function through study of behavior changes following experimental brain damage. Without going into details which are reviewed elsewhere (e.g., Teitelbaum, 1967; Grossman, 1968; Stevenson, 1969; Morgane & Jacobs, 1969; Finger & Mook, 1971; Hoebel, 1971; and in particular, Epstein, 1971) lateral hypothalamic lesions cause a loss of appetite with accompanying symptoms ranging from initial hypokinesis, sensory neglect, and abhorrence for all but the best-tasting food, to a permanent loss of drinking in the face of osmotic challenge and loss of feeding response in the face of dangerously low blood sugar. This collage of symptoms is properly called a syndrome. It is a syndrome not only because the symptoms occur together, but because they recover in a sequence that is always the same (Teitelbaum, 1961). Moreover, they can be produced by chemically induced lesions as well as the classical techniques (Fibiger, Zis, & McGeer, 1973; Zigmond & Striker, 1973; Myers & Martin, 1973; Marshall & Teitelbaum, 1973). Thus there must be underlying causes which unify the various symptoms in this syndrome of self-starvation. One which relates particularly to the theme of this paper is the role of taste in generating approach or withdrawal. Ellison (1968) observed that lateral-lesioned rats actively reject food placed in the mouth; but if their ventromedial hypothalamus is included in an island of deactivated brain tissue, the starving rats will passively accept and swallow food. Approach and withdrawal on the basis of taste apparently depends on the balance of activity in lateral and medial hypothalamic tissue.

Damage to the medial hypothalamic region alone causes a syndrome marked by overeating and may also cause hyperreactivity to taste. Under certain circumstances both types of finicky eaters will partake of only palatable food, spurning any diet that is even slightly bitter, salty, diluted, or stale. Teitelbaum (1961) reviewed the evidence that these two syndromes reflect a change in feeding that cannot be explained solely as deficits in simple reflexes. The lateral-lesioned rat fails to eat when it could and normally would; the ventromedial rat overeats even if an instrumental response is required for the food. This suggested that complex feeding responses are controlled in part by a dual hypothalamic system in which the lateral hypothalamus elicits feeding and the ventromedial hypothalamus inhibits it. We in this laboratory have been concerned with the ventromedial hypothalamic syndrome, seeking to find and dissect out the underlying factors which make it up.

*Weight control.* According to the original reports, ventromedial lesions disinhibit feeding, and the emphasis was on "hypothalamic hyperphagia," implying that the primary effect of the lesion was hyperphagia, which leads secondarily to obesity (Brobeck, Tepperman, & Long, 1943).

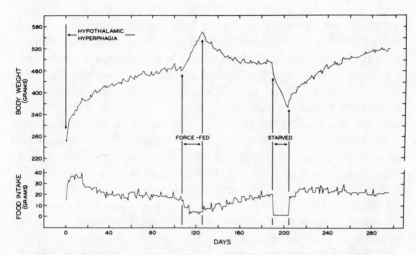

FIG. 1. Ventromedial hypothalamic lesions (at left) cause hyperphagia (bottom curve) leading to obesity (top curve). The rat maintains this new obese weight level in spite of force feeding or starvation. (From Hoebel & Teitelbaum, 1966.)

We knew, however, that normal rats regulate their food intake in accordance with their body weight. Rats made to overeat by daily injections of long-acting insulin became obese and subseqently ate less than normal. When insulin treatment stopped, they remained anorectic until body weight declined (Hoebel & Teitelbaum, 1966).

Teitelbaum suggested that rats suffering from hypothalamic hyperphagia might similarly regulate their eating to maintain an obese body weight. We found this true. If the animals were made sufficiently obese prior to the ventromedial lesions, they failed to become hyperphagic, but instead ate just enough to remain at the obese level. Likewise, ventromedial-lesioned rats allowed to become obese and then force fed to superobesity actually curbed their intake until their body weight fell to the preferred obese plateau. Thus the term *hypothalamic hyperphagia* could be misleading. The lesion causes a shift in the level of weight control (Hoebel & Teitelbaum, 1966), not necessarily hyperphagia. The weight of these brain-damaged animals is abnormal, but their food intake may be normal.

When I made successive lesions it was clear that one could produce a plateau at higher and higher levels as one destroyed more and more tissue. If at any time the rat was starved back down to a normal body weight, then allowed to eat freely again, it would go through another phase of overeating and its body weight would go up about to where it had been before (Hoebel, 1969). Apparently the weight plateau depends on how much of the hypothalamus is destroyed. Gold (1973) has recently collected the histology to show this. Although massive damage is sufficient for maximal obesity, it is not a necessary condition. Razor-thin knife cuts will do the same thing if they are in the right place (Sclafani & Grossman, 1969; Gold, 1970).

We concluded that some stimulus correlated with obesity controls food intake. After ventromedial damage, a higher weight level is required to inhibit feeding by activating the remaining tissue (Hoebel & Teitelbaum, 1966). The term *weight regulation* is often used, although it is understood that weight is controlled indirectly, not regulated. The actual stimulus that is regulated must be some correlate of body weight.

Other researchers have extended the weight-regulation idea in new directions; I will mention four of them. Powley and Keesey (1970) demonstrated that weight regulation at subnormal levels is an element in the lateral hypothalamic syndrome; thus lateral lesions do not necessarily cause anorexia any more than medial lesions necessarily cause hyperphagia. Body weight is critical.

Nisbett (1972) has pointed out that many "overweight" people may actually be underweight relative to their own preferential weight level. He suggests that some of their personality characteristics relate therefore to being underweight, not overweight as Schacter (1971) had proposed. The issue of personality changes in relation to weight is still an open and exciting question, but in any case we would suggest from the rat data that people who are overweight according to insurance company statistics might be expected to display some characteristics of underweight if they are below their hypothalamically determined preferred weight. In particular they would be expected to overeat even though somewhat fat already.

Le Magnen and his coworkers (1973) suggested that our findings corroborate their evidence of a lipostatic mechanism which they find operative within a diurnal cycle. The breakdown of fat occurs during the animal's sleep period and inhibits feeding. Lipogenesis, on the other hand, occurs during the animal's waking period when most eating occurs.

As a result of studies which emphasize weight control, it is now common to refer to the "set-point" at which an animal maintains its weight. Ventromedial lesions shift the set-point upwards, lateral lesions shift it downwards. An animal below its set-point eats excessively; an animal above it is anorectic. Sclafani and Kluge (1974) suggest that rats with ventromedial lesions control their "appetite" at a new higher weight set-point, but that "hunger" induced through food deprivation has another set-point which is unaffected by the lesion. Thus they propose not one, but two, lipstatic set-points.

*The irritation question.* Not everyone agreed with the basic premise for this work. Reynolds (1963) and later Rabin and Smith (1968) reported failure to obtain obesity following ventromedial hypothalamic electrocauterization by radio frequency current. They proposed that electrocauterization avoided electrolytic deposition of iron from the electrode and thereby avoided irritation to the nearby lateral hypothalamic feeding system. Lateral irritation might elicit hyperphagia. Although this finding was indeed a fair warning against the use of steel electrodes, it seemed an unlikely explanation for classical hypothalamic obesity because hyperphagia could be produced in other ways. For example, temporary hyperphagia resulted from ventromedial procaine injections (Epstein, 1960; Hoebel, 1968). My attempts to confirm Reynold's finding failed when we made radio frequency lesions through platinum iridium electrodes in female rats (Hoebel, 1965). They became obese. I have reviewed elsewhere the several lines of research which were spurred by this controversy (Hoebel, 1971). A number of interesting factors were discovered. Each was important in its own right and led to further series of experiments, but none of them explained away hypothalamic obesity.

Ventromedial-lesioned rats show a tremendous burst of continuous eating immediately after the lesion is made and then settle down to a pattern of big meals (Teitelbaum & Campbell, 1958; Balagura & Davenport, 1970; Le Magnen, 1971; Becker & Kissileff, 1974). This is so large an effect that we routinely remove food for 24 hours after the lesion so the rat cannot eat to the point of suffocation and death. Harrell and Remley (1973) have revived the irritation hypothesis to explain this initial burst of uncontrolled eating. They point to extreme hyperactivity, hyperreactivity and hyperglycemia in the first few postlesion hours as evidence for lateral hypothalamic excitation. The hyperglycemia may be secondary to overeating; but in general this interpretation makes good sense, particularly when the lesions are designed to cause irritation, as in their study, by the use of stainless steel insect pins for electrodes. It may even be true of any kind of lesion, judging from Wolf and DiCara's (1969) report of local swelling in the hours after a lesion is made. Behavioral evidence for spread of damage following lesions has also been reported (Van Sommers & Teitelbaum, 1974). Whether irritation can explain voracious eating seen within 2 minutes after a platinum electrode lesion (Hoebel, 1965) is not clear. We also do not yet know if the immediate hyperphagia will follow knife cuts or arcuate nucleus lesions which cause long-term hyperphagia and weight gain with minimal lateral hypothalamic impingement.

In summary, irritation to a feeding system may augment hyperphagia, particularly postsurgical gluttony, but irritation does not account for longer-term hyperphagia leading to obesity.

I hope any neurosurgeon who might happen to read this will make note of these problems in technique, side effects, and variations in the time course of effects which can occur. Platinum-iridium electrodes to avoid iron deposits, electrocauterization to seal blood vessels, or knife cuts that can avoid blood vessels would seem to be indicated in any brain surgery. Hypothalamotomy, however, is completely contraindicated by the rat work because of the frequent multiple effects on feeding, drinking, emotion, various kinds of aggression, mating, and pituitary functions, as will become clear in the remainder of this paper. Our animal studies also involve unreported deaths due to cerebral edema probably associated with ventricular damage, plus an undocumented number of hemorrhages. Anyone who thinks such warnings are unnecessary, as I used to, will find Chorover's (1974) presentations and Valenstein's (1973a) book enlightening. Hopefully the research I am discussing will lead to pharmacological techniques for helping people with diseases involving the hypothalamus, techniques that will at least be reversible.

*Three more facets of the syndrome.* From both the research and the clinical point of view there is a need for new techniques for studying hyperphagia which will not produce so many symptoms at once. In addition to changes in weight control, the three major symptoms of particular concern to our work are as follows: (a) Ventromedial lesions increase positive and negative feeding reactions to good and bad tastes, a reaction called "finickiness." (b) The ventromedial lesions fail to diminish amphetamine-induced anorexia as one might expect from damage to a satiety system (Epstein, 1959). Instead, it is the lateral hypothalamic lesions that interfere with amphetamine anorexia (Carlisle, 1964). (c) Ventromedial-lesioned rats display metabolic anomalies. They engage in lipogenesis in the day as well as all night (Le Magnen, et al., 1973). They also gain slightly more weight than normals on the same amount of food (Han, 1968). One might suspect pituitary involvement in the lesion effects. However, Friedman (1972), working in this laboratory, has shown that insulin release after the lesions does not account for the hyperphagia, and hypophysectomy does not block hyperphagia or obesity (Hetherington, 1941; Cox, Kakolewski, & Valenstein, 1968); therefore, the main aspects of the syndrome are not primarily due to damage to the hypothalamic-pituitary system. In fact, early workers could find no evidence of metabolic disruption at all (Brobeck, Tepperman, & Long, 1943; Brooks, 1946), which suggests that metabolic changes observed recently may be secondary to changes in meal pattern or diurnal rhythms which could cause different researchers to get different results depending on the feeding schedule and sampling time.

Our studies of each of these three issues will be discussed in turn. First, the abnormalities in taste reaction suggested that further study might help us in our efforts to understand the neural substrates that control approach and withdrawal in feeding behavior. Second, the paradoxical amphetamine story suggested that a pharmacological and neurochemical approach to the brain would be necessary to unravel the satiety mechanisms. Third, the metabolic anomalies pointed to the need for a physiological analysis of satiety deficits. In particular, Le Magnen's new findings offer renewed hope that analysis of hyperphagia might clarify the role of the hypothalamus in controlling or responding to metabolic signals.

*Taste finickiness: A separable factor.* Everyone would agree that the taste of food influences how much we eat, and that over the long term, food palatability can influence body weight. In animal experiments, normal animals eating a bad-tasting diet lose some weight, but on a highly palatable diet they eat excessively and become heavier (Corbit & Stellar, 1964). This effect is magnified in the ventromedial-lesioned rats. They are unusually finicky about their food (Teitelbaum, 1955). A finicky eater is one that increases its intake of a sweet diet more than a normal animal would and decreases intake of a bitter diet more than normal. In short, it overreacts to taste.

Jacobs and Sharma (1969) showed that even normal animals are unusually reactive to food tastes if they are food-deprived. Just as ventromedial hypothalamic lesions make rats eat as if they were underweight, perhaps ventromedial rats are finicky partly because they are under their preferred weight level. But there must be more to finickiness than this, because Teitelbaum (1955) found that ventromedial rats are more measurably finicky when they are close to the static level of obesity than soon after the lesion. A fat lesioned rat may even stop eating rather than eat a diet slightly adulterated with quinine. Therefore, Teitelbaum emphasized that the rats were finicky because they were obese. Recent evidence supports aspects of both views — underweight finickiness, and obesity finickness — by suggesting that finickiness in ventromedial rats is not a unitary phenomenon. Positive overreaction to palatable food is best seen when the rat is tested at normal body weight, i.e., below the preferred weight level; whereas negative overreaction to quinine is manifest when the rat becomes obese. Thus the quality of the finickiness can vary with weight (Sclafani, Springer & Kluge, submitted for publication). In a similar vein, Keesey and Boyle (1973) report that even though rats with small lateral lesions typically show a quinine overreaction at normal weight, they lose the quinine finickiness when tested after they have lost weight to a new, low weight plateau. Thus the two faces of finickiness, overeating good food and undereating bad food, are each influenced by body weight. In addition, some lesions may accentuate one or both aspects of finickiness regardless of body weight; it is difficult to tell from the data available. The simpler question to which we addressed ourselves is whether or not weight regulation and finickiness can be experimentally separated.

Early reports from several laboratories suggested a disassociation of a variety of "motivational" factors from changes in feeding per se. Graff and Stellar (1962) found obesity after ventromedial lesions was not necessary for finickiness to occur. Morgane (1967) suggested that rats starving after lesions in the far-lateral hypothalamus had a lasting feeding regulation problem that transcended transient motivational disorders. Ellison (1968) combined both medial and lateral lesions using a hypothalamic island procedure. Like Morgane, Ellison found rats could be made extremely aphagic; however, those animals with medial hypothalamic isolation as well as lateral damage were not finicky. They would passively swallow food put on the tongue, food that a lateral-lesioned rat would vigorously reject if its ventromedial region were intact. All of these lesion studies pointed to the possibility of separable neuroanatomical substrates for feeding and for taste hyperreaction.

In my laboratory, Bevan (1973) has confirmed and extended Graff and Stellar's work and defined a critical area for finickiness as precisely as he could with electrolytic lesions. The lesions were below the fornix about midway between the usual medial and lateral hypothalamic lesion sites. These rats displayed overreaction to adulteration of powdered chow with sugar or quinine. They also performed subnormally on a variable interval (VI-60) schedule and on a progressive, fixed-ratio schedule of pellet reinforcement. In spite of finickiness they did not get fat. However, as Graff and Stellar noted, it is not clear whether such lesions really have no effect on food intake mechanisms or whether they cause equal damage to lateral and medial systems, giving a balanced, net zero effect of feeding and body weight.

We learn more from the rats that become obese without finickiness. Graff and Stellar tended to find this in rats with large lesions of the ventromedial nucleus or posterior hypothalamus. Bevan found it in rats with lesions about the size of the ventromedial nucleus but located on its ventrolateral border. His rats were tested 2 weeks after the operation, before they reached a static weight level. They were fat but did not overreact to sugar or quinine (Bevan, 1973).

To summarize so far, my first point was that food intake depends on body weight in both normal and ventromedial-lesioned rats. Then I made the point that various aspects of finickiness can be observed as a function of body weight in normal rats or ventromedial-lesioned rats, and now I am making the point that finickiness can be disassociated from the overeating and obesity.

Some authors suggest that taste overreaction is one of a constellation of symptoms involving changes in affectiveness (Grossman, 1966), emotionality (Singh, 1973; Wampler, 1973), or general inhibitory functions (Sclafani & Grossman, 1971). It is very difficult to judge how best to classify finickiness when it occurs, because a number of studies have discovered that in addition to body weight the results depend on pretraining (Hamilton & Brobeck, 1964; Singh, 1973; King & Gaston, 1973); deprivation conditions, liquid vs. solid food, test session duration (Beatty, 1973); time of day (Le Magnen, 1971); and reinforcement schedule effects, including reinforcement density, delay, and contrast effects (Falk, 1961; Jaffe, 1973; Kent &

Peters, 1973). Sclafani and Kluge (1974) suggest that their dual lipo-stat model with an upper "appetite" set-point and a lower "hunger" set-point can explain most of these effects. In any case, I suggest that overreaction to food tastes can be anatomically separated from hyperphagia and obesity. Thus, this much of the classical syndrome can be split off for separate study.

In real life, the two symptoms, finickiness and hyperphagia, are often coupled, as in diabetic or infant rats. Diabetic rats eat tremendous amounts, probably for lack of insulin to transport satiety signals into satiety receptors. They never get fat, because without insulin they can not store fat. Hernandez and Briese (1972) discovered they are also hyperreactive to food tastes. Thus, they are hyperphagic, underweight, and finicky. Hernandez and Briese refer to them as animals with "functional lesions" of the ven-tromedial hypothalamus. In immature rats one may see the same thing. The ventromedial satiety system is blocked, this time possibly by growth hormone, and the young animal is both hyperphagic and finicky (Teitelbaum, Cheng, & Rozin, 1969; Kurtz, Rozin, & Teitelbaum, 1972). Hyperphagia and hyperreaction to food taste seem to go together so often that I would be hesitant to claim a sepa-rate system for inhibition and disinhibition of feeding, per se, if we did not have further evidence from the neurochemical studies to follow.

*Amphetamine action and new approaches to the neurochemistry of satiety.* An electrode which makes an indiscriminate hole in the brain is very likely to produce some symptoms which reflect damage to very disparate, perhaps unrelated neural systems. This may be a good thing if one is trying to duplicate the effects of tumor damage, but for research and therapeutic aims one would prefer a lesion that is selective along lines of brain circuitry. The neurochemical and pharmacological approaches based on chemical differences among neural systems offer this advantage. In our efforts to analyze lesion-induced hyperphagia and the underlying satiety systems, we turned first to chemical-induced satiety and the well-known appetite-suppressant drug amphetamine.

Amphetamine is a mixed blessing, as anyone who has used it in research knows. Recently, however, its multiple effects on the brain have begun to be deciphered and a fascinating, clinically im-portant picture is emerging. Amphetamine would be expected to act at synapses, whereas lesions destroy both axons and synapses; thus differences with the two tools are to be expected. Nevertheless, it came as a surprise and paradox that amphetamine-induced satiety is augmented by ventromedial lesions (Stowe & Miller, 1957; Epstein, 1959) and blocked by lesions in the lateral feeding region (Carlisle, 1964; Fibiger, Zis & McGeer, 1973). This suggested that a satiety pathway enters the lateral hypothalamus, where its neurons must intermix or synapse with the feeding system. Amphetamine is thought to act at synapses indirectly through endogenous stores of cathecholamine neurotransmitters, norepinephrine and dopamine (Taylor & Snyder, 1970). This is confirmed by the observation that blocking catecholamine synthesis antagonizes amphetamine anorexia (Weissman, Koe, & Tenen, 1966; Glowinski, Axelrod, & Iversen, 1966). Therefore, this amphetamine-sensitive satiety system which is dependent on lateral hypothalamic tissue is likely to be noradrenergic or dopaminergic.

The suggestion that norepinephrine might be involved in satiety ran counter to the pioneering studies with intrahypothalamic injection from Miller's laboratory in which Grossman (1960) and later Booth (1967) and others found that norepinephrine injections produced eating instead of satiety. A similar effect occurred with intraventricular norepinephrine which could cause eating (Myers & Yaksh, 1968) and rapid recovery of feeding after lateral hypothalamic lesions (Berger, Wise, & Stein, 1971). Booth (1968) got around the problem by suggesting that amphetamine overstimulated the noradrenergic feeding system and thereby depressed it.

Meanwhile, work on drinking from Lehr's laboratory suggested that drugs known to characterize alpha and beta adrenergic receptor types in the peripheral nervous system could distinguish dual receptor types in the brain as well (Lehr, Mallow, & Krukowski, 1967). Using systemic injections of appropriate adrenergic stimulants and blockers, they found evidence for a central satiety mechanism of the beta-adrenergic type. They proposed that alpha and beta receptors play contrasting roles in brain control of food intake (Conte, Lehr, Goldman, & Krukowski, 1968).

However when Margules (1969, 1970) injected alpha and beta drugs into the hypothalamus he discovered not one satiety system, but two. They were the same two we were discussing earlier, inhibition by postingestional factors and inhibition by taste. He reported alpha adrenergic (i.e., noradrenergic) inhibition of milk ingestion and beta adrenergic suppression of feeding by taste factors. Amphetamine, he suggested, acts at the alpha adrenergic satiety synapses.

Leibowitz (1970b) proposed a different resolution to the amphetamine problem. Amphetamine produced feeding when cannulated into the medial hypothalamic region, where she demonstrated an alpha-adrenergic feeding system, whereas amphetamine produced satiety when cannulated into the lateral hypothalamus, where she localized a beta-adrenergic satiety system. The normal neurotransmitter at beta-type synapses is not known.

Some details of the controversy over norepinephrine's role in feeding and/or satiety as of 1971 are described in my review. Since then, Margules and his coworkers (1972) have found that cannulated norepinephrine can have reverse effects within a diurnal cycle. Norepinephrine causes eating during daytime sleeping hours and satiety during the wakeful eating period at night. However, alpha adrenergic blockade with phentolamamine disinhibits feeding day or night, and the rats appear to overeat for both taste and calories (Margules & Dragovich, 1973). This is in direct opposition to the classical noradrenergic feeding effect which Leibowitz (1974) has recently localized in the paraventricular nucleus, using small doses which approach normal concentrations for hypothalamic tissue.

Intrahypothalamic cannulation is clearly a useful tool, but with the present state of the art cannulated norepinephrine is giving too many conflicting results. This calls for a variety of approaches to the problem as stressed by a number of authors (Myers, 1966; Routtenberg, 1972; Booth, 1972; Ahlskog, in press). The problem is to manipulate normal concentrations of norepinephrine at synapses that actually use it for neurotransmission in normal circumstances.

A different approach to the problem is to deplete norepinephrine from its normal stores and see what behavior deficits occur. Recently this has become possible. We find a new obesity syndrome giving evidence of a noradrenergic satiety system.

Studies with fluorescence histochemistry demonstrated that most hypothalamic noradrenergic terminals derive from cells in the hind brain (Anden, Dahlstrom, Fuxe, Larsson, Olsson, & Ungerstedt, 1966). This is a technique in which sections of brain tissue are viewed microscopically with ultraviolet light, which causes the catecholamines reacted with formaldehyde vapor to fluoresce in beautiful tones of yellow. By examining the brain in serial sections the

Swedish group saw that the norepinephrine-containing axons join to form a ventral bundle which projects to the hypothalamus and basal forebrain. There is also a dorsal noradrenergic bundle arising in the locus coeruleus and passing through the lateral hypothalamus, but it has relatively few synapses and projects onward and upward to the cortex, hippocampus, and other higher forebrain structures.

These facts suggested to Ahlskog, then a graduate student in the laboratory, that the ventral noradrenergic bundle might serve as the substrate for amphetamine-induced anorexia and might be important in the regulation of food intake. If so, selective destruction of this nerve bundle should produce overeating leading to obesity, and amphetamine should lose its effectiveness as an anorectic. This idea was generated by the work of Ungerstedt (1971b), who used the fluorescence histochemistry technique to chart dopamine and noradrenergic pathways, and then used a selective neurotoxin, 6-hydroxydopamine to destroy the dopamine pathway. The result was aphagia (Ungerstedt, 1971a). However, behavioral functions of the noradrenergic pathways were still unknown.

We have used 6-hydroxydopamine to destroy the noradrenergic pathways. The result of ventral noradrenergic bundle lesions was hyperphagia and obesity (Ahlskog & Hoebel, 1972, 1973). This new syndrome has important differences from the old. As a preview, these rats are not as fat, not hyperreactive to food tastes, and are subnormally responsive to amphetamine and dependent on the pituitary to manifest hyperphagia and obesity.

*Hyperphagia from noradrenergic depletion.* Ahlskog perfected the stereotaxic placement of cannulas so as to inject 6-hydroxydopamine into the noradrenergic bundles while sparing the dopaminergic nigrostriatal tract. The neurotoxin must be injected in the midbrain tegmentum posterior to the substantia nigra. He could destroy the dorsal bundle alone or both dorsal and ventral bundles, depending on cannula depth. To hit the ventral bundle alone, electrolytic lesions were used.

Fluorescence histochemical analysis comparing normal and lesioned rats showed that loss of noradrenaline in the ventral bundle, not the dorsal bundle, was necessary for hyperphagia. The control rats and rats pretreated with desmethylimipramine (DMI) to block uptake of the neurotoxin failed to show norepinephrine depletion and failed to show hyperphagia (Ahlskog & Hoebel, 1973).

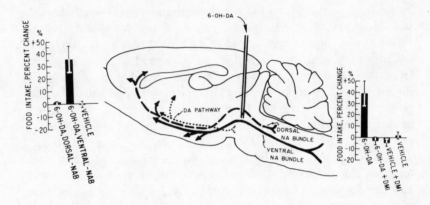

FIG. 2. (a) The selective neurotoxin 6-hydroxydopamine (6-OH-DA) depleted the brain of norepinephrine and caused hyperphagia as shown at the left, but only when injected into the ventral, not dorsal, noradrenergic bundle. (b) Side view of the brain showing the ventral and dorsal noradrenergic (NA) bundles and the dopamine (DA) nigrostriatal pathway. (After Ungerstedt, 1971b.) (c) Hyperphagia is prevented by pretreatment with the noradrenergic uptake blocker desmethylimipramine (DMI), which protects the ventral noradrenergic bundle from 6-hydroxydopamine. (From Ahlskog & Hoebel, 1973, and Ahlskog, submitted.)

Dopamine fluorescence was normal in the striatum of all animals. Assays of diencephalic-telencephalic dopamine and serotonin verified normal levels of these neurotransmitters in the hyperphagic rats; whereas assays revealed that norepinephrine was reduced to 15% of normal or less.

Our results are very much in keeping with earlier norepinephrine satiety theories (Margules, 1970). The results make it very unlikely that norepinephrine elicits feeding directly, because if it did our norepinephrine-depleted rats would have starved. However, recent norepinephrine feeding theories suggest that norepinephrine causes eating by inhibiting a satiety system (Leibowitz, 1970a; Herberg & Franklin, 1972). This indirect effect is not ruled out by our results; if we depleted a major satiety system as well as a feeding disinhibitory system, the loss of satiety could predominate.

We conclude from observing hyperphagia and obesity that when this neural system is intact, it functions in part to produce satiety. The logic is the same as applied to classic ventromedial hypothalamic lesions. Loss of neural function disinhibits feeding. But with this new technique, we can go much further and conclude that the neural path involved in this case is the ventral noradrenergic bundle with its known cell bodies of origin, known trajectory, and known neurotransmitter.

*New and old hyperphagia syndromes contrasted.* Earlier I emphasized three facets of classical hyperphagia: finickiness, amphetamine actions, and the noneffect of hypophysectomy even though there are metabolic changes following ventromedial lesions. A similar analysis of the new hyperphagia reveals interesting differences in all three respects. For this discussion the term *ventromedial hypothalamus* will be abbreviated to VMH and *ventral noradrenergic bundle* as VNAB.

Although fat, the VNAB chemically-lesioned rats were not finicky. Tests of food consumption when moderately obese, using a high-fat diet laced with quinine or saccharine, gave results indistinguishable from those obtained with normal rats. Adjustment to the high calorie diet was also normal, even though it took an unusually long time (Ahlskog, 1973). Additional tests with standard diets are called for, but the data so far substantiate the earlier argument that a satiety system can be isolated from the nerves involved with taste overreaction. It is logical to surmise that in Graff and Stellar's rats and Bevan's rats, lesions which caused VMH hyperphagia without finickiness avoided some of the neural structures for taste hyperreaction that we avoided with neurochemically specific lesions.

Amphetamine lost about half of its potency in 6-hydroxydopamine-treated, norepinephrine-depleted animals. This was with a 4-hr. daily feeding schedule which gave similar food intake baselines for the experimental and control groups. Therefore, the noradrenergic satiety system is one of the substrates for amphetamine anorexia (Ahlskog & Hoebel, 1973; Ahlskog, in press). This helps explain why lateral hypothalamic lesions which probably damage this pathway caused a similar loss of amphetamine potency.

Gold (1973) has suggested that hyperphagia following knife cuts is tantamount to VMH hyperphagia, that his knife cuts interrupt the VNAB, and therefore VMH hyperphagia may be largely attributed to VNAB damage. To the contrary, our evidence so far emphasizes that hyperphagia following VMH lesion and VNAB depletion are different. Notably, total hypophysectomy eliminated VNAB hyperphagia (Ahlskog, Hoebel, & Breisch, 1974). Apparently, pituitary function is necessary for the VNAB effect but not the VMH effect. In addition, the VNAB rats, although significantly hyperphagic and obese, do not on the average show as great an effect as seen with VMH lesions. Thus the classical VMH syndrome may in part be brought about by VNAB destruction, but there is more involved here than we can explain on the basis of VNAB depletion with 6-hydroxydopamine.

In summary, we now have a new tool for selectively destroying one or both noradrenergic bundles, a new hyperphagia syndrome to analyze, and an opportunity to extend knowledge of the neuroanatomy and neurochemistry of satiety. Where the classical lesion techniques showed what would happen when a hole is made in the ventromedial hypothalamus, the new neurochemical techniques show what happens when one depletes a given pathway of known origin, known destination, and known neurotransmitter. The conclusions, albeit tentative at this early date, are (a) that a function of the VNAB is to inhibit feeding, (b) that norepinephrine is the neurotransmitter that exerts this inhibition, (c) that amphetamine's ability to suppress appetite is partly due to the facilitation of this noradrenergic function, and (d) that the pituitary is somehow directly or indirectly an important intermediary in this satiety system. This noradrenergic satiety system passes into and through the lateral hypothalamus with projections into the medial region. Damage to this system by electrolytic lesions may account for (a) some part of the classical ventromedial "hypothalamic hyperphagia" syndrome, (b) the lateral hypothalamic loss-of-amphetamine-anorexia effect, and (c) perhaps some of the metabolic disorders that have been noted. With regard to finickiness or excessive affective responses, we have no evidence yet to suggest that this pathway is involved in either positive or negative overreactions to taste. As far as we have been able to see to date, destruction of this path simply makes rats eat more and put on weight. The fact that our VNAB-depleted rats are less hyperphagic and less obese than rats with classical VMH lesions or knife cuts could be due to a number of factors; for example, (a) 6-hydroxydopamine lesions may be less effective than VMH lesions or knife cuts in depleting norepinephrine in the projection areas critical for satiety, (b) VMH lesions may destroy additional and/or different satiety systems, (c) taste overreaction after VMH lesions may cause some of the added hyperphagia and obesity, and (d) VNAB lesions may cause pituitary-linked abnormalities that affect hyperphagia. The point is that we have a new hyperphagia syndrome. It may account for part of the classical one, but there are differences. With luck the differences will soon tell us more about brain organization of satiety mechanisms.

*Hyperphagia associated with serotonin depletion.* Parachlorphenylalanine (PCPA) injected into the ventricle of rats caused hyperphagia (Breisch & Hoebel, in preparation). This new discovery hinged on the use of intraventricular instead of intraperitoneal (i.p.) injections. Earlier studies using i.p. injection showed either no effect (Sheard, 1969), a decrease in food intake (Funderburk, Hazelwood, Ruckart, & Ward, 1971), or a very slight hyperphagia (Mouret, Bobillier, & Jouvet, 1968).

PCPA depletes serotonin although the time course of this effect and various side effects is complicated. Another problem with i.p. injections is the depletion of serotonin in blood and peripheral organs (Koe & Weisman, 1966) which could easily make the animal too sick to show any increase in behavior. Similarly a negative result after depletion of brain serotonin by reticular formation lesions (Samanin, Ghezzi, Valzelli, & Garattini, 1972) tells us what is happening to serotonin, but not what serotonin does for behavior. However, the appetite-suppressant property of fenfluramine, which has as one of its effects a serotonergic action, suggested that serotonin depletion might increase feeding behavior.

To deplete brain serotonin without peripheral depletion, Breisch injected the PCPA intraventricularly. To take advantage of the reported time course of PCPA action in interpreting the results, food intake was measured daily for $2\frac{1}{2}$ weeks. Brody (1970) reported that behavior changes could be correlated with known neurochemical changes after PCPA. Maximal serotonin depletion occurred 3 days after PCPA administration when PCPA itself and phenylalanine had largely been cleared from the system and norepinephrine levels were normal. There are all the usual problems in interpretation stemming from imcomplete depletion, supersensitivity, and possible lack of specificity, but when we leaped into the fray and used intraventricular injections, hyperphagia turned up in 19 out of 19 rats. Overeating began on the second day, reached a maximum on the fourth day, and gradually returned to normal in about 2 weeks. There was an increase in tilt-cage activity, but it began sooner than hyperphagia and did not last as long. Injection of 5-HTP, the precursor of serotonin, to bypass the synthesis block on the second day after PCPA caused the predicted behavior change. Hyperphagia was mitigated.

Tests of amphetamine anorexia in PCPA-treated hyperphagic rats are very interesting in the light of the early discussion of norepinephrine-depleted hyperphagics. Recall that classical ventromedial-lesioned (VMH) rats respond normally to amphetamine by curbing their food intake, but norepinephrine-depleted (VNAB) rats do not. The third and newest type of hyperphagia is like classical VMH hyperphagia. Amphetamine retained its potency in PCPA hyperphagic rats.

It may be that VMH lesions cause hyperphagia which is a combination of norepinephrine and serotonin depletion effects. At least we would not want to attribute hypothalamic hyperphagia entirely to one or the other until more is known. In particular we are not yet confident that PCPA acts by way of serotonin, but at least PCPA hyperphagia appears different from VNAB hyperphagia.

We turn now to the effects of hypothalamic stimulation. Instead of disinhibiting feeding, we will elicit it. The goal is to bring feeding under direct experimental control and then to study self-stimulation and stimulation escape with the same electrodes and the same experimental manipulations. Instead of making a lesion and seeing long-term changes in feeding, we will see feeding and associated neural reinforcement controlled from moment to moment in a rat with an intact brain.

## 2. Electrically Induced Feeding

*Elicited behaviors.* It is often found that a single electrode will both induce behavior such as feeding and also support self-stimulation. I suspected that electrically elicited behavior might be a clue to which electrodes would give self-stimulation related to a particular behavior. For example, electrically induced feeding suggested that self-stimulation at that electrode might be related to feeding. This was later substantiated. In the hope of finding electrode sites related to other behaviors, we searched for and found electrically elicited copulation in the posterior hypothalamus (Caggiula & Hoebel, 1966), including elicited bar pressing for the opportunity to copulate (Caggiula, 1967); electrically elicited wheel running (Rosenquist & Hoebel, 1968), including elicited bar pressing for the opportunity to run; and electrically elicited mouse killing (King & Hoebel, 1968).

Induced feeding is remarkable to see. I have seen a rat begin sniffing and start eating within seconds of stimulus onset the first time ever stimulated with a given electrode, then stand with one paw on the food cup, dip into the mash with the other forepaw each time the current came on, and when the current went off drop a pawful of food midway to the mouth. It goes without saying that electrically elicited copulation and killing are also dramatic.

In these early studies we assumed that Hess's view of elicited behavior was correct. He suggested that specific behavioral functions are correlated with circumscribed regions of the diencephalon, but with a good deal of overlapping and intermingling (Hess, 1957). Elicited behavior was like normal behavior. For example, Miller (1958) and his coworkers found that electrically induced eating had properties of normal eating, including sensitivity to bitter (Tenen & Miller, 1964) and sweet tastes (Chisholm & Trowill, 1972). Steinbaum and Miller (1965) reported that prolonged hours of lateral hypothalamic stimulation could cause enough eating to induce obesity. This was confirmed as part of one of our experiments in which rats self-stimulated most of the day with a lever which also delivered food pellets. The result was self-induced hyperphagia leading to obesity (Hoebel & Thompson, 1969).

*Emergence of new behaviors.* Studies by Valenstein, Cox, and Kakolewski (1969) showed that elicited eating can shift to include elicited drinking or gnawing when the food is removed and stimulation continued. Perhaps the most surprising instance was a rat that ate pellets when stimulated, but then switched to another behavior rather than eat the same food ground to a powder. This led Valenstein to question the idea that elicited eating reflected normal hunger; he suggested it can be understood better in the context of learning and a behavior prepotency hypothesis (Valenstein, 1973b). Roberts (1969), on the basis of his work with the opossum, advocates systems with overlapping anatomy that may be nonspecific at some levels and specific at others. The problem becomes one of finding the anatomical, physiological, and pharmacological conditions of specificity and nonspecificity.

*Stabilization of elicited feeding and drinking.* When Milgram was in my laboratory as a postdoctoral fellow, he and two other students confirmed and extended Valenstein's findings. They found that rats would shift from eating to drinking spontaneously, that is, without removal of the food. The relative amount of elicited eating and drinking in any given test then stabilized so that they were the same from day to day (Milgram, Devor, & Server, 1971). This was interesting, but particularly valuable to us because it gave us rats with a stable baseline of elicited eating and drinking on which we could measure the effects of food and water intake.

*Selective physiological inhibition.* Even though more than one behavior could be elicited from a given electrode, it seemed reasonable that the behaviors would still be under normal physiological control, as I had seen for self-stimulation. To test this idea, we teamed up with Wise, in Canada, who was planning similar experiments. The question was whether or not the postingestional factors associated with food intake would exert inhibition over elicited feeding without curbing drinking too. That is what we found. Food in the stomach inhibited the elicited eating component and raised the electrical threshold for eating; water ingestion inhibited the drinking component and raised the drinking threshold (Devor, Wise, Milgram, & Hoebel, 1970). The results therefore demonstrated appropriate physiological control of elicited feeding and drinking.

*Selective pharmacological inhibition.* Knowing that elicited feeding is under independent inhibitory controls, it follows that drugs which specifically block free feeding should also specifically block electrically elicited feeding. It should be possible to identify and separate the underlying mechanisms for elicited behaviors according to their pharmacology.

Amphetamine is the best-known appetite suppressant and as such it should block elicited feeding. This was found by Miller and Coons (Miller, 1960) and Stark and Totty (1967). On the other hand, amphetamine is also a stimulant and tends to augment any behavior.

To avoid this problem we tested phenylpropanolamine (propadrine). This is the same molecule as amphetamine but with a hydroxyl group on the beta carbon atom. It is a very mild stimulant, as shown by lack of EEG activation and relative lack of efficacy in keeping people awake (Goodman & Gilman, 1965). Epstein (1959) found that phenylpropanolamine curbs food intake in rats without overt signs of a change in activity level.

Phenylpropanolamine suppressed elicited eating without suppressing elicited drinking (Hoebel, 1971). Evidently, elicited feeding and elicited drinking have pharmacologically separable substrates at some level in the brain.

Evidence for separate substrates at the hypothalamic level comes from three sources. First, pure feeding or drinking responses can sometimes be elicited by unusually small diameter electrodes (Huang & Mogenson, 1972). Second, in some cases different stimulation frequencies elicit different behaviors from the same electrode (Mogenson, Gentil, & Stevenson, 1971; Hess, 1957). Third, cannula-injected drugs can induce feeding without drinking and vice versa (Grossman, 1960; Leibowitz, 1970; Margules & Dragovich, 1973; Fisher, 1969).

Within the realm of feeding itself, it is possible to have selective inhibition. Wise and Albin (1973) demonstrated that electrically induced feeding reflected normal food preferences established by prior learned-aversion training in which the taste of a certain food was paired with gastric illness. Stimulated rats ate regular food but not the food that had been associated with illness. Apparently, elicited feeding behavior is capable of reflecting much of the exquisite finickiness of a rat's normal feeding habits. This is evidence par excellence for Valenstein's (1973) view that environmental conditions are sometimes implicated in the association of hypothalamic stimulation with a particular behavior. Valenstein's other main point, that elicited feeding does not generalize along a dimension expected of hunger, is not a problem if we assume that elicited eating reflects all aspects of normal eating as opposed to reflecting deprivation-induced hunger. Rats and other animals eat in response to many kinds of stimuli. The learned-aversion experiment is an example of taste stimuli taking priority over deprivation-induced stimuli. In short, hypothalamic-elicited feeding reflects taste factors as well as deprivation. Thus we are proceeding on the assumption that elicited feeding behavior reflects a rat's normal feeding habits, and that the underlying systems are separable, and in that sense specific.

At the same time, it has become clear that lateral hypothalamic stimulation can be expected to activate a variety of behaviors in addition to feeding. Our neurochemical studies indicate that electrodes in the lateral hypothalamus near the ventral noradrenergic bundle can also be expected to induce satiety. Feeding predominates, but sensitive tests should reveal satiety as well. Peripheral sensory systems will also be excited, for example the systems for mouth and face sensitivity shown to exist in the lateral hypothalamus by stimulation experiments in the cat (MacDonnell & Flynn, 1966) and by lesion experiments in the rat (Marshall, Turner, & Teitelbaum, 1971). Lateral hypothalamic stimulation would also, depending on exact electrode placement, activate the nigrostriatal dopamine pathway and the sub fornix nerves we said were involved in lesion-produced finickiness. The list of other paths of unknown function which pass through this region is extensive (Morgane, 1961). A variety of depleters, blockers, and lesions combined with lateral hypothalamic stimulation will have to be used before being able to understand which substrates are necessary for eliciting or inhibiting eating, or for controlling the many other behaviors we have seen. That we have been able to make progress using gross electrical stimulation testifies to the brain's ability to channel or funnel the effects of vague stimulation into sharper signals leading to surprisingly discrete responses. Teitelbaum (1974) reminds us that this is standard operating procedure for sensory systems according to the principles laid out by Bekesy (1967).

The main point of our current studies is that the feeding induced by stimulation is under normal physiological and pharmacological control. For this conclusion it does not matter that the electrode induces more than one behavior; in fact, it gives us a built-in control to see one behavior changing and not the other. The interesting fact is that when induced feeding was inhibited, it occurred predictably and selectively.

*Nonspecific arousal.* Stimulation of the lateral hypothalamus makes a rat active. We measured electrically induced arousal as increased tilt-cage activity in experiments that also revealed stimulation-induced wheel running (Rosenquist & Hoebel, 1968). Wise and Erdmann (1973) and Wise (1974) suggest that induced arousal involving emotionality can sometimes account for differences in electrically induced feeding and deprivation-induced feeding. Valenstein (1973b) suggests that elicited object-carrying in a shuttle box is due to arousal in the neighborhood of the objects coupled with current off-go and calming where the objects are deposited. Similarly, Mendelson (1972) suggests that rats carry objects because it can be calming. The neural recording studies of Rolls and Kelly (1972) point to lateral hypothalamic involvement in a reticular arousal system, and Gallistel (1973) reviews evidence that a hypothalamic system distinguished by its neural refractory period and temporal decay properties serves a nonspecific arousal, or "priming," function. All the above measures of "arousal" are probably not actually measuring the same thing, but there is no question that some kind of arousal plays an important role in what we see during lateral hypothalamic stimulation.

On the other hand, Campbell and Baez (in press) have shown a disassociation of arousal and regulatory behaviors after lateral hypothalamic lesions. Amphetamine still caused arousal, although it no longer suppressed feeding. Our studies suggest that general arousal cannot account for control systems that govern hypothalamically elicited behaviors such as feeding and drinking. We have shown that elicited feeding and elicited drinking are separable functions. As long as elicited feeding reflects normal food intake, as we have shown, then I suspect we are still on a path to understanding the mechanism that the animal's brain actually uses to start and stop feeding in the control of energy balance.

*Summary.* It is interesting that the conclusion to this section bears similarities to the conclusion to our earlier discussion of hypothalamic hyperphagia. In both hyperphagia from medial lesions and hyperphagia from lateral stimulation, we have eliminated anomalous results and sidestepped theories based on all-encompassing emotion or motivational changes by using procedures designed to avoid or control for overall arousal. This is not meant to minimize the great importance of arousal in feeding, but to try to see the changes in feeding that can occur without dependence on arousal level.

On the basis of evidence cited in the first two sections a list of the functions that have been dissected apart includes the following: (1) A feeding function that is inhibited by postingestional factors and correlates of body weight acting in part via the ventromedial hypothalamus, and also inhibited by the ventral noradrenergic bundle. We can guess that this might be the same feeding function that is activated by lateral hypothalamic stimulation, because it, too, is inhibited by food intake and by a putative noradrenergic agonist, phenylpropanolamine. (2) A taste hyperreactivity function that may also be influenced by food intake and body weight that involves hypothalamic tissue below the fornix and apparently does not involve the ventral noradrenergic bundle. (3) A separable drinking function. (4) An activity function involving the lateral hypothalamus and manifest as wheel running. (5) A general arousal function for which lateral hypothalamic stimulation is sufficient but not necessary. One aspect of arousal is possibly related to "emotionality," that is, behavior which is diminished by practice, familiarity, or a minor tranquilizer. Item 2, taste hyperreactivity, may fall into this class.

These are not functions suggested by a theory of behavior. They simply try to summarize the recurring themes in the empirical results that have been discussed above in the context of lesion-induced feeding and stimulation-induced feeding. Item 1, the feeding response, is the core of our problem. Items 2-5 are related phenomena that may occur in connection with hypothalamic manipulations of feeding but that can be studied separately.

The final series of experiments relates self-stimulation and stimulation escape to the basic feeding responses. The other factors will enter into the results, but having found out how to isolate them or eliminate them, it should be possible to examine self-stimulation in relation to feeding, pure and simple.

3. Self-Stimulation and Stimulation-Escape

Research using the technique of brain stimulation through implanted electrodes was given impetus in a new direction when Olds and Milner (1954) discovered that presentation of the brain stimulus could be a reward which was effectively controlled by the recipient animal itself. Just as an animal can be trained to perform a response for food, so can the animal be trained to respond for brain stimulation. Rats, for example, will press a switch three thousand times an hour for several hours without stopping, if each switch closure triggers electrical stimulation to an appropriate site in the brain.

In contrast to the self-stimulation phenomenon, at some brain regions, often the same ones, stimulation causes an animal to work for termination of the stimulus. Therefore brain stimulation can induce motivation which is positive or negative, i.e., causing the animal to approach the stimulus, escape it, or both (Roberts, 1958; Olds & Olds, 1962; Margules, 1966).

The main thrust of work from this laboratory has been concerned with these systems, inquiring as to their normal function and the means by which they act and are controlled. Specifically, we began by investigating the relation between electrical self-stimulation and feeding behavior.

*Feeding related to self-stimulation.* Electrical stimulation of the lateral hypothalamus induced rats to eat. Then self-stimulation was obtained from the same electrodes without changing the current intensity. This could have been a coincidence, just two unrelated systems both lying near the electrode. Or the elicited feeding could be a clue as the natural role of the self-stimulation mechanism.

Electrolytic lesions through the self-stimulation electrodes caused starvation, and subsequent stimulation elicited the first eating and drinking during recovery. This again tentatively suggested that the self-stimulation might be involved in feeding. If so, the systems which inhibit feeding should also inhibit self-stimulation.

To investigate the possibility that the ventromedial hypothalamus inhibits self-stimulation, it was necessary to devise a method for controlling the activity of the medial and lateral hypothalamus simultaneously and bilaterally in a given rat. This was done by means of four insulated platinum tubes which served as either electrodes or cannulas for electrical or chemical treatments of each hypothalamic site. Solid electrodes were made from platinum-iridium wire (Hoebel, 1964). The current we use is a 100 Hz, monophasic pulse passed through an isolation transformer for zero net current flow. Each bar press for self-stimulation delivers a 0.5-sec. non-overlapping train of pulses.

The rate of lateral hypothalamic self-stimulation was decreased by ventromedial stimulation. This suggested that the ventromedial region inhibits self-stimulation; however, the next experiment was necessary to show that the effect was not entirely due to aversive aspects of medial stimulation which might simply disrupt any ongoing behavior.

Electrolytic lesions or local anesthetization of the ventromedial region accelerated self-stimulation. If food was available, the animal began to eat. When Reynolds (1963) questioned the traditional view of a "satiety center" on the grounds that ventromedial hypothalamic lesions made by electrocauterization with radio frequency current often failed to produce obesity in male rats, we repeated the experiment; lesions made with radio frequency current disinhibited not only feeding, but also lateral hypothalamic self-stimulation (Hoebel, 1965). These were all short-run experiments measuring self-stimulation and feeding for a half hour before and after ventromedial suppression. Since deactivation of ventromedial tissue by destruction or anesthetization augmented both feeding and self-stimulation, it was assumed that active ventromedial tissue inhibits both feeding and self-stimulation. However, Ferguson and Keesey 1971) found that the increase in self-stimulation after ventromedial lesions does not last, but instead the self-stimulation rate reverts to a new low level. We have confirmed this and are now testing the effect of lesions which disinhibit feeding without causing damage immediately adjacent to the self-stimulation electrode. PCPA treatment has already been shown to increase self-stimulation (Poschel & Ninteman, 1971), and insulin diabetes increases self-stimulation perhaps by way of the ventromedial hypothalamus, as I will describe further on.

Keesey and Powley (1973) have done a similar experiment but with lateral hypothalamic lesions. Midbrain self-stimulation decreased, and then it partially recovered at the same time the rats reached a low, stable body weight. They suggest that body weight, in combination with other long-term changes, is reflected in the self-stimulation they observed. Another approach, with yet another result, comes from the recent knife cut experiments of Sclafani, Gale, and Maul (submitted for publication). Cuts between the medial and lateral hypothalamus caused hyperphagia and obesity, but self-stimulation neither increased as in the Hoebel and Teitelbaum (1962) study nor decreased as in the Ferguson and Keesey (1971) study.

In each of our earlier experiments, manipulations which were known to have a given effect of feeding were reproduced and shown to have a similar effect on self-stimulation of the lateral hypothalamus, but not all of the parallel effects were sustained over long periods, and all are only correlations. Critical, therefore, are the next experiments performed to see if there is a direct interaction between food intake and self-stimulation.

Food placed directly into the stomach did depress the rate of self-stimulation, so a new question was asked. Which of the various food-related stimuli play a role in the control of self-stimulation? To begin with, three postingestional factors were chosen for test: carbohydrate nutrition, osmotic factors, and gastric distention.

Intragastric injections of glucose or saline inhibited self-stimulation in proportion to their concentration. Equiosmotic glucose and saline had roughly equal inhibitory effects, which could be attributed to either tonicity or gastric distention. 

To analyze this finding, gastric distention was tested alone. A new intragastric balloon was devised for this purpose. The balloon was placed on the end of a nasal-esophageal tube so that no gastric surgery was involved (Hoebel, 1967). This technique eliminated wounds which might be painful when the balloon was inflated. Distention of the stomach depressed self-stimulation. This was shown both by measuring rate of self-stimulation and by a modified, self-selected threshold procedure which controlled for disability. Nevertheless gastric distention alone was not sufficient to account for the effects of glucose or saline, as shown by the next phase of the experiment.

*Osmotic control of self-stimulation.* The same glucose and saline solutions previously tested intragastrically were now injected intravenously. A chronic jugular vein catheter was used to deliver the solution directly to the heart while the rat was pressing a bar for lateral hypothalamic stimulation. With this technique, bypassing the stomach completely, 0.5 cc. of either hypertonic glucose or hypertonic saline depressed self-stimulation. Water accelerated it (Hoebel, 1968). Smith (1966) reported simultaneously that intravenous solutions have similar effects on food intake. Hypertonic solutions cause satiety; water, which dilutes body fluids, causes feeding. Therefore, it was suggested that tonicity may play a major role in the control of lateral hypothalamic self-stimulation and feeding.

Balagura (1968) went on to show a caloric effect independent of osmotic factors by demonstrating that inhibition of self-stimulation after hypertonic saline is reversed by water intake, whereas inhibition of self-stimulation by hypertonic glucose persists long after the rat has satisfied its thirst. Thus the calories in the glucose appeared to inhibit self-stimulation independent of osmotic factors.

*Glucostatic control of self-stimulation.* Mayer (1953) was the main proponent of glucostatic control of feeding, and recently Le Magnen (1971) has made it an integral part of his diurnal lipostatic-glucostatic theory. Almost every researcher in the field has called on this theory in one context or another. My work in this regard began in 1957 with Teitelbaum when we confirmed that repeated injection of long-acting insulin could cause rats to become obese (MacKay, Callaway, & Barnes, 1940; Hoebel & Teitelbaum, 1966). The dose of insulin was critical; I had to keep the rats chronically hypoglycemic without killing them. When this was accomplished they overate. Presumably hyperphagia was the result of low blood sugar, which activated glucoreceptors. Two types of glucoreceptors have been proposed: the ventromedial hypothalamic gluco-satiety receptor which fires when utilization is elevated, and what Epstein (1971) has called the "glucoprivic" receptor in the lateral hypo-thalamus which fires when utilization is low. Oomura (1973) reports recording the activity of both types of receptor cells.

Lateral hypothalamic self-stimulation increased, like feeding, when Balagura and I (1967) injected rats with insulin. Again, dose was critical. Because no food was available, we used very small doses to prevent coma or lethargy, then the self-stimulation increase was seen. Because feeding and self-stimulation covaried and because the complementary hormone, glucagon, had the opposite effect, I interpreted this as support for the feeding-reward theory of lateral hypothalamic self-stimulation.

Hernandez and Briese (1971) used higher doses of insulin and found the opposite result; nevertheless, they also interpreted their result as support for the same theory. They proposed that insulin in their procedure acted not by way of hypoglycemia and low blood sugar utilization, but by increasing the passage of glucose into gluco-satiety receptors and thereby inhibiting self-stimulation. They supported this view with the finding that diabetic rats, lacking insulin, self-stimulated at increased rates. Diabetic rats given insulin then self-stimulated more slowly.

The fact that stands out in the work from the two laboratories is that procedures which increased food intake also increased self-stimulation. Balagura and Hoebel confirmed that the insulin dose they used caused transient hyperphagia, and Hernandez and Briese stress that their diabetic rats were permanently hyperphagic. In both cases self-stimulation increased accordingly.

Hernandez and Briese proposed that rats which lack insulin have a blocked ventromedial hypothalamus, thereby disinhibiting both feeding and self-stimulation. If this is correct it is extremely important evidence for the feeding-reward theory of self-stimulation. Recall that lesions of the ventromedial hypothalamus by electrolytic (Hoebel & Teitelbaum, 1962) or radio frequency current (Hoebel, 1965) increase self-stimulation almost immediately, but Ferguson and Keesey (1971) report that the effect of the lesions reverses after about a day. Self-stimulation reverts to normal or subnormal levels even though feeding is still excessive. Note, however, that in the Hernandez and Briese study with "functional lesions," self-stimulation does not revert but remains elevated. In these rats lacking insulin, feeding and self-stimulation both increase and both stay that way. The evidence pointing to the ventromedial hypothalamus is very indirect, relying on gold-thio-glucose and insulin studies in mice (Debons, Krimsky, From, & Cloutier, 1969). However, the evidence does support the idea that some glucostatic, or insulin-sensitive, satiety system inhibits both feeding and self-stimulation.

The implication of this series of studies was clear. Factors that inhibit feeding seem to inhibit self-stimulation, and factors which increase feeding, increase self-stimulation. It began to look as if postingestional factors might control feedings by controlling the hypothalamic mechanism we monitor through self-stimulation.

If this view is correct, then as a control we should be able to find self-stimulation sites that are not related to feeding in this way. We prepared animals with electrodes in the septal region as well as the lateral hypothalamus to compare the effects of food intake on self-stimulation at both sites. The animals self-stimulated for 5-min. periods at the hypothalamic site and septal site in alteration. The current was adjusted initially so that hypothalamic self-stimulation was the more rapid of the two. A half hour was allotted to obtain baseline rates and then the animals were tube fed liquid diet. After tube feeding, lateral hypothalamic self-stimulation decreased markedly, while self-stimulation in the septal region did not. We confirmed this result with a second technique in which the hypothalamic and septal self-stimulation levers were simultaneously active. Rats were fed by a remote syringe connected to a water-tight swivel joint leading to an Epstein type nasopharyngeal-gastric tube. Tube feeding in this manner shifted the animal's preference for self-stimulation from the lateral hypothalamus to the lateral septal region. The shift could not be explained as a decrease in activity or generalized responsiveness, nor as a response to distraction, because both responses were comparable in their physical requirement. It appeared that food intake either inhibits an arousal system not shared by the septal region or actually inhibits reward in the lateral hypothalamus more than in this particular septal site (Hoebel, 1968). Similarly Miliaressis and Cardo (1973) found hypothalamic self-stimulation more sensitive to food intake than was tegmental self-stimulation. Gallistel and Beagley (1971) showed that rats in a T-maze would prefer one electrode when food-deprived and another when water-deprived, suggesting specificity of reward mechanisms.

We were convinced that there was some special link between food intake and lateral hypothalamic self-stimulation. The next step followed logically. In the first section of this paper I described the evidence that obesity inhibits feeding. Will obesity inhibit self-stimulation? Donald MacNeil, when he was a graduate student in this laboratory, found that experimentally induced obesity does inhibit self-stimulation. This was true in obese rats even when voluntary food intake was subnormal (Hoebel, 1969; MacNeil, 1974). In summary, physiological factors correlated with food intake and with body weight appeared to exert a corresponding control over feeding and self-stimulation. This suggested that hypothalamic self-stimulation is like eating; hypothalamic reward is like food reward.

An interesting prediction follows from this "feeding-reward theory." If the hypothalamic stimulation is like food to the rat, stimulation should become aversive after a huge meal.

*Satiety related to stimulation-escape.* Rats with lateral hypothalamic electrodes perform a great deal of licking and chewing. A dramatic change in this behavior sometimes occurs after excessive force feeding. The animal then tends to run its chin along the floor or bob its head up and down. These are signs of distaste such as seen when quinine is tasted. This was most noticeable immediately after stimulation. It appeared to the observer that feeding caused the stimulus to become aversive. If the feeding-reward theory and this

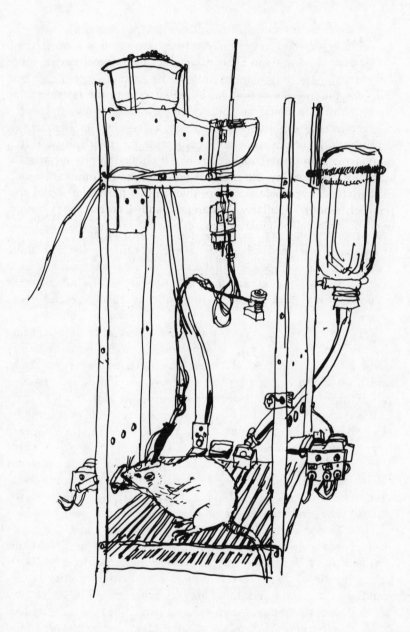

FIG. 3. Apparatus for testing self-stimulation (left lever) and escape from automatic stimulation (right lever). The lever at the back delivers food pellets in some experiments. (From Hoebel & Thompson, 1969.)

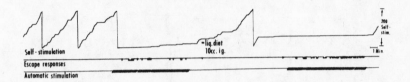

FIG. 4. Self-stimulation decreases by one third (top line, cumulative response record) and stimulation-escape triples (middle line, event marker) after this rat is tube fed liquid diet. The bottom trace shows when the current is turned on automatically for the escape test.

observation are correct, the rat should perform an instrumental response to escape stimulation after excessive feeding.

Rats were used in which electrodes elicited eating, self-stimulation, and stimulation-escape. Stimulation-escape means responding on a lever to turn off the stimulator for 5 seconds. If the rat does not respond, stimulation turns on automatically for ½ second every second.

Rats responded more to escape-stimulation after tube feeding than before. This new finding showed that postingestional factors could cause a shift toward "lateral hypothalamic aversion." The effect lasted 1–2 hours, after which it reversed and escape response rate returned to normal (Hoebel & Thompson, 1969).

It was stated earlier that osmotic factors play a role in controlling self-stimulation. To determine whether osmotic factors influence hypothalamic aversion, rats were first given a stomach load of food, and then later a load of water, while we alternately measured self-stimulation and escape. In some rats, water consistently reversed the effects of food. That is, stimulation-escape increased after feeding, and then decreased after the subsequent water load.

The question naturally arose whether obesity would cause a shift to increased aversion. To perform this experiment a new technique was used to produce experimental obesity. Instead of injecting long-acting insulin or daily force feeding, a combination of stimulation-induced eating and self-stimulation was programmed in such a way as to cause self-induced hyperphagia which led to self-induced obesity. Self-stimulation and stimulation-escape were measured daily in these animals.

The rats escaped more when fat than when at a normal body weight. In our best animal, self-stimulation fell from 3,500 responses

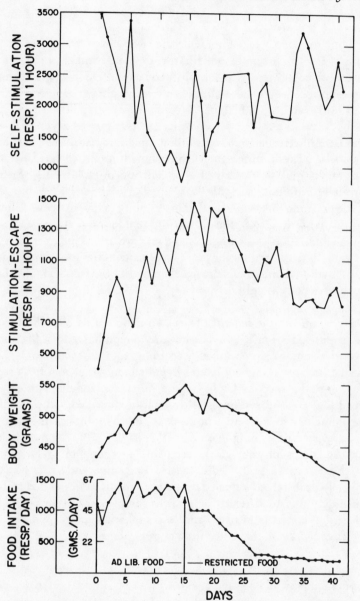

FIG. 5. Our best record of a rat that made itself obese by pressing a lever for prolonged (30-sec.) stimulation, which caused overeating (bottom curve). Daily 1-hr. tests of self-stimulation (top curve) and stimulation-escape (second from top) show that as the rat gained weight self-stimulation decreased and stimulation-escape increased. Restricting food intake reversed the process. (From Hoebel & Thompson, 1969.)

an hour to 1,000 when the rat became 100 gm. overweight. At the same time and in spite of lethargy or sluggishness, stimulation-escape response rose dramatically from 500 responses in an hour when normal weight to 1,500 when overweight. When food intake was restricted, the effect persisted until the animals lost weight. As body weight returned to normal the two curves reversed. Self-stimulation went back up to its initial rapid rate and escape subsided (Hoebel & Thompson, 1969). Thus something about lateral hypo-thalamic stimulation changed as a function of unidentified factors correlated with body weight.

We presume that whatever factors inhibit feeding in obese animals are also inhibiting self-stimulation. But more than that, these factors make stimulation exceedingly aversive if we are to judge from a fat rat waddling up to press the "off" lever 1,000 times more than usual. Thus hypothalamic aversion is related to both excess food intake and excess body weight.

*The beginning of a general theory.* To include this idea the theory has expanded from a "feeding-reward" hypothesis to a "feeding-reward-aversion" hypothesis. According to this view, there is a mechanism involving the lateral hypothalamus that monitors signs of energy balance and adjusts the animal's tendency to eat by rewarding feeding responses when energy is needed and punishing the animal for overeating. The beauty of this hypothetical mechanism is that we are describing instrumental behavior. This is a mechanism that translates physiological needs into instrumental behavior on the part of the rat. This mechanism apparently senses the physiological state as signaled by energy- and osmotic-related factors and then links food-related stimuli to complex approach responses when the animal is in need, and to complex escape response when surfeited. More on this later; first, more evidence.

*Appetite suppressants: Phenethylamines and estrogen.* Appetite suppressants would be predicted to cause self-stimulation to decrease and escape to increase. This should be true unless activity changes mask the results. In addition to amphetamine, we have studied two other appetite suppressants, phenylpropanolamine and fenfluramine. All three share the same basic phenethylamine skeleton but with major differences in pharmacological properties. Amphetamine is a

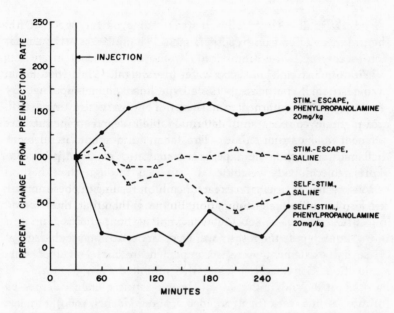

FIG. 6. Group data in which i.p. injection of the amphetamine analogue phenylpropanolamine decreased self-stimulation and increased stimulation-escape. This drug also decreases food intake and inhibits electrically induced feeding in rats. (After Hoebel & McClelland, submitted.)

stimulant, but phenylpropanolamine and fenfluramine are not (Goodman & Gilman, 1965; Ziance, Sipes, Kinnard, & Buckley, 1971). Amphetamine is best known for its facilitation of catecholamines (Taylor & Snyder, 1970); phenylpropanolamine's action is relatively unstudied; fenfluramine is known to release and eventually deplete serotonin and cause sedation (Johnson, Funderburk, Ruckart, & Ward, 1972). In sum, all three are anorectics, but amphetamine is a stimulant and fenfluramine a mild sedative.

Amphetamine increases both self-stimulation (Stein & Wise, 1970) and stimulation-escape, but increases may be artifacts. Phenylpropanolamine, on the other hand, caused a decrease in self-stimulation and an increase in escape (Hoebel, 1971; Hoebel & McClelland, submitted). Extending this work in our laboratory, Kornblith (1974) has obtained similar results and shown that fenfluramine decreases both self-stimulation and escape while causing general inactivity. Thus, phenylpropanolamine, the same drug we used to selectively inhibit electrically elicited feeding, is the one that has the predicted effects on hypothalamic self-stimulation and stimulation-escape.

With the help of Thomas Scott, feeding and rate of self-stimulation in the lateral hypothalamus were experimentally manipulated by estrogen administration in female rats. They were also tested with proven male copulators to determine their degree of sexual excitement, and vaginal smears were taken to identify the phase of their estrous cycle. The experiment consisted of three parts: (a) Some subjects were permitted to proceed through their natural estrous cycles, (b) others were artifically put into heat by injecting sex hormones subcutaneously, and (c) a third group was placed into chronic estrous by subcutaneous implantations of estrogen-laden tubes. In each case the results were similar: estrus and high degrees of sexual excitement were accompanied by high rates of self-stimulation. Conversely, feeding was inhibited during natural and induced estrus, and, in the case of chronic estrus, remained depressed for more than a week (Scott & Hoebel, 1966; Hoebel, 1969). Because rats become hyperactive during estrogen administration (Mook, Kenney, Roberts, Nussbaum & Rodier, 1972), we suspect the increase in self-stimulation reflects activity, as was the case with amphetamine.

*Appetite whetting.* A taste of food near the self-stimulation lever can whet the animal's appetite for self-stimulation in the sense that self-stimulation increases (Poschel, 1968; Mendelson, 1970; Mogenson & Kaplinsky, 1970) just as the first tastes of food accelerate free feeding at the beginning of a meal (Le Magnen, 1971). I found that sucrose dripped on the tongue by an indwelling mouth cannula increased self-stimulation (Hoebel, 1969) with the opposite effect on escape. This is exactly what would be predicted, but quinine dripped on the tongue had inconsistent effects, so the effects of quinine are not in complete accord with the theory.

In sum, postingestional factors, experimental obesity, and phenylpropanolamine decrease self-stimulation and increase stimulation-escape, whereas the taste of palatable food has the opposite effect. Thus self-stimulation rate goes down with satiety and stimulation-escape goes up; conversely, when the animal's appetite is whetted, self-stimulation increases while escape decreases.

A THEORY OF BRAIN CONTROL OF
APPETITIVE BEHAVIOR

Feeding Reward and Aversion

Our new results suggest a possible role for the aversive component of lateral hypothalamic activity in the control of feeding behavior. Rats regulate their daily food intake very accurately by eating discrete meals with predictable intermeal intervals (Teitelbaum & Campbell, 1958; Le Magnen, 1971; Panksepp, 1973; Becker & Kissileff, 1974) depending on food composition and availability (Collier, 1973). The net result of this ingestion pattern is a relatively constant body weight. If rats are forced to become obese, they become anorectic until body weight returns to normal (Hoebel & Teitelbaum, 1966). The experiments described above show that neural activity in the lateral hypothalamus is aversive to an overfed or overweight rat; therefore, it is logical to suppose that this aversion system contributes to the maintenance of normal meal size and normal body weight by causing aversion which would serve as a deterrent when normal bounds are exceeded. An animal would then abstain from eating until the physiological signals associated with digestive processes and body weight were again within normal limits.

Stated another way (Hoebel & Thompson, 1969; Hoebel, 1971), lateral hypothalamic activity generates a combination of reward and aversion which shifts along a continuum depending on the animal's homeostatic balance. When the animal is hungry, lateral hypothalamic stimulation is a potent reward; when satiated, the same stimulus is less rewarding and more aversive; and when cloyed, stimulation is noxious.

The essential elements of this theory are three. (a) There occurs a "translation" of physiological stimuli into behavior, or what Mogenson and Huang (1973) call the functional coupling of endocrine, autonomic, and somatic efferent systems. (b) This translation involves the integration or gating of internal and external stimuli so as to control food intake, sexual activity, and the like. (c) This integrative gating process is organized so that a given stimulus which generates approach will cause withdrawal instead after sufficient consummatory behavior. Two more principles are implied although not always necessary: (a) the introduction of some

**Table 1**
*Summary*

| | | Feeding | Self-stim. | Stim-escape |
|---|---|:---:|:---:|:---:|
| Postingest. factors: | meal | ↓————↓ | | |
| | stomach disten. | ↓————↓ | | |
| | i.g. glucose | ↓————↓ | | |
| | i.g. NaCl | ↓————↓ | | |
| | i.v. glucose | ↓————↓ | | |
| | i.v. NaCl | ↓————↓ | | |
| | i.v. water | ↑————↑ | | |
| | i.g. liquid diet | ↓————↓ | ————↑ | |
| Taste factors: | sweet taste | ↑————↑ | ————↓ | |
| | bitter taste | ↓ | ↑ | ↑ |
| Weight factors: | excess body weight | ↓————↓ | ————↑ | |
| | food deprivation[1] | ↑————↑ | | |
| Hormonal factors: | i.p. insulin | ↑————↑ | | |
| | i.p. glucagon | ↓————↓ | | |
| | i.p. insulin[2] | | ↓ | |
| | insulin diabetes[2] | ↑————↑ | | |
| | antidiabetic[2] | ↓————↓ | | |
| | estrogen | ↓ | ↑ | |
| Anorectic drugs: | amphetamine | ↓ | ↑ | ↑ |
| | fenfluramine | ↓ | ↓ | ↓ |
| | propadrine | ↓————↓ | ————↑ | |
| Exp. hyperphagia: | VMH lesion | ↑ | ↑↓ | |
| | VNAB lesion | ↑ | | |
| | i. vtr. PCPA | ↑ | | |

| | | Mating | Self-stim. | Stim-escape |
|---|---|:---:|:---:|:---:|
| Hormonal factors: | castration | ↓————↓ | ————↑ | |
| Behavioral factors: | ejaculation | ↓————↓ | ————↑ | |

1. Margules & Olds, 1962.
2. Hernandez & Briese, 1971.
Other references are given along with the discussion in the text. Arrows indicate the direction of behavior change, increase or decrease. Horizontal lines between arrows indicate that the change is in the direction expected from the reward-aversion theory as presented in the text.

"reward" and/or "aversion" capable of working beyond the bounds of fixed reflexes, i.e., capable of measurement in terms of instrumental responses and (b) the assignment of affect or subjective hedonism when it can be measured as in human reports of pleasure or displeasure. Further discussion will clarify these points.

If this hypothesis has merit, it should generalize to other kinds of behavior. We sought a reward-aversion mechanism for sexual behavior.

Reward and Aversion in Mating: A Test of the Theory

It was important to determine whether the relation between feeding and self-stimulation was unique. One way to approach the problem of specificity was to look for a reward site that was related to some motivated behavior other than feeding. It had previously been shown by Herberg (1963) that self-stimulation of a site in the posterior hypothalamus of male rats is accompanied by ejaculation. When Anthony Caggiula was a graduate student here, we confirmed this result, and found in addition that stimulation of the same brain site can elicit copulation with an estrous female. Continuous stimulation of the posterior hypothalamic site in male rats elicited immediate copulation. The males would even press a bar to open a door for access to the female.

The site that elicited copulation was also a self-stimulation site. The rate of self-stimulation increased after systemic injection of testosterone as also reported by Herberg (1963). Therefore, stimulation at this site in males is like normal sexual stimulation; it elicits responses to reach the female; it induces copulation; it is rewarding, and the reward varies with the amount of sex hormone (Caggiula & Hoebel, 1966).

Caggiula went on to discern a separation between sex and feeding reward systems in the same animal. In rats with both female and food available as stimulus objects, lateral stimulation elicited eating, but when stimulation was changed to the posterior electrode the male stopped eating and started to mate. When returned to lateral stimulation, the male jilted the female and resumed eating.

Physiological manipulations demonstrated specificity of reward at the sex electrode. Self-stimulation at the posterior site decreased

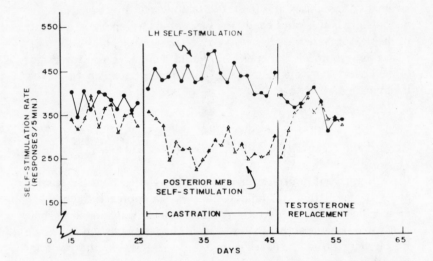

FIG. 7. This male rat had both lateral hypothalamic (LH) and posterior hypothalamic (PH) electrodes for self-stimulation. Daily tests before castration, after castration, and after hormone replacement therapy suggest that PH self-stimulation was related to sex hormone level, but LH self-stimulation was unaffected or perhaps oppositely affected. (From Caggiula, 1967.)

after castration and increased again after testosterone therapy, whereas lateral hypothalamic self-stimulation in the same animals was unaffected, or in one case oppositely affected (Caggiula, 1967). I consider it important to the argument that the underlying neural systems for various behavior patterns can be physiologically distinguished in this way.

If one accepts that self-stimulation at the posterior hypothalamic site reflects approach tendencies in mating, then by analogy with our feeding studies, we can predict that stimulation-escape might reflect sexual withdrawal during the postejaculatory refractory phase. We find as predicted that rewarding stimulation shifts to aversion during the 10 minutes after ejaculation (Hoebel, Cardell, & Coblentz, 1974).

The experimental series described above is providing evidence for the hypothesized reward-aversion system for mating. The results directly parallel the findings in the reward-aversion system for

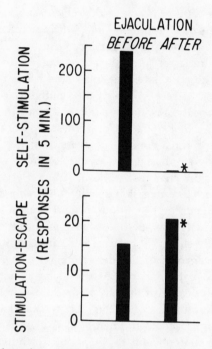

FIG. 8. Group data showing that PH self-stimulation in male rats stopped after ejaculation, but stimulation-escape increased. (From Hoebel, Cardell, & Coblentz, 1974.)

feeding. In turn, this suggests that a dual mechanism of this type may be found for several other appetitive behaviors.

There are problems inherent in interpreting an escape response as being a sign of aversion (Hodos, 1965; Deutsch & DiCara, 1967; Ball, 1972; Szabo, 1972; Atrens, 1973). We have made this inference because a decrease in self-stimulation coupled with a simultaneous increase in escape cannot be attributed to overall changes in activity level, nor can an increase in escape under those conditions be attributed to increased work for reward. That is to say, the rat does not increase the number of responses to turn the current off just to have it come on again, because responses to self-stimulate are decreased, not increased (as after ejaculation or a meal). Moreover, it is often impossible to prime the rat into self-stimulation when escape rate is elevated. Therefore, I believe we are correct in assuming that escape is not just a form of self-stimulation. The strongest note of caution is sounded by Deutsch's (1973) evidence that reward neurons gradually stop firing during prolonged stimulation just like peripheral sensory neurons. This adaptation theory suggests that a rat turns the current off in order to disadapt the system so as to stimulate it again. Deutsch has not applied the theory to the present case in which the relative frequency of self-stimulation and escape responses shift as a result of physiological manipulations. It is not apparent how the adaptation theory could eliminate the need for a concept of aversion in this case, but the theory does rightly emphasize that we do not know whether reward changes or aversion changes or both. The observation that our measures of reward and aversion usually vary reciprocally suggests they are at two ends of a continuum, and that our physiological and pharmacological manipulations cause shifts along this continuum. The neurophysiological basis of this shift is unknown.

Reward and aversion as I use the terms must always be thought of in the context of the measurements we use. The papers in this symposium which deal with the physiological psychology of reward illustrate the importance of this point. Gallistel takes the psychophysical approach to the neurophysiology of reward; Routtenberg takes the anatomical path; Stein puts forth his great insights and pharmacological experiments which promise new comprehension of mental illness; and Valenstein reviews brain-stimulation reward from the point of view of patients' subjective responses. We are probably not all measuring the same thing, even though we all have some concept of self-stimulation "reward." For example, Stein describes hypothalamic self-stimulation as part of a general, noradrenergic reward system, but it is not clear how the general system might be linked to the separately controlled reward systems for feeding and mating that I have described. Likewise, my use of "reward" is too general for Gallistel's techniques where hypothalamic self-stimulation is seen to include not only a reward component but also a priming component. Thus each of us uses the concept of reward in slightly different ways as tied to our techniques for manipulating self-stimulation. Some of the theoretical implications of various interpretations have been reviewed (Trowill, Panksepp, & Gandelman, 1969; Bindra, 1968), but new findings and new ways of measuring reward continue to complicate the puzzle without filling in the details; therefore strict adherence to operational definitions is necessary.

One more caution is in order. With regard to the findings which led to the reward-aversion theory presented here, it should be clearly recognized that the phenomena I have described, such as the new hyperphagia syndromes and physiological control of self-stimulation and stimulation-escape, are all descriptions of *sufficient* conditions for obtaining the effects. I do not want to imply that these are the only conditions or even necessary conditions for producing the phenomena.

Value of the Theory

The reward-aversion theory has been very useful in predicting experiments that give positive results. The feeding-reward idea predicted feeding aversion; this in turn predicted the reward and aversion effects related to mating. In this sense it has been a good theory.

The theory was generated by showing that factors known to control feeding and mating exert a corresponding control over self-stimulation and escape at appropriate brain sites. Now that the theory has proved useful and to this extent validated, we can begin to turn the tables and predict facts about feeding and mating that have not yet been recognized experimentally. We can deduce from the fact that rats will escape the brain stimulation that they will work to escape the natural conditions which affect that part of the brain. Specifically, conditions which increase stimulation-escape should also cause animals to escape food or sexual contact.

For example, the increased escape from brain stimulation we observe after ejaculation suggests that the rat should display increased escape from natural sexual stimulation. Current literature says mating is "inhibited" after ejaculation (Kurtz & Adler, 1973). I am suggesting that mating is more than inhibited, it is aversive. The male should work to escape sexual contact under appropriate conditions such as right after ejaculation.

Stated broadly, the theory stresses that appetitive behavior is controlled by a process that does more than facilitate and inhibit responses, it facilitates approach and *escape*. What looks like inhibited responding or nonresponding may show itself as escape if the experiment is designed to measure it.

Conceived in this way, the theory is useful to anyone concerned with affect as P. T. Young was, and also to anyone working with simpler animals where the anthropomorphism of a hedonistic description is more of a hinderance than a help. I will briefly discuss the theory from each of these points of view.

The Complex Level

Research in humans makes hedonism obvious and directly measurable. Cabanac, Duclaux, and Spector (1971) performed an experiment which fits directly into the reward-aversion theory. They showed that the taste of a sucrose solution that subjects rated "pleasant" shifted to "unpleasant" after a large meal of the sucrose. Thus the reward of sugar gave way to aversion as a result of postingestional factors, just as self-stimulation gave way to stimulation-escape in our rats.

It is conceivable that the anorectic drugs which shifted reward to aversion in rats would do so in people. This would depend on people's having a satiety system neurochemically comparable to that of rats, and that is unknown. However, we chose the rat anorectic drugs not only because we knew they should act on the noradrenergic satiety pathway, but because they suppress appetite in people. It is not unreasonable, therefore, to predict a drug-induced shift from pleasure to displeasure in people.

Phenylpropanolamine was the drug of choice instead of amphetamine or fenfluramine because it selectively depressed electrically induced feeding and caused a decrease in self-stimulation coupled with an increase in stimulation-escape.

We had 32 people take a pill before an ad libitum lunch of chocolate Metrecal liquid diet for each of 10 days. They sucked the diet from an unseen reservoir as in the Jordan (1969) technique. On 5 of the days, randomly selected, they received phenylpropanolamine and on the other 5, a placebo. As a result they ate less of the diet on propadrine days, and also rated the diet as subjectively tasting less good (Hoebel, Cooper, Kamin, & Willard, submitted).

In sum, caloric intake and phenylpropanolamine can cause a change from pleasure towards displeasure in people's reaction to food. Thus the reward-aversion theory generated from our rat work fits Cabanac's data with humans and accurately predicted a shift in the subjective responses with a specific appetite-suppressant drug.

FIG. 9. The person drinks an ad libitum lunch of liquid diet (Metrecal) from a hidden reservoir starting 30 min. after taking phenylpropanolamine (nonprescription amphetamine analogue) or a placebo. (After the technique of Jordan, 1969; from Hoebel, Cooper, Kamin, & Willard, submitted.)

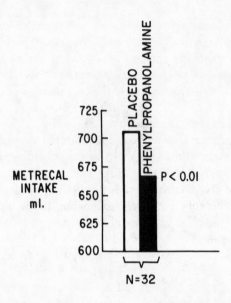

FIG. 10. Group data demonstrating that phenylpropanolamine taken orally reduces food intake in humans under the conditions of this test.

Thus in the realm of feeding in humans the theory could be described as "homeostatic hedonism." However, it is more than just homeostatic because in rats it applies to sexual behavior as well as feeding, and it is more than hedonism because it may well apply to the behavior of simpler animals to which few would attribute pleasure or displeasure.

The Simple Level

The reward-aversion theory does not require an animal capable of hedonism or a hedonistic interpretation in animals that do have such feelings. Animals low on the evolutionary scale may be guided in feeding and mating by reward and aversion systems such as I have described. Schneirla proposed a biphasic approach-withdrawal theory which is very similar, except that his view of simple creatures linked approach to weak stimuli and withdrawal to strong stimuli (Schneirla, 1959; Jaynes, 1973). The neural mechanisms under discussion may have started out that way and evolved to include

(a) a central excitatory state controlling preference threshold, (b) a central mechanism for instrumental behavior, and (c) affective sensations. However, the concept of a reward-aversion mechanism as it has grown out of our rat work postulates that stimuli generate approach or withdrawal according to the combination of physiological signals within the animal, not just the strength of peripheral stimulation. Therefore, the notion as I use it is only helpful at a level of neural organization complex enough to permit internal stimuli to gate other stimuli so that the animal responds to a given stimulus with approach at one time and escape at another. For example, in the fly, Dethier (1968, 1970) has shown exactly this process if one accepts proboscis extension to be approach and proboscis withdrawal as escape. He found that food deprivation acting via the central nervous system caused a behavioral change such that an NaCl solution which produced proboscis retraction, "rejection," when the fly was deprived only 24 hours later produced extension, "acceptance," when the fly was deprived more than 24 hours. Therefore I suspect that an approach-withdrawal mechanism for feeding exists in the fly brain along the same lines as in the rat brain. The fact that instrumental responses have been difficult to demonstrate in the fly just means that the fly is perhaps less complex in this regard. If we were to stimulate the fly with an appropriate frequency in that part of the brain which is normally excited by sweet tastes, stimulation would be expected to produce an approach response such as proboscis extension when the gut is empty, and proboscis withdrawal when full. In other words, one will see just simple stimulation-induced feeding. Complex stimulation-induced feeding in which an instrumental response is interposed is not expected in this creature until someone learns to train flies to work for food. Then we should see the more complex elicited feeding and also self-stimulation. Then we will be back in the realm of "rewards" and "aversions." Until then it will be better to speak simply of approach and withdrawal.

Glickman and Schiff (1967) suggest that lateral hypothalamic stimulation triggers repetition of natural motor sequences. This fits into the present formulation at the "simple" level I have been describing. Some of the evidence presented in this paper could be taken as evidence for their theory that animals tend to repeat behaviors that are contiguous with elicitation of naturalistic behavior patterns. That would bring us a step up in complexity above the fly proboscis example, from a motor act to a motor pattern. My emphasis, however, would again be on the shift from approach to withdrawal patterns that occurs as a function of physiological changes that channel the animal's sensory input and/or motor output so as to maintain homeostasis in the case of feeding and maintain the species in the case of mating.

Like the example of proboscis motor control, Glickman and Schiff's examples of species-typical motor sequences are adequately, but minimally, described in terms of approach and withdrawal. But when the behavior under study reaches the level of complexity where an arbitrarily chosen act is interposed in the behavior chain, then following Teitelbaum's (1967) argument, a higher level of complexity is involved.

In animals that can and do perform instrumental responses we need terms such as reward and aversion, and in animals that talk we need the concept of pleasure and displeasure. Some aspects of the underlying neural mechanisms at all three levels may be rather similar in their essential features. If electrically induced eating can be taken as a model of the simple approach system, and if electrically induced instrumental responses and self-stimulation are taken as models of more complex reward systems, and we use human reports as the most complex pleasure system, then indeed we already have a tiny glimmer of evidence for a common mechanism, because food intake and phenylpropanolamine administration shifted all three. The food and drug selectively blocked elicited approach to food, shifted electrical reward towards aversion, and changed a pleasurable taste into a less pleasurable one. The reward-aversion theory points to the brain processes that underlie these changes and suggests that we may find these processes faster if they are looked at in this way.

FINAL SUMMARY

We started this discussion with Young's hedonistic theory of behavior control, brought to bear Skinnerian techniques as used by Olds for measuring reward and aversion in the brain, then applied Teitelbaum's approach to the analysis of feeding, and have generated a reward-aversion theory for brain control of feeding and other basic behavior patterns. This has been a process of discovering factors that enter into neural control of feeding and then determining their effects on self-stimulation and stimulation-escape.

Analysis of hypothalamic hyperphagia revealed a weight-control process. Neurochemical studies revealed a noradrenergic component to satiety which served as a substrate for amphetamine anorexia. Applying these findings to brain stimulation, we found physiological and pharmacological manipulations had systematic effects on electrically induced feeding, and on self-stimulation and stimulation-escape. The factors that augmented food intake increased self-stimulation and decreased escape; conversely, satiety factors caused a shift from "reward" to "aversion." The results were sufficiently predictable to warrant proposing a feeding reward-aversion theory which contends that hypothalamic reward is involved in rewarding eating when the animal needs food, and hypothalamic aversion is involved in aversion to food when the animal is satiated. Thus it is possible to use the animal's own responses for brain stimulation to monitor brain mechanisms that translate physiological stimuli into behavioral action by generating approach responses when energy balance is low and withdrawal responses when energy balance is high.

A reward-aversion mechanism was then predicted for mating control and was demonstrated on the basis of systematic changes in self-stimulation and stimulation-escape with sex hormone manipulation and copulation. The ability of the theory to predict positive results suggests it is a good working hypothesis and leads to the proposal that all basic behavior patterns are controlled by brain reward-aversion mechanisms that generate approach to a given stimulus at one time and withdrawal at another, depending on the relevant physiological signals. As a theory of behavior control, this idea fits a wide variety of phenomena which are illustrated, from the approach and withdrawal behavior of the fly to the subjective pleasure and displeasure responses of humans.

It is concluded that self-stimulation and stimulation-escape can reflect neural mechanisms for approach and withdrawal and can demonstrate for us how these mechanisms are controlled by internal and external stimuli.

REFERENCES

Ahlskog, J. E. Brain norepinephrine and its involvement in the regulation of food consumption. Ph.D. dissertation, Princeton University, 1973.

Ahlskog, J. E. Food intake and amphetamine anorexia after selective forebrain norepinephrine loss. *Brain Research*, in press.

Ahlskog. J. E., & Hoebel, B. G. Hyperphagia resulting from selective destruction of an ascending adrenergic pathway in the rat brain. *Federation Proccedings*, 1972, **31**, 377.

Ahlskog, J. E., & Hoebel, B. G. Overeating and obesity from damage to a noradrenergic system in the brain. *Science*, 1973, **182**, 166-169.

Ahlskog, J. E., Hoebel, B. G., & Breisch, S. T. Hyperphagia following lesions of the noradrenergic pathway is prevented by hypophysectomy. *Federation Proceedings*, 1974, **33**, 463.

Anden, N. E., Dahlstrom, A., Fuxe, K., Larsson, K., Olsson, L., and Ungerstedt, U. Ascending monoamine neurons to the telencephalon and diencephalon. *Acta Physiologica Scandinavica*, 1966, **67**, 313-326.

Atrens, D. M. A reinforcement analysis of rat hypothalamus. *American Journal of Physiology*, 1973, **224**, 62-65.

Balagura, S. Influence of osmotic and caloric loads upon lateral hypothalamic self-stimulation. *Journal of Comparative and Physiological Psychology*, 1968, **66**, 325-328.

Balagura, S., & Davenport, L. D. Feeding patterns of normal and ventromedial hypothalamic lesioned male and female rats. *Journal of Comparative and Physiological Psychology*, 1970, **71**, 357-364.

Balagura, S., & Hoebel, B. G. Self-stimulation of the hypothalamic "feeding-reward system" modified by insulin and glucagon. *Physiology and Behavior*, 1967, **2**, 337-340.

Ball, G. G. Self-stimulation in the ventromedial hypothalamus. *Science*, 1972, **178**, 72-73.

Beatty, W. W. Influence of type of reinforcement on operant responding by rats with ventromedial lesions. *Physiology and Behavior*, 1973, **10**, 841-846.

Becker, E. E., & Kissileff, H. R. Inhibitory controls of feeding by the ventromedial hypothalamus. *American Journal of Physiology*, 1974, **226**, 383-396.

Bekesy, G. von. *Sensory Inhibition*. Princeton, N.J.: Princeton University Press, 1967.

Berger, B. D., Wise, C. D., & Stein, L. Norepinephrine-reversal of anorexia in rats with lateral hypothalamic damage. *Science*, 1971, **172**, 281-284.

Bevan, T. E. Experimental disassociation of hypothalamic finickiness and motivational deficits from hyperphagia and from hyperemotionality. Ph.D. dissertation, Princeton University, 1973.

Bindra, D. Neurophysiological interpretations of the effects of drive and incentive-motivation on general activity and instrumental behavior. *Psychological Review*, 1968, **75**, 1-22.

Booth, D. A. Localization of the adrenergic feeding system in the rat diencephalon. *Science*, 1967, **158**, 515-517.

Booth, D. A. Amphetamine anorexia by direct action on the adrenergic feeding system of rat hypothalamus. *Nature*, 1968, **217**, 869-870.

Booth, D. A. Unlearned and learned effects of intrahypothalamic cyclic AMP injection on feeding. *Nature New Biology*, 1972, **237**, 222-224.

Breisch, S. T., & Hoebel, B. G. Hyperphagia and obesity following intraventricular parachlorophenylalanine (PCPA). In preparation.

Brobeck, J. R., Tepperman, J., & Long, C.N.H. Experimental hypothalamic hyperphagia in the rat. *Yale Journal of Biology and Medicine*, 1943, **15**, 831-853.

Brody, J. F. Behavioral effects of serotonin depletion and of p-chlorophenylalanine (a serotonin depleter) in rats. *Psychopharmacologia*, 1970, **17**, 14-33.

Brooks, C. McC. A study of the respiratory quotient in experimental hypothalamic obesity. *American Journal of Physiology*, 1946, **147**, 727-734.

Cabanac, M., Duclaux, R., & Spector, N. H. Sensory feedback in regulation of body weight: Is there a ponderostat? *Nature*, 1971, **229**, 125-127.

Caggiula, A. R. Specificity of copulation-reward systems in the posterior hypothalamus. *Preceedings of the 75th Annual American Psychological Association Convention*, 1967.

Caggiula, A. R., & Hoebel, B. G. A "copulation-reward" site in the posterior hypothalamus. *Science*, 1966, **153**, 1284-1285.

Campbell, B. A., & Baez, L. A. Dissociation of arousal and regulatory behaviors following lesions of the lateral hypothalamus. *Journal of Comparative and Physiological Psychology*, in press.

Carlisle, H. J. Differential effects of amphetamine on food and water intake in rats with lateral hypothalamic lesions. *Journal of Comparative and Physiological Psychology*, 1964, **58**, 47-54.

Chisholm, D. C., & Trowill, J. A. The effects of incentive shifts on stimulus-bound licking in rats. *Physiology and Behavior*, 1972, **9**, 277-279.

Chorover, S. Symposium on psychosurgery. *Boston University Law Review*, 1974, **54**, 231-248.

Collier, G., Hirsol, E., & Hamlin, P. H. The Ecological determinants of reinforcement in the rat. *Physiology and Behavior*, 1972, **9**, 705-716.

Conte, M., Lehr, D., Goldman, W., Krukowski, M. Inhibition of food intake by beta-adrenergic stimulation. *Pharmacologist*, 1968, **10**, 180.

Corbit, J. D., & Stellar, E. Palatability, food intake, and obesity in normal and hyperphagic rats. *Journal of Comparative and Physiological Psychology*, 1964, **58**, 63-67.

Cox, V. C., Kakolewski, J. W., & Valenstein, E. S. Effects of ventromedial hypothalamic damage in hypophysectomized rats. *Journal of Comparative and Physiological Psychology*, 1968, **65**, 145-148.

Debons, A. F., Krimsky, I., From, A., & Cloutier, R. J. Rapid effects of insulin on the hypothalamic satiety center. *American Journal of Physiology*, 1969, **217**, 1114-1118.

Delgado, J.M.R., Roberts, W. W., & Miller, N. E. Learning motivated by electrical stimulation of the brain. *American Journal of Physiology*, 1954, **179**, 587-593.

Dethier, V. G. Chemosensory input and taste discrimination in the blowfly. *Science*, 1968, **161**, 389-391.

Dethier, V. G. Feeding and drinking behavior of invertebrates. *Handbook of Physiology: Alimentary Canal*, 1970. Ch. 6, p. 79.

Deutsch, J. A. Prolonged rewarding brain stimulation. *Psychology of Learning and Motivation*, 1973, **7**, 297-311.

Deutsch, J. A., & DiCara, L. Hunger and extinction in intracranial self-stimulation. *Journal of Comparative and Physiological Psychology*, 1967, **63**, 344-347.

Devor, M. G., Wise, R. A., Milgram, N. W., & Hoebel, B. G. Physiological control of hypothalamically elicited feeding and drinking. *Journal of Comparative and Physiological Psychology*, 1970, **73**, 226-232.

Ellison, G. D. Appetitive behavior in rats after circumsection of the hypothalamus. *Physiology and Behavior*, 1968, **3**, 221-226.

Epstein, A. N. Suppression of eating and drinking by amphetamine and other drugs in normal and hyperphagic rats. *Journal of Comparative and Physiological Psychology*, 1959, **52**, 37-45.

Epstein, A. N. Reciprocal changes in feeding behavior produced by intrahypothalamic chemical injections. *American Journal of Physiology*, 1960, **199**, 969-974.

Epstein, A. N. The lateral hypothalamic syndrome: Its implications for the physiological psychology of hunger and thirst. *Progress in physiological psychology*, 1971. Vol. 4, pp. 263-317.

Falk, J. L. Comments on Dr. Teitelbaum's paper. In M. R. Jones (Ed.), *Nebraska symposium on motivation*, **1961**. Lincoln: University of Nebraska Press, 1961. Pp. 65-68.

Ferguson, N.B.L., & Keesey, R. E. Comparison of ventromedial hypothalamic lesion effects upon feeding and lateral hypothalamic self-stimulation in the female rat. *Journal of Comparative and Physiological Psychology*, 1971, **74**, 263-271.

Fibiger, H. C., Zis, A. P., & McGeer, E. G. Feeding and drinking deficits after 6-hydroxydopamine administration in rat: Similarities to the lateral hypothalamic syndrome. *Brain Research*, 1973, **55**, 135-148.

Finger, F. W., & Mook, D. G. Basic drives. *Annual Review of Psychology*, 1971, **22**, 1-38.

Fisher, A. E. The role of limbic structures in the central regulation of feeding and drinking behavior. *Annals of the New York Academy of Sciences*, 1969, **157** (R2), 844-901.

Friedman, M. I. Effects of alloxan diabetes on hypothalamic hyperphagia and obesity. *American Journal of Physiology*, 1972, **222**, 174-178.

Funderburk, W. H., Hazelwood, J. C., Ruckart, R. T., & Ward, J. W. Is 5-hydroxytryptamine involved in the mechanism of action of fenfluramine? *Journal of Pharmacy and Pharmacology*, 1971, **23**, 468-469.

Gallistel, C. R. Self-stimulation: The neurophysiology of reward and motivation. In J. A. Deutsch (Ed.), *The physiological basis of memory*. New York: Academic Press, 1973.

Gallistel, C. R., & Beagley, G. Specificity of brain stimulation reward in the rat. *Journal of Comparative and Physiological Psychology*, 1971, **76**, 199-205.

Glickman, S. E., & Schiff, B. B. A biological theory of reinforcement. *Psychological Review*, 1967, **74**, 81-109.

Glowinski, J., Iversen, L. L., & Axelrod, J. Storage and synthesis of norepinephrine in the reserpine-treated rat brain. *Journal of Pharmacology and Experimental Therapeutics*, 1966, **151**, 385-399.

Gold, R. M. Hypothalamic hyperphagia produced by parasagittal knife cuts. *Physiology and Behavior*, 1970, **5**, 23-25.

Gold, R. M. Hypothalamic obesity: The myth of the ventromedial nucleus. *Science*, 1973, **182**, 488-490.

Goodman, L. S., & Gilman, A. (Eds.) *The Pharmacological Basis of Therapeutics*. (3rd ed.) New York: Macmillan, 1965. Pp. 478-486.

Graff, H., & Stellar, E. Hyperphagia, obesity and finickiness. *Journal of Comparative and Physiological Psychology*, 1962, **55**, 418-424.

Grossman, S. P. Eating or drinking elicited by direct adrenergic or cholinergic stimulation of the hypothalamus. *Science*, 1960, **132**, 301-302.

Grossman, S. P. The VMH: A center for affective reactions, satiety, or both? *Physiology and Behavior*, 1966, **1**, 1-10.

Grossman, S. P. Hypothalamic and limbic influences on food intake. *Federation Proceedings*, 1968, **27**, 1349-1360.

Hamilton, C. L., & Brobeck, J. R. Hypothalamic hyperphagia in the monkey. *Journal of Comparative and Physiological Psychology*, 1964, **57**, 271-278.

Han, P. W. Energy metabolism of tube-fed hypophysectomized rats bearing hypothalamic lesions. *American Journal of Physiology*, 1968, **215**, 1343-1350.

Harrell, E. H., & Remley, N. R. The immediate development of behavioral and biochemical changes following ventromedial hypothalamic lesions in rats. *Behavioral Biology*, 1973, **9**, 49-63.

Herberg, L. J. Seminal ejaculation following positively reinforcing electrical stimulation of the rat hypothalamus. *Journal of Comparative and Physiological Psychology*, 1963, **56**, 679-685.

Herberg, L. J., & Franklin, K. B. J. Adrenergic feeding: Its blockade or reversal by posterior VMH lesions; and a new hypothesis. *Physiology and Behavior*, 1972, **8**, 1029-1034.

Hernandez, L., & Briese, E. Insulin inhibition of hypothalamic self-stimulation. *Acta Physiologica Latinoamericana*, 1971, **21**, 57-63.

Hernandez, L., & Briese, E. Analysis of diabetic hyperphagia and polydipsia. *Physiology and Behavior*, 1972, **9**, 741-746.

Hess, W. R. *Functional Organization of the Diencephalon*. Ed. J. R. Hughes. New York: Grune & Stratton, 1957.

Hetherington, A. W. The relation of various hypothalamic lesions to adiposity and other phenomena in the rat. *American Journal of Physiology*, 1941, **133**, 326-327.

Hodos, W. Motivational properties of long durations of rewarding brain stimulation. *Journal of Comparative and Physiological Psychology*, 1965, **59**, 219-224.

Hoebel, B. G. Electrode-cannulas for electrical or chemical treatment of multiple brain sites. *Journal of Encephalography and Clinical Neurophysiology*, 1964, **16**, 399-402.

Hoebel, B. G. Hypothalamic lesions by electrocauterization: Disinhibition of feeding and self-stimulation. *Science*, 1965, **149**, 452-453.

Hoebel, B. G. Intragastric balloon without gastric surgery for the rat. *Journal of Applied Psychology*, 1967, **22**, 189-190.

Hoebel, B. G. Inhibition and disinhibition of self-stimulation and feeding: Hypothalamic control and postingestional factors. *Journal of Comparative and Physiological Psychology*, 1968, **66**, 89-100.

Hoebel, B. G. Feeding and self-stimulation in neural regulation of food and water intake. *Annals of the New York Academy of Sciences*, 1969, **157** (R2), 758-778.

Hoebel, B. G. Feeding: Neural control of intake. *Annual Review of Physiology*, 1971, **33**, 533-568.

Hoebel, B. G., Cardell, K. L., & Coblentz, J. E. Sexual inhibition is reflected in aversion to posterior hypothalamic stimulation. Paper presented at *Eastern Psychological Association Meeting*, 1974 (also submitted for publication).

Hoebel, B. G., Cooper, J., Kamin, M. C., & Willard, D. Food intake decreased by phenylpropanolamine in humans. Submitted for publication.

Hoebel, B. G., & McClelland, S. J. The effects of amphetamine and phenylpropanolamine on hypothalamic reward and aversion. Submitted for publication.

Hoebel, B. G., & Teitelbaum, P. Hypothalamic control of feeding and self-stimulation. *Science*, 1962, **135**, 375-377.

Hoebel, B. G., & Teitelbaum, P. Weight regulation in normal and hypothalamic hyperphagic rats. *Journal of Comparative and Physiological Psychology*, 1966, **61**, 189-193.

Hoebel, B. G., & Thompson, R. D. Aversion to lateral hypothalamic stimulation caused by intragastric feeding or obesity. *Journal of Comparative and Physiological Psychology*, 1969, **68**, 536-543.

Huang, Y. H., & Mogenson, G. J. Neural pathways mediating drinking and feeding in rats. *Experimental Neurology*, 1972, **37**, 269-286.

Jacobs, H. L., & Sharma, K. N. Taste versus calories: Sensory and metabolic signals in the control of food intake. *Annals of the New York Academy of Sciences*, 1969, **157** (R2), 1084-1125.

Jaffe, M. L. The effects of lesions in the ventromedial nucleus of the hypothalamus on behavioral contrast in rats. *Physiological Psychology*, 1973, **1**, 191-198.

Jaynes, J. A long way from genes to behavior and molecules to man. *Contemporary Psychology*, 1973, **18**, 611-613.

Johnson, D. H., Funderburk, W. H., Ruckart, R. T., & Ward, J. W. Contrasting effects of two 5-hydroxytryptamine-depleting drugs on sleep patterns in cats. *European Journal of Pharmacology*, 1972, **20**, 80-84.

Jordan, H. A. Voluntary intragastric feeding: Oral and gastric contributions to food intake and hunger in man. *Journal of Comparative and Physiological Psychology*, 1969, **68**, 498-506.

Keesey, R. E., & Boyle, P. C. Effects of quinine adulteration upon body weight of LH-lesioned and intact male rats. *Journal of Comparative and Physiological Psychology*, 1973, **84**, 38-46.

Keesey, R. E., & Powley, T. L. Self-stimulation and body weight in rats with lateral hypothalamic lesions. *American Journal of Physiology*, 1973, **224**, 970-978.

Koe, B., & Weissman, A. P-chlorophenylalanine: A specific depletor of brain serotonin. *Journal of Pharmacology and Experimental Therapeutics*, 1966, **154**, 499-516.

Kent, M. A., & Peters, R. H. Effects of ventromedial hypothalamic lesions on hunger-motivated behavior in rats. *Journal of Comparative and Physiological Psychology*, 1973, **83**, 92-97.

106

NEBRASKA SYMPOSIUM ON MOTIVATION, 1974

King, B. M., & Gaston, M. G. The effects of pretraining on the bar-
pressing performance of VMH-lesioned rats. *Physiology and Behavior*,
1973, **11**, 161-166.

King, M. B., & Hoebel, B. G. Killing elicited by brain stimulation in rats.
*Communications in Behavioral Biology*, 1968, **2**, Part A, 173-177.

Kornblith, C. Effects of anorexic drugs on food intake, self-stimulation
and stimulation-escape. Paper presented at Eastern Psychological
Association Meeting, 1974.

Kurtz, R. G., & Adler, N. T. Electrophysiological correlates of copulatory
behavior in the male rat: Evidence for a sexual inhibitory process.
*Journal of Comparative and Physiological Psychology*, 1973, **84**, 225-239.

Kurtz, R. G., Rozin, P., & Teitelbaum, P. Ventromedial hypothalamic
hyperphagia in the hypophysectomized weaning rat. *Journal of Comparative and Physiological Psychology*, 1972, **80**, 19-25.

Lehr, D., Mallow, J., & Krukowski, M. Copious drinking and simultaneous
inhibition of urine flow elicited by beta-adrenergic stimulation and
contrary effect of alpha-adrenergic stimulation. *Journal of Pharmacology and Experimental Therapeutics*, 1967, **158**, 150-163.

Leibowitz, S. F. A hypothalamic beta-adrenergic "satiety" system antagonizes an alpha-adrenergic "hunger" system in the rat. *Nature*,
1970, **226**, 963-964. (a)

Leibowitz, S. F. Reciprocal hunger-regulating circuits involving alpha- and
beta-adrenergic receptors located, respectively, in the ventromedial
and lateral hypothalamus. *Proceedings of the National Academy of
Sciences*, 1970, **67**, 1063-1070. (b)

Leibowitz, S. F. Paraventricular nucleus: A primary site mediating
adrenergic feeding elicitation. Paper presented at Eastern Psychological
Association Meeting, 1974.

Le Magnen, J. Advances in studies on the physiological control and
regulation of food intake. *Progress in physiological psychology*, 1971.
Vol. 4.

Le Magnen, J., Devos, M., Guadilliere, J. P., Louis-Sylvestre, J., & Tallon, S.
Role of lipostatic mechanism in regulation by feeding of energy balance
in rats. *Journal of Comparative and Physiological Psychology*, 1973, **84**, 1.

MacDonnell, M. F., & Flynn, J. P. Control of sensory fields by stimulation
of hypothalamus. *Science*, 1966, **152**, 1406-1408.

MacKay, E. M., Callaway, J. W., & Barnes, R. H. Hyperalimentation
in normal animals produced by protamine insulin. *Journal of Nutrition*,
1940, **20**, 59-66.

MacNeil, D. Lateral hypothalamic self-stimulation: Effect of excess body
weight. *Physiological Psychology*, 1974, **2**, 51-53.

Margules, D. L. Separation of positive and negative reinforcing systems
in the diencephalon of the rat. *American Journal of Psychology*, 1966,
**79**, 205-216.

Margules, D. L. Noradrenergic synapses for the suppression of feeding behavior. *Life Science,* 1969, **8,** 693-704.

Margules, D. L. Alpha-adrenergic receptors in hypothalamus for the suppression of feeding by satiety. *Journal of Comparative and Physiological Psychology,* 1970, **73,** 1-12.

Margules, D. L., & Dragovich, J. A. Studies on phentolamine-induced overeating and finickiness. *Journal of Comparative and Physiological Psychology,* 1973, **84,** 644-651.

Margules, D. L., Lewis, M. J., Dragovich, J. A., & Margules, A. S. Hypothalamic norepinephrine: Circadian rhythms and the control of feeding behavior. *Science,* 1972, **178,** 640-643.

Margules, D. L., & Olds, J. Identical "feeding" and "rewarding" systems in the lateral hypothalamus of rats. *Science,* 1962, **135,** 374-375.

Marshall, J. F., & Teitelbaum, P. A comparison of the eating in response to hypothalamic and glucoprivic challenges after nigral 6-hydroxy-dopamine and lateral hypothalamic electrolytic lesions in rats. *Brain Research,* 1973, **55,** 229-233.

Marshall, J. F., Turner, B. H., & Teitelbaum, P. Sensory neglect produced by lateral hypothalamic damage. *Science,* 1971, **174,** 523-525.

Mayer, J. Glucostatic regulation of food intake. *New England Journal of Medicine,* 1953, **249,** 13.

Mendelson, J. Self-induced drinking in rats: The qualitative identity of drive and reward systems in the lateral hypothalamus. *Physiology and Behavior,* 1970, **5,** 925-930.

Mendelson, J. Ecological modulation of brain stimulation effects. *International Journal of Psychobiology,* 1972, **2,** 285-304.

Milgram, N. W., Devor, M., & Server, A. C. Spontaneous changes in behaviors induced by electrical stimulation of lateral hypothalamus in rats. *Journal of Comparative and Physiological Psychology,* 1971, **75,** 491-499.

Miliaressis, E., & Cardo, B. Self-stimulation versus food reinforcement: Comparative study of two different nervous structures, the lateral hypothalamus and the ventral tegmental area of the mesencephalon. *Brain Research,* 1973, **57,** 75-83.

Miller, N. E. Central stimulation and other new approaches to motivation and reward. *American Psychologist,* 1958, **13,** 100-108.

Miller, N. E. Motivating effects of brain stimulation and drugs. *Federation Proceedings,* 1960, **19,** 846-854.

Mogenson, G. J., Gentil, C. G., & Stevenson, J.A.F. Feeding and drinking elicited by low and high frequencies of hypothalamic stimulation. *Brain Research,* 1971, **33,** 127-137.

Mogenson, G. J., & Huang, Y. H. The neurobiology of motivated behavior. *Progress in Neurobiology,* 1973, **1,** 53-83.

Mogenson, G. J., & Kaplinsky, M. Brain self-stimulation and mechanisms of reinforcement. *Learning and Motivation*, 1970, **1**, 186-198.

Mook, D. G., Kenney, N. J., Roberts, S., Nussbaum, A. I., & Rodier, W. I. Ovarian-adrenal interaction in regulation of body weight by female rats. *Journal of Comparative and Physiological Psychology*, 1972, **81**, 198-211.

Morgane, P. J. Medial forebrain bundle and "feeding centers" of the hypothalamus. *Journal of Comparative Neurology*, 1961, **117**, 1-18.

Morgane, P. J. Metabolic and regulatory feeding deficiencies produced by central nervous lesions in rats. *Clinical Research*, 1967, **15**, 326.

Morgane, P. J., & Jacobs, H. L. Hunger and satiety. *World Review of Nutrition Dietetics*, 1969, **10**, 100-213.

Mouret, J., Bobillier, P., & Jouvet, M. Insomnia following parachlorophenylalanine in the rat. *European Journal of Pharmacology*, 1968, **5**, 17-22.

Myers, R. D. Injection of solutions into cerebral tissue: Relation between volume and diffusion. *Physiology and Behavior*, 1966, **1**, 171-174.

Myers, R. D., & Martin, G. E. 6-hydroxydopamine lesions of the hypothalamus: Interaction of aphagia, food palatability, set-point for weight regulation, and recovery of feeding. *Pharmacology, Biochemistry and Behavior*, 1973, **1**, 329-345.

Myers, R. D., & Yaksh, T. L. Feeding and temperature responses in the unrestrained rat after injections of cholinergic and aminergic substances into the cerebral ventricles. *Physiology and Behavior*, 1968, **3**, 917-928.

Nisbett, R. E. Eating behavior and obesity in men and animals. *Advances in Psychosomatic Medicine*, 1972, **7**, 173-193.

Olds, J. Physiological mechanism of reward. In M. R. Jones (Ed.), *Nebraska symposium on motivation*, **1955**. Lincoln: University of Nebraska Press, 1955. Pp. 73-139.

Olds, J., & Milner, P. Positive reinforcement produced by electrical stimulation of septal area and other regions of rat brain. *Journal of Comparative and Physiological Psychology*, 1954, **47**, 419.

Olds, M. E., & Olds, J. Approach-escape interactions in rat brain. *American Journal of Physiology*, 1962, **203**, 803-810.

Oomura, Y. Lateral hypothalamic glucosensitive neurons, ventromedial hypothalamic glucoreceptors. Paper given at International Symposium on Hunger and Regulation of Energy Balance, Ermonville, France, 1973.

Panksepp, J. Reanalysis of feeding patterns in the rat. *Journal of Comparative and Physiological Psychology*, 1973, **82**, 78-94.

Poschel, B.P.H. Do biological reinforcers act via the self-stimulation areas of the brain? *Physiology and Behavior*, 1968, **3**, 53-60.

Poschel, B.P.H., & Ninteman, F. W. Intracranial reward and forebrain's serotonergic mechanism: Studies employing para-chlorophenylalanine and para-chloroamphetamine. *Physiology and Behavior*, 1971, 7, 39-46.

Powley, T. L., & Keesey, R. E. Relationship of body weight to the lateral hypothalamic feeding syndrome. *Journal of Comparative and Physiological Psychology*, 1970, 70, 25-36.

Rabin, B. M., & Smith, C. J. Behavioral comparison of the effectiveness of irritative and non-irritative lesions in producing hypothalamic hyperphagia. *Physiology and Behavior*, 1968, 3, 417-420.

Reynolds, R. W. Ventromedial hypothalamic lesions without hyperphagia. *American Journal of Physiology*, 1963, 204, 60-62.

Roberts, W. W. Both rewarding and punishing effects from stimulation of posterior hypothalamus of cat with same electrode at same intensity. *Journal of Comparative and Physiological Psychology*, 1958, 51, 400-407.

Roberts, W. W. Are hypothalamic motivational mechanisms functionally and anatomically specific? *Brain Behavior and Evolution*, 1969, 2, 317-342.

Rolls, E. T., & Kelly, P. M. Neural basis of stimulus-bound locomotor activity in the rat. *Journal of Comparative and Physiological Psychology*, 1972, 81, 173-182.

Rosenquist, A. C., & Hoebel, B. G. Wheelrunning elicited by electrical stimulation of the brain. *Physiology and Behavior*, 1968, 3, 563-566.

Routtenberg, A. Intracranial chemical injection and behavior: A critical review. *Behavioral Biology*, 1972, 7, 601-641.

Samanin, R., Ghezzi, D., Valzelli, L., & Garattini, S. The effects of selective lesioning of brain serotonin or catecholamine containing neurones on the anorectic activity of fenfluramine and amphetamine. *European Journal of Pharmacology*, 1972, 19, 318-322.

Schachter, S. Some extraordinary facts about obese humans and rats. *American Psychologist*, 1971, 26, 129.

Schneirla, T. C. An evolutionary and developmental theory of biphasic processes underlying approach and withdrawal. In M. R. Jones (Ed.), *Nebraska symposium on motivation, 1959*. Lincoln: University of Nebraska Press, 1959. Pp. 1-42.

Sclafani, A., Gale, S. K., & Maul, G. The effects of knife cuts between the medial and lateral hypothalamus on feeding and LH self-stimulation in the rat. Submitted for publication.

Sclafani, A., & Grossman, S. P. Hyperphagia produced by knife cuts between the medial and lateral hypothalamus in the rat. *Physiology and Behavior*, 1969, 4, 533-537.

Sclafani, A., & Grossman, S. P. Reactivity of hyperphagic and normal rats to quinine and electric shock. *Journal of Comparative and Physiological Psychology*, 1971, 74, 157-166.

Sclafani, A., & Kluge, L. Food motivation and body weight levels in hypothalamic hyperphagic rats: A dual lipostatic model of hunger and appetite. *Journal of Comparative and Physiological Psychology*, 1974, 86, 28-46.

Sclafani, A., Springer, D., & Kluge, L. Effects of diet palatability on the body weight of hypothalamic hyperphagic rats. Submitted for publication.

Scott, T. R., & Hoebel, B. G. Effect of sex hormones on lateral hypothalamic self-stimulation and feeding. *American Zoologist*, 1966, 6, Abstr. no. 144.

Sheard, M. The effect of p-chlorophenylalanine on behavior in rats: Relation to brain serotonin and 5-hydroxyindoleacetic acid. *Brain Research*, 1969, 15, 524-528.

Singh, D. Effects of preoperative training on food-motivated behavior of hypothalamic hyperphagic rats. *Journal of Comparative and Physiological Psychology*, 1973, 84, 47-52.

Smith, M. H. Effects of intravenous injections on eating. *Journal of Comparative and Physiological Psychology*, 1966, 61, 11-14.

Stark, P., & Totty, C. W. Effects of amphetamines on eating elicited by hypothalamic stimulation. *Journal of Pharmacology and Experimental Therapeutics*, 1967, 158, 272-278.

Stein, L., & Wise, C. D. Mechanism of the facilitating effects of amphetamine on behavior. In D. H. Efron (Ed.), *Psychotominetic drugs*. New York: Raven, 1970. Pp. 123-149.

Steinbaum, E. A., & Miller, N. E. Obesity from eating elicited by daily stimulation of hypothalamus. *American Journal of Physiology*, 1965, 208, 1-5.

Stevenson, J.A.F. Mechanisms in the control of food and water intake. *Annals of the New York Academy of Sciences*, 1969, 157 (R2), 1069-1083.

Stowe, F. R., & Miller, A. T. The effect of amphetamine on food intake in rats with hypothalamic hyperphagia. *Experientia*, 1957, 13, 114-115.

Szabo, I. Drive-decay theory of instrumental self-stimulation: Motor correlates. *Acta Physiol. Acad. Sci. Hungary*, 1972, 42, 255-265.

Taylor, K. M., & Snyder, S. H. Amphetamine: Differentiation by d- and l-isomers of behavior involving brain norepinephrine or dopamine. *Science*, 1970, 168, 1487-1489.

Teitelbaum, P. Sensory control of hypothalamic hyperphagia. *Journal of Comparative and Physiological Psychology*, 1955, 48, 156-163.

Teitelbaum, P. Disturbances in feeding and drinking behavior after hypothalamic lesions. In M. R. Jones (Ed.), *Nebraska symposium on motivation, 1961*. Lincoln: University of Nebraska Press, 1961. Pp. 39-69.

Teitelbaum, P. The biology of drive. In G. C. Quarton, T. Melnichuk, and F. O. Schmitt (Eds.), *The neuro-sciences: A study program*. New York: Rockefeller University Press, 1967.

Teitelbaum, P. On the use of electrical stimulation to study hypothalamic structure and function. In A. N. Epstein, H. R. Kissileff, and E. Stellar (Eds.), *The neuropsychology of thirst*. New York: Winston, 1974. Pp. 143-154.

Teitelbaum, P., & Campbell, B. A. Ingestion patterns in hyperphagic and normal rats. *Journal of Comparative and Physiological Psychology*, 1958, **51**, 135-141.

Teitelbaum, P., Cheng, M. F., & Rozin, P. Development of feeding parallels its recovery after hypothalamic damage. *Journal of Comparative and Physiological Psychology*, 1969, **67**, 430-441.

Tenen, S. S., & Miller, N. E. Strength of electrical stimulation of lateral hypothalamus, food deprivation and tolerance for quinine in food. *Journal of Comparative and Physiological Psychology*, 1964, **58**, 55-62.

Trowill, J. A., Panksepp, J., & Gandelman, R. An incentive model of rewarding brain stimulation. *Psychological Review*, 1969, **76**, 264-281.

Ungerstedt, U. Adipsia and aphagia after 6-hydroxydopamine induced degeration of the nigro-striatal dopamine system. *Acta Physiologica Scandinavica*, 1971. Suppl. 367. (a)

Ungerstedt, U. Stereotaxic mapping of the monoamine pathways in the rat brain. *Acta Physiologica Scandinavica*, 1971. Suppl. 367. (b)

Valenstein, E. S. *Brain Control: A Critical Examination of Brain Stimulation and Psychosurgery*. New York: Wiley, 1973. (a)

Valenstein, E. S. *Brain Stimulation and Motivation*. Glenview, Ill.: Scott, Foresman, 1973. (b)

Valenstein, E. S., Cox, V. C., & Kakolewski, J. W. The hypothalamus and motivated behavior. In J. T. Tapp (Ed.), *Reinforcement and behavior*. New York & London: Academic Press, 1969. Pp. 242-287.

Van Sommers, P., & Teitelbaum, P. Spread of damage produced by electrolytic lesions in hypothalamus. *Journal of Comparative and Physiological Psychology*, 1974, **86**, 288-299.

Wampler R. S. Increased motivation in rats with ventromedial hypothalamic lesions. *Journal of Comparative and Physiological Psychology*, 1973, **84**, 275-285.

Weissman, A., Koe, B. K., & Tenen, S. S. Antiamphetamine effects following inhibition of tyrosine hydroxylase. *Journal of Pharmacology and Experimental Therapeutics*, 1966, **151**, 339-352.

Wise, R. A. Lateral hypothalamic electrical stimulation: Does it make animals "hungry"? 1974, in press.

Wise, R. A., & Albin, J. Stimulation-induced eating disrupted by conditional taste aversion. *Behavioral Biology*, 1973, **9**, 289-297.

Wise, R. A., & Erdmann, E. Emotionality, hunger and normal eating: Implications for interpretation of electrically induced behavior. *Behavioral Biology*, 1973, **8**, 519-531.

Wolf, G., & DiCara, L. V. Progressive morphologic changes in electrolytic brain lesions. *Experimental Neurology*, 1969, **23**, 529-536.

Young, P. T. The role of hedonic process in motivation. In M. R. Jones (Ed.), *Nebraska symposium on motivation, 1955*. Lincoln: University of Nebraska Press, 1955. Pp. 193-238.

Zigmond, M. J., & Stricker, E. M. Recovery of feeding and drinking by rats after intraventricular 6-hydroxydopamine or lateral hypothalamic lesions. *Science*, 1973, **182**, 717-719.

Ziance, R. J., Sipes, I. G., Kinnard, W. J., Jr., & Buckley, J. P. Central nervous system effects of fenfluramine hydrochloride. *Journal of Pharmacology and Experimental Therapeutics*, 1971, **180**, 110-117.

# Norepinephrine Reward Pathways: Role in Self-Stimulation, Memory Consolidation, and Schizophrenia

## Larry Stein[1]

*Wyeth Laboratories,*
*Philadelphia, Pennsylvania*

*T*he idea that the brain's reward system may be made up of norepinephrine (NE)-containing neurons has guided our research for more than a decade (Stein & Seifter, 1961; Stein, 1962). In the first part of this review, we consider the evidence that NE pathways are involved in self-stimulation of the brain. Special emphasis is placed on the question of the relative importance of NE and dopamine (DA) systems in the mediation of this behavior. In the second section, we report new studies which suggest that NE systems are also involved in learning and long-term memory. Finally, we speculate on the implications of these findings for the pathogenesis of schizophrenia.

SELF-STIMULATION

Analysis of the structure of the reward system has been facilitated by the discovery that animals will electrically self-stimulate certain regions of their own brains (Olds & Milner, 1954). Like all operant behavior, self-stimulation requires a source of reinforcement for its maintenance. In the absence of other sources of positive reinforcement, the reward for self-stimulation must arise from the neuronal activity that is excited by the electrical stimulus. Although such centrally elicited reinforcement could be an artifact, it more plausibly represents a direct activation of the brain's normal reward

1. The work which provided the basis for this paper was done in collaboration with Drs. C. David Wise, James D. Belluzzi, and Sue Ritter, who generously contributed ideas and data in the preparation of this presentation.

system (Deutsch, 1960; Olds, 1962; Stein, 1964a; Gallistel, 1973). If so, identification of the pathways that subserve self-stimulation would reveal the pathways that subserve reward.

Because the field of stimulation contains diverse neural elements, identification of those neurons which are actually responsible for self-stimulation is largely a matter of inference. Solutions may be based on mapping studies which demonstrate self-stimulation in anatomically coherent systems, and on pharmacological studies which implicate specific neurotransmitters. Anatomical and pharmacological evidence of this kind has produced widespread agreement that NE-containing neurons in the brain play a critical role in self-stimulation (Stein, 1962, 1968; Poschel & Ninteman, 1963; Arbuthnott, Fuxe, & Ungerstedt, 1971; Stinus & Thierry, 1973; Phillips & Fibiger, 1973; Wise, Berger, & Stein, 1973). More recently, it has been suggested that DA neurons also may be activated to yield self-stimulation (Crow, 1972a, 1972b; Clavier & Routtenberg, 1974; German & Bowden, 1974). The DA hypothesis has generated a lively controversy, and new evidence which bears on its validity is described in detail below.

Pharmacological Evidence Implicating Norepinephrine

In early studies, it was found that self-stimulation behavior is selectively affected by drugs that influence central catecholamine transmission (Stein, 1962, 1964b). Substances that release catecholamines rapidly from functional stores (such as amphetamine or phenethylamine in combination with a monoamine oxidase inhibitor) facilitate self-stimulation. Conversely, drugs that deplete catecholamine stores (reserpine) or inhibit catecholamine synthesis ($\alpha$-methyl-$p$-tyrosine) or block catecholamine receptors (chlorpromazine, haloperidol) suppress self-stimulation. Later work suggested that the relevant catecholamine is NE (Wise & Stein, 1969, 1970). Selective blockade of NE synthesis by inhibition of dopamine-$\beta$-hydroxylase (DBH), the enzyme that converts DA to NE, abolished self-stimulation and eliminated the rate-enhancing action of amphetamine. Intraventricular administration of $l$-NE after DBH inhibition reinstated self-stimulation and restored the facilitatory action of amphetamine; in control experiments, similar injections of $d$-NE and DA were ineffective. Central injections of NE also

*Norepinephrine Reward Pathways*

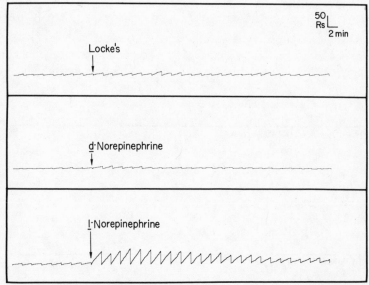

FIG. 1. Facilitation of lateral hypothalamic self-stimulation by *l*-norepin-ephrine (10 µg.). The drug was dissolved in 10 µl. of Ringer-Locke solution and injected in the lateral ventricle. Control injections of Ringer-Locke solution or *d*-norepinephrine hydrochloride (10 µg.) had negligible effects. Pen cumulates self-stimulation responses and resets automatically every 2 minutes (see key in upper right-hand corner). (From Wise, Berger, & Stein, 1973.)

facilitate self-stimulation in undrugged rats, presumably by enrich-ing the presynaptic stores of transmitter (fig. 1).

The NE receptor involved in behavioral reinforcement appears to be of the α-type (Wise, Berger, & Stein, 1973). Intraventricular administration of the α-NE antagonist phentolamine, but not the β-antagonist propranolol, reduced the rate of self-stimulation and blocked the facilitatory effect of amphetamine (fig. 2). In other experiments, rewarding brain stimulation or moderate doses of amphetamine given to freely moving rats with permanently indwel-ling cannulas released NE and its metabolites into brain perfusates (Stein & Wise, 1969). Both treatments caused shifts in the pattern of metabolites toward *O*-methylated products (see also Glowinski & Axelrod, 1965).

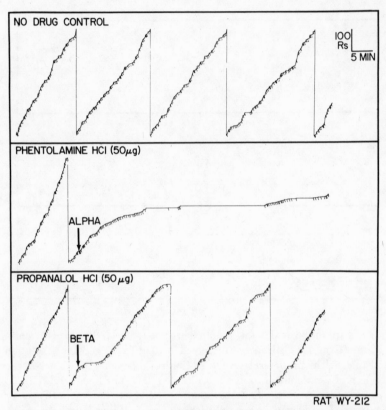

FIG. 2. Selective suppression of self-stimulation by central α-noradrenergic blockade. Phentolamine (α-antagonist) and propranolol (β-antagonist) were injected in the lateral ventricle 15 minutes after the start of a 75-minute test. Pen resets automatically after 500 responses. Variable interval reinforcement schedule. (From Wise, Berger, & Stein, 1973.)

Anatomical Evidence Implicating Norepinephrine

These pharmacological observations fit nicely with the results of self-stimulation mapping studies on the one hand and histochemical maps of NE pathways on the other. This histochemical work presently demonstrates three major ascending NE fiber systems in the rat brainstem (Fuxe, Hökfelt, & Ungerstedt, 1970; Ungerstedt, 1971b; Jacobowitz, 1973; Lindvall & Björklund, 1974) A *dorsal* pathway originates mainly in the principal locus coeruleus (NE cell group A6 in the classification of Dahlström & Fuxe, 1964) and

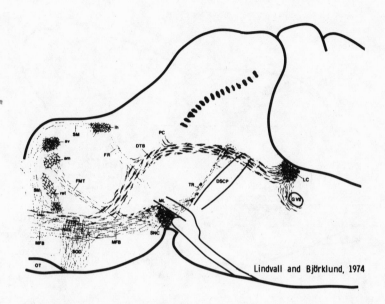

Lindvall and Björklund, 1974

FIG. 3a. Semidiagrammatic representation of the dorsal noradrenergic bundle (DTB), originating in the locus coeruleus (LC), and its projections in the diencephalon. The medial part of the medial forebrain bundle (MFB) and cells in the pars compacta of the substantia nigra (SNC) are also included. For other abbreviations, see Lindvall and Björklund (1974).

innervates neocortex, cerebellum, hippocampus, and thalamus, (fig. 3a). A *ventral* pathway originates more heterogeneously and mainly from NE cell groups in the medulla oblongata and pons (A1, A2, A5, A6, and A7) and innervates hypothalamus and ventral parts of the limbic system (fig. 3c). And a newly discovered *periventricular* pathway originates in part from disseminated NE cell bodies in the central gray matter and innervates medial regions of thalamus and hypothalamus (fig. 3b). All three NE systems may subserve self-stimulation. Detailed mapping studies and supporting pharmacological evidence indicate that electrodes in the dorsal pathway or its cells of origin in the locus coeruleus support high rates of self-stimulation (Crow, Spear, & Arbuthnott, 1972; Ritter & Stein, 1973). High rates of self-stimulation also have been obtained from ventrocaudal sites in the mesencephalic central gray in the region of

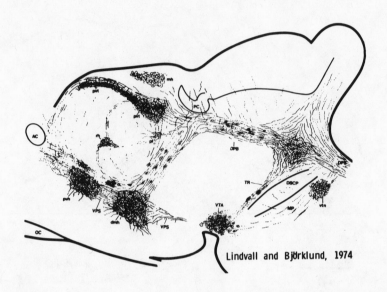

Lindvall and Björklund, 1974

FIG. 3b. Semidiagrammatic representation of the periventricular noradrenergic bundle (DPB) rostral to the lócus coeruleus, the medial fiber flow of the tegmental radiations (TR), and the catecholamine fibers of the mamillary peduncle (MP). For other abbreviations, see Lindvall and Björklund (1974).

the dorsal raphe nucleus (Margules, 1969; Routtenberg & Malsbury, 1969; Liebman, Mayer, & Liebeskind, 1973) or just rostral to the locus coeruleus (Ritter & Stein, 1973). Although self-stimulation generally is not obtained and mostly aversive effects are reported in more rostral central gray sites (Liebman, Mayer, & Liebeskind, 1973), these reports can now be taken as evidence that activation of at least some components of the periventricular NE system also yields positive reinforcement.

The role of the ventral NE pathway in self-stimulation, however, is still disputed. Arbuthnott, Fuxe, and Ungerstedt (1971) obtained self-stimulation from five electrodes in the ventral bundle at the level of the interpeduncular nucleus; furthermore, they observed in all positive cases (but not in 15 out of 16 non-self-stimulators) an increased turnover of NE on the stimulated side in hypothalamic and limbic system areas innervated by terminals of the ventral bundle. Similar results with slightly more rostral reward placements

## THREE MAJOR ASCENDING NE PATHWAYS IN RAT BRAIN STEM

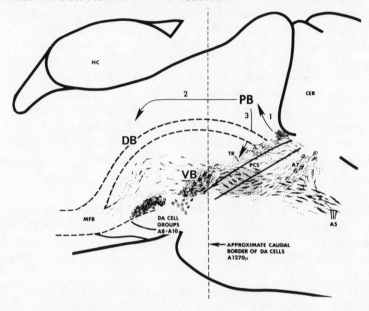

FIG. 3c. Semidiagrammatic representation of the ventral noradrenergic bundle (VB) in relation to the principal dopamine (DA) cell groups (after Lindvall & Björklund, 1974). Dorsal and periventricular noradrenergic pathways (DB and PB, respectively) follow more medial courses and are depicted schematically. Composite drawing of different sagittal planes. The VB was mapped for self-stimulation throughout the region of its separation from the DB. Stippled rectangle shows approximate location of 11 self-stimulation electrodes in a region of VB caudal to all known DA cell groups (also see fig. 4). Other abbreviations: 1 = caudal PB; 2 = dorsal PB; 3 = ventral PB; A7 = subcoeruleus noradrenergic cell group; CER = cerebellum; HC = hippocampus; MFB = medial forebrain bundle; PCS = superior cerebellar peduncle; TR = tegmental radiations. (From Ritter & Stein, 1974.)

in the area ventralis tegmenti also have been reported (Stinus et al., 1973). On the other hand, Anlezark et al. (1974) and Clavier and Routtenberg (1974) failed to obtain self-stimulation either from within the A1 or A2 areas or from the ascending fibers of the ventral bundle at the level of the locus coeruleus; both groups concluded that their experiments do not support the contention that the ventral bundle of NE neurons is involved in electrical self-stimulation.

Recently, Ritter and Stein (1974) mapped the trajectory of the ventral bundle for self-stimulation throughout the region of its separation from the dorsal bundle in the mesencephalon of the rat. Eleven rewarding electrodes were localized in the ventral bundle at sites clearly caudal to all known DA cell groups (fig. 4). Since activation of DA neurons or other NE systems by current spread could be ruled out, the positive reinforcement was attributed to NE fibers in the ventral bundle itself. The cells of origin of these positive fibers were not identified, but NE neurons in rostrally located cell groups (A6 and A7) were thought to be more likely candidates than those in caudally located groups (A1, A2, and A5). Only nonrewarding electrodes have thus far been found in the area of the three caudal cell groups or in the trajectory of the ventral bundle posterior to the level of the locus coeruleus (Anlezark et al., 1974; Clavier & Routtenberg, 1974). On the other hand, cell groups A6 and A7 supply an important inflow of fibers to the ventral bundle anterior to the locus coeruleus (Lindvall & Björklund, 1974), and electrodes in the region of both A6 and A7 support high rates of self-stimulation (Crow, Spear, & Arbuthnott, 1972; Ritter & Stein, 1973).

If NE fibers in the ventral bundle in fact support self-stimulation, then it would appear that activation of all three major ascending NE systems in the brain yields positive reinforcement. The evolutionary selection of the NE neuron for reward functions raises interesting questions about the neurochemical characteristics that suit it for this role and the anatomical organization that permits its fulfillment. It is also interesting to consider in what ways reward functions may be differentiated or specialized among the three systems. The innervation of neocortex, hippocampus, thalamus, and cerebellum by the dorsal pathway suggests its involvement in associative thinking and learning (Anlezark, Crow, & Greenway, 1973; Kety, 1970, 1972a; Ritter & Stein, 1973; Stein & Wise, 1971); the capacity of neurons in this pathway for regeneration and new growth (Stenevi et al., 1974), and hence for reorganization, supports this suggestion. The innervation of hypothalamus and limbic system by the ventral pathway suggests involvement in motivation, mood, and neuroendocrine function (Olson & Fuxe, 1972; Stein & Wise, 1971; Stein, Wise, & Berger, 1972). And the periventricular system's innervations of medial hypothalamus and mesencephalic central gray suggests, respectively, an involvement in feeding (Leibowitz, 1972)

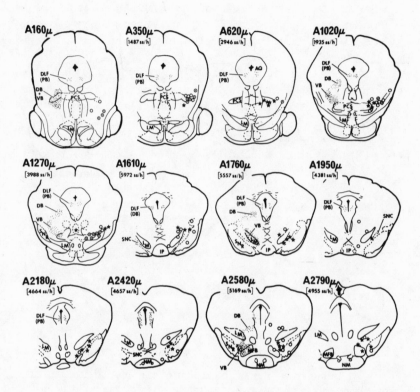

FIG. 4. Summary of electrode placements on frontal sections of rat brainstem from the atlas of König and Klippel (1963). Locations of ventral noradrenergic bundle (VB) and dorsal noradrenergic bundle (DB) were taken from the atlas of Ungerstedt 1971b). Explanation of symbols: ★ positive for self-stimulation; O negative for self-stimulation; ⊙ escape. Eleven positive VB cases, appearing in the sections in the top row, are located caudally to the principal dopaminergic cell groups. Uppermost numbers refer to the distance in μ anterior (A) to the zero plane of the König and Klippel atlas. Numbers in brackets indicate the mean response rate of the positive self-stimulators at each level. Key to abbreviations: AQ = cerebral aqueduct; DLF (PB) = dorsal longitudinal fasciculus (periventricular noradrenergic bundle); IP = interpeduncular nucleus; LM = medial lemniscus; MFB = medial forebrain bundle; NM = mammillary nucleus; PCS = superior cerebellar peduncle; SNC = substantia nigra, zona compacta (dopamine cell group A6); SNR = substantia nigra, zona reticulata; SS/h = self-stimulations per hour. (From Ritter & Stein, 1974.)

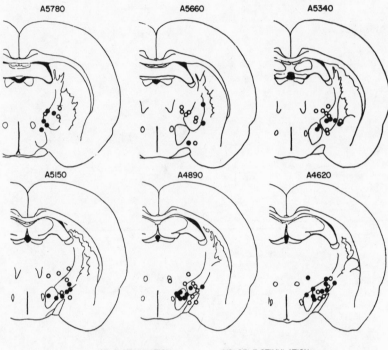

● SELF-STIMULATION     ○ NO SELF-STIMULATION

FIG. 5. Self-stimulation sites in the region of the internal capsule. Electrode placements are shown on frontal sections of rat brain from the atlas of König and Klippel (1963). Uppermost numbers refer to the distance in μ anterior (A) to the zero plane of the atlas. Positive electrodes fall in the medial forebrain bundle, the ansa lenticularis (A5150), in the region surrounding the tip of the crus cerebri, and the ento-peduncular nucleus (A5340). (After Kojima et al., unpublished data.)

and interactions with pain and punishment systems (Mayer & Liebeskind, 1974; Stein, Wise, & Berger, 1973).

Self-Stimulation and Brain Dopamine

While it is evident that NE is crucially involved in self-stimulation, the role of DA is still unclear. Mapping studies suggest that the DA tracts in the medial forebrain bundle and internal capsule can support self-stimulation, but this evidence is inconclusive because of the close proximity of NE tracts. Thus, Kojima et. al. (cited in

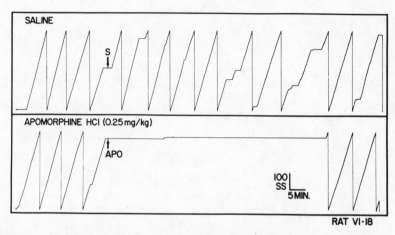

FIG. 6. Suppression of internal capsule self-stimulation by apomorphine (APO). (After Kojima et al., unpublished data.)

Stein & Wise, 1973) obtained self-stimulation from some electrodes in the internal capsule, particularly from sites surrounding the tip of the crus cerebri (fig. 5); however, maximum rates were only about 20 percent of the maximum rates obtained from medial forebrain bundle electrodes. The most reinforcing internal capsule placements were located either in medial sites that border on the NE fiber system in the medial forebrain bundle, or in ventrolateral sites just dorsal to the NE projection into the amygdala. Internal capsule self-stimulation was facilitated by *d*- and *l*-amphetamine but *d*-amphetamine was about nine times more potent.

High doses of amphetamine induce a stereotyped behavior pattern that appears to be mediated by the release of DA (Randrup & Munkvad, 1967, 1970); however, at these high doses of amphetamine, self-stimulation is usually suppressed rather than facilitated (Stein & Wise, 1970). Apomorphine, a centrally active DA receptor stimulant, also suppresses self-stimulation, even when electrodes are located in the internal capsule (fig. 6) (Liebman & Butcher, 1973; Stein & Wise, 1973; but also see St.-Laurent et al., 1973, and Wauquier & Niemegeers, 1973). This observation can be interpreted in various ways. On the one hand, if internal capsule self-stimulation were reinforced by the activation of DA neurons, the intense DA stimulation caused by apomorphine could render the behavior superfluous. On the other hand, apomorphine may simply induce

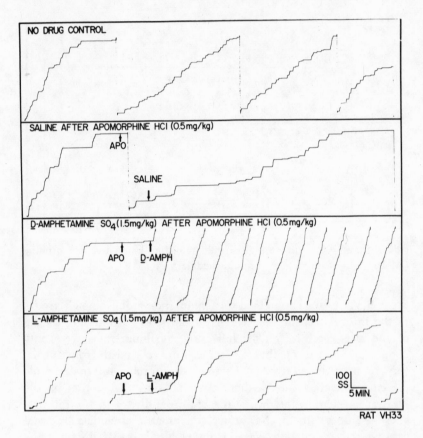

FIG. 7. Suppression of internal capsule self-stimulation by apomorphine (APO) and reversal by d-amphetamine. The same dose of l-amphetamine has only a small effect. (After Kojima et al., unpublished data.)

a stereotyped response pattern that competes with and disrupts NE-mediated goal-directed behavior. The second interpretation implies that it might be possible to antagonize apomorphine's suppressant action by administration of NE-enhancing drugs. Such seems to be the case. In moderate doses, amphetamine readily reverses apomorphine-induced suppression of self-stimulation (fig. 7).

The effects of NE and DA on self-stimulation were directly examined by injecting these agents into the lateral ventricle via permanently indwelling cannulas. l-NE facilitated medial forebrain bundle self-stimulation at low doses and suppressed it at high doses

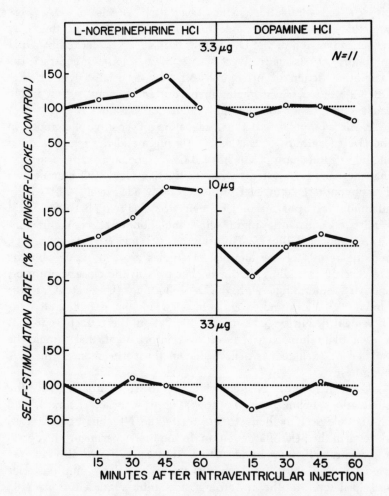

FIG. 8. Facilitation of self-stimulation by norepinephrine and suppression by dopamine. The catecholamines were dissolved in 10 μl. of Ringer-Locke solution and injected into the lateral ventricle one-half hour after the start of the 90-minute test. Averaged data of 11 rats with electrodes in the medial forebrain bundle (level of posterior hypothalamus). (From Stein & Wise, 1973.)

(Stein & Wise, 1973) (fig. 8). Similar doses of DA generally suppressed self-stimulation. Mild facilitating effects of DA were sometimes observed after a delay of several minutes, and thus may reflect conversion of the DA to NE. If this step is blocked by DBH inhibitors, DA is ineffective (Wise & Stein, 1969). In contrast, the facilitating action of exogenous NE was especially evident after DBH inhibition, since depletion of the endogenous stores of NE causes suppression of the self-stimulation baseline.

As already indicated, the localization of positive electrodes in the DA cell groups of the substantia nigra and the region around the interpeduncular nucleus has led Crow (1972a, 1972b) to suggest that there are DA systems whose activation yields self-stimulation. This hypothesis, however, has not been adequately verified by anatomical and pharmacological evidence. The two pharmacological studies of substantia nigra self-stimulation offer conflicting interpretations (Phillips & Fibiger, 1973; Stinus & Thierry, 1973), and the results of the anatomical studies are confounded by the presence of ascending NE tracts that pass in the close vicinity of, and partly intermingle with, the DA cell groups (Ungerstedt, 1971b; Lindvall & Björklund, 1974). In view of the demonstrated involvement of NE systems in self-stimulation, these tracts represent a potentially important source of reinforcement that should be isolated or excluded as a first step in the verification of the DA hypothesis.

To evaluate the NE contribution to substantia nigra self-stimulation, Belluzzi et al. (1975) used surgical, chemical, and pharmacological methods to inactivate the NE, but not the DA, systems in the field of stimulation. In the first experiment, the dorsal and ventral NE fiber bundles were transected by a knife cut just caudal to the interpeduncular nucleus, at a level 2.5 mm. posterior and ipsilateral to the rewarding substantia nigra electrode (fig. 9). This level is caudal to all known central DA systems (Ungerstedt, 1971b). Only an ipsilateral cut was thought to be necessary because the NE fibers are mostly uncrossed (Ungerstedt, 1971b); for the same reason, contralateral knife cuts were expected to be largely ineffective and were placed in control rats to assess any nonspecific effects of the brain damage. A retracting, 150-μm. stainless steel wire knife was used to transect deep structures with minimum damage to overlying structures (Sclafani & Grossman, 1969; Gold, Kapatos, & Carey, 1973).

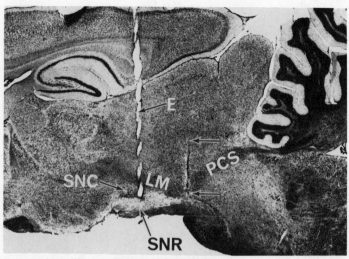

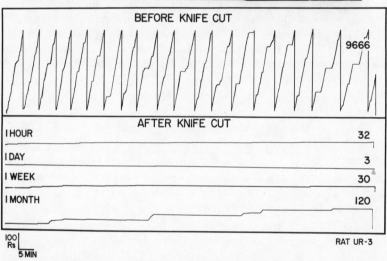

FIG. 9. *A.* Sagittal section of rat brain showing knife cut (dorsoventral extent marked by arrows) and electrode track (E) terminating in dopamine cells of substantia nigra. Other abbreviations are substantia nigra, zona compacta (SNC); substantia nigra, zona reticulata (SNR); medial lemniscus (LM) and superior cerebellar peduncle (PCS). Klüver-Barrera (1953) stain. *B.* Curves of substantia nigra self-stimulation for the rat whose histology is shown above. Priming, reshaping, and increases of current failed to restore self-stimulation after the knife cut in this case. Numbers indicate self-stimulations in the 2-hour tests. (After Belluzzi et al., 1975.)

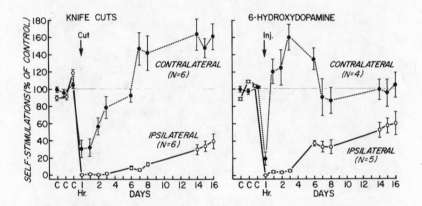

FIG. 10. Daily rates of substantia nigra self-stimulation after unilateral damage to ascending noradrenergic tracts by knife cuts or local injections of 6-hydroxydopamine, both placed caudally to the principal dopamine cell groups. Self-stimulation rates are expressed as percentages of 3-day control means. Bars indicate standard errors of mean. C, control days before treatments. (From Belluzzi et al., 1975.)

Ipsilateral knife cuts through the dorsal and ventral NE bundles virtually abolished substantia nigra self-stimulation for three days, starting within one hour after the operation (fig. 10). Self-stimulation remained suppressed over the next several weeks, although varying degrees of partial recovery were observed in most cases. In a few cases, no recovery was obtained despite efforts to restore the response by priming, reshaping, and increases of current. In contrast, contralateral knife cuts caused only partial suppression of self-stimulation behavior during the first three days, and recovery occured rapidly. Indeed, by the end of the first week, the response rate in the contralateral group had significantly exceeded that prior to surgery, and, by the end of the second week, had stabilized at about 160 percent of control.

In both groups, spontaneous circling away from the cut side was observed in almost every case. The circling started immediately after the operation and persisted for at least several days. In about one-third of the rats, feeding was disrupted for a few days.

In a second experiment, the dorsal and ventral NE bundles were chemically lesioned, at the same caudal level as before, by local

**Table 1**

*Mean Concentrations of Brain Catecholamines* (µg./g.) ± S.E.M.
*after Completion of Behavioral Tests (Approximately 1 Month after Treatments)*

| Treatment | Forebrain Minus Striatum* | | | | Striatal Dopamine | |
|---|---|---|---|---|---|---|
| | Norepinephrine | | Dopamine | | Dopamine | |
| | Treated Side | Untreated Side | Treated Side | Untreated Side | Treated Side | Untreated Side |
| Ascorbate | 0.523 | 0.554 | 0.534 | 0.458 | 4.935 | 6.324 |
| Control | ±0.030 | ±0.039 | ±0.050 | ±0.021 | ±0.632 | ±0.329 |
| (N = 5) | | | | | | |
| Knife Cut | 0.290† | 0.551 | 0.639 | 0.630 | 5.780 | 6.164 |
| (N = 7) | ±0.029 | ±0.050 | ±0.064 | ±0.065 | ±0.470 | ±0.525 |
| | (54.9)‡ | (99.5) | (119.6) | (137.6) | (117.1) | (97.5) |
| | | | | | | |
| 6-Hydroxy- | 0.134† | 0.443 | 0.440 | 0.591 | 3.633 | 5.314 |
| dopamine | ±0.022 | ±0.024 | ±0.058 | ±0.032 | ±0.533 | ±0.262 |
| (N = 9) | (25.4) | (80.0) | (82.3) | (129.1) | (73.6) | (84.0) |

*Source:* Belluzzi et al., 1975.

*Brains were dissected by a vertical transection through the rostral diencephalon at a level approximately 3 mm anterior to the substantia nigra electrode.

† Significantly different from ascorbate control, P < .001.

‡ Numbers in parentheses indicate percent of ascorbate control.

applications of 6-hydroxydopamine (10 µg. in 1 µl. of saline). Because the toxic drug is selectively taken up and concentrated in catecholamine neurons (Ungerstedt, 1971a), the injections were expected to cause a more specific degeneration of the NE fiber bundles than can be produced by knife cuts. Again, ipsilateral damage to NE systems caused an almost immediate suppression of substantia nigra self-stimulation that persisted, with only partial recovery, throughout the observation period (fig. 10). The effects of contralaterally injected 6-hydroxydopamine similarly resembled those of the contralateral knife cuts; however, the initial suppressant effect was observed only on the day of injection, and the phase of supranormal response, which again peaked at about 160 percent of control, appeared several days earlier. In contrast to the persistent

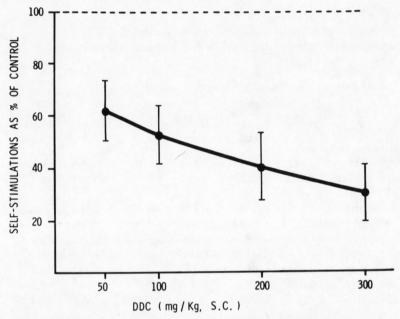

FIG. 11. Suppression of substantia nigra self-stimulation by subcutaneous administration of diethyldithiocarbamate (DDC) 1 hour prior to the 2-hour test. Tests at the different doses were spaced 2 weeks apart. (From Ritter et al., unpublished data).

contraversive turning which was caused by the knife cuts, only transient ipsiversive turning was observed after the administration of 6-hydroxydopamine. Also, unlike the knife cuts, the drug injections did not disrupt feeding.

Brain catecholamines were analyzed for representative rats in both experiments (table 1). The knife cuts caused a selective 45 percent reduction in forebrain NE on the treated side, but no reduction of forebrain or striatal DA on either side. The 6-hydroxydopamine injections decreased NE levels by 75 percent on the treated side and by 20 percent on the untreated side; striatal and nonstriatal DA on the treated side was also reduced by 26 and 18 percent, respectively. Although the 6-hydroxydopamine injections thus appeared to cause some injury to DA neurons, the biochemical analysis generally confirms that both manipulations produced largely

**Table 2**

*Summary Data of Diethyldithiocarbamate (DDC)-
Reversal Experiments*

| Treatment | Dose (μg.) | Number of Rats | Self-Stimulations (% of undrugged control) | |
|---|---|---|---|---|
| | | | Before Treatment | After Treatment |
| Ringer-Locke solution | — | 5 | $15.1\pm11.8$ | $11.4\pm11.4$ |
| Dopamine | 10 | 4 | $10.2\pm7.2$ | $7.6\pm7.5$ |
| Clonidine† | 0.5 or 1 | 5 | $11.4\pm11.4$ | $6.3\pm6.3$ |
| Norepinephrine | 10 | 8 | $8.3\pm4.5$ | $114.8\pm27.9*$ |

*Source*: Ritter et al., unpublished data.

*Note*: Substantia nigra self-stimulation was suppressed by subcutaneous administration of diethyldithiocarbamate (200 or 300 mg./kg.). Two to 3 hours later, intraventricular injections of the indicated substances were made in an attempt to reinstate the suppressed behavior. Scores indicate self-stimulation rates in the 15-minute periods just before and after intraventricular injections as a percent of the undrugged rate in the same time period on a preceding control day. The mean undrugged rate for all rats was $798.8\pm116.2$ self-stimulations/15 min. See figure 12 for an illustrative experiment.

\* Different from all other treatments, $p < .01$.

† Tested after Ringer-Locke solution.

selective damage to NE pathways on the treated side as intended. Furthermore, while total brain levels provide only a crude measure of the relevant catecholamine stores, final self-stimulation rates in both groups correlated significantly with ipsilateral levels of NE (rho = 0.61, $p < .02$), but not striatal DA (rho = 0.12, $p > 0.1$) nor nonstriatal DA (rho = 0.18, $p < 0.1$).

In a related experiment by Ritter et al. (cited in Belluzzi et al., 1975) the involvement of NE systems in substantia nigra self-stimulation was analyzed pharmacologically by the use of diethyldithiocarbamate (DDC), an inhibitor of DBH. DDC thus decreases the synthesis and the brain concentration of NE, while the concentration of DA remains unchanged or is slightly increased (Goldstein & Nakajima, 1967). Subcutaneous injections of DDC (50

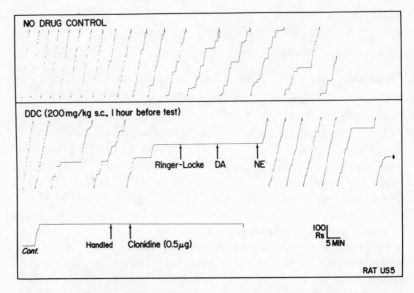

FIG. 12. Suppression of substantia nigra self-stimulation after inhibition of norepinephrine synthesis by diethyldithiocarbamate (DDC) and its selective reinstatement by an injection of *l*-norepinephrine hydrochloride (NE, 10 μg.) in the lateral ventricle. Similar injections of Ringer-Locke solution and dopamine (DA, 10 μg.) were ineffective. In other animals, similar results were obtained when the sequence of norepinephrine and dopamine injections was reversed. Direct stimulation of noradrenergic receptors by intraventricularly injected clonidine also was without effect, which suggests that presynaptic uptake and replenishment of functional stores of norepinephrine, and not simply restoration of central noradrenergic "tone," is required for the reinstatement of self-stimulation. (From Ritter et al., unpublished data.)


to 300 mg./kg.) in 21 rats caused dose-related decreases in the rate of substantia nigra self-stimulation, with nearly complete suppression in most cases within one to three hours after the higher doses (fig. 11.) During this time the animals were hypoactive but not asleep. Reversal experiments demonstrated that the suppression of self-stimulation by DDC was due to its inhibitory action on DBH and the consequent depletion of NE, and not to some other action unrelated to the metabolism of NE. Intraventricular administration of 10 μg. of *l*-NE hydrochloride, which rapidly replenishes depleted stores of the transmitter, restored the suppressed behavior of 8 rats within the first 15 minutes after injection to 114.8 ± 27.9 percent of control (e.g., fig. 12). Similar injections of Ringer-Locke solution, DA, or clonidine were ineffective (table 2).

Belluzzi's and Ritter's experiments thus show that electrodes in the substantia nigra lose their ability to support self-stimulation after surgical, chemical, or pharmacological treatments that inactivate NE systems, but leave DA systems relatively unaffected. These findings and the fact that three different approaches produced convergent results strongly suggest that ipsilateral NE fibers of passage play an essential role in the mediation of substantia nigra self-stimulation. The origin of these fibers cannot yet be specified with certainty, but it is probable from recent histochemical evidence (Lindvall & Björklund, 1974) that they mainly involve those components of the dorsal, ventral, and periventricular NE fiber systems which enter the ventral mesencephalon via the tegmental radiations and intermingle with the DA cell bodies and their outgoing fibers.

The role of the DA systems, and their relationship to NE systems, remains to be clarified. Ritter and Stein (1974) found that rostrally placed electrodes in the ventral NE bundle (in regions of NE and DA overlap) yielded higher maximum self-stimulation rates than more caudal ventral bundle electrodes in relatively "pure" NE sites (fig. 4). It was suggested, among other explanations, that self-stimulation at the rostral sites may have been enhanced by the simultaneous activation of NE and DA neurons. The possibility that both catecholamines may be involved in rostral mesencephalic self-stimulation may be considered a "weak" form of the DA hypothesis, an idea which is consistent with anatomical and pharmacological evidence (Crow, 1972b; Liebman & Butcher, 1973; Lippa et al., 1973; Wauquier & Niemegeers, 1972). The "strong" form of the DA hypothesis holds that the activation of DA neurons alone will yield self-stimulation (Crow, 1972a). Although this idea is indirectly supported by the demonstration that rats will intravenously self-inject the DA receptor stimulant apomorphine (Baxter et al., 1974), it is clearly contradicted by the previously described studies of Belluzi et al. (1975) and Ritter et al. (unpublished data). New methods for the selective stimulation and inactivation of DA systems are needed to help sort out these apparently discrepant findings.

Noradrenergic Control of Feeding:
Operant vs. Respondent Regulation

Considerable evidence confirms and extends Grossman's (1960) observation that feeding is enhanced by direct noradrenergic stimulation of the brain. Injection of NE (or NE derivatives with α-receptor stimulating activity) in a variety of diencephalic and limbic forebrain sites increases the food intake of satiated rats; conversely, central or systemic administration of α-NE blocking agents suppresses feeding and antagonizes the facilitating effects of NE (Booth, 1967; Grossman, 1968; Slangen & Miller, 1969; Broekkamp & Van Rossum, 1972; Leibowitz, 1972). Early physiological work (Von Brügger, 1943; Anand & Brobeck, 1951) showed that feeding is enhanced by stimulation or suppressed by damage to the lateral hypothalamus—a region in which catecholamine fiber tracts are localized (Hillarp, Fuxe, & Dahlström, 1966). Since intraventricular administration of NE reverses the anorexia caused by hypothalamic damage, and since injections of nerve growth factor (a protein that promotes the regeneration of damaged NE fibers in the brain [Björklund & Stenevi, 1972]) increases the rate of recovery from the anorexic syndrome, it has been assumed that the lateral hypothalamic syndrome arises at least in part from damage to NE neurons (Berger, Wise, & Stein, 1971, 1973). If so, then many physiological and neurochemical facts about feeding would appear to be consistent with the view that NE is a transmitter in a central feeding system.

Recent experiments by Ritter, Wise, and Stein (1975) may shed some light on the mechanisms by which NE systems influence feeding. Two modes of regulation were considered. A hypothesis of "operant" regulation holds that feeding is reinforced by the activation of NE systems, in much the same way that such activity is presumed to reinforce self-stimulation or other operant behavior. Thus, an animal feeds or electrically self-stimulates its brain in order to release NE onto reward receptors. To explain the facilitation of either behavior by central administrations of NE, it must be assumed (a) that the injected material is taken up presynaptically and thus produces enrichment of the transmitter stores and (b) as a consequence, more NE is released by each food or brain stimulation reinforcement. Furthermore, since there would be no incentive to feed or self-stimulate if the reward receptors were

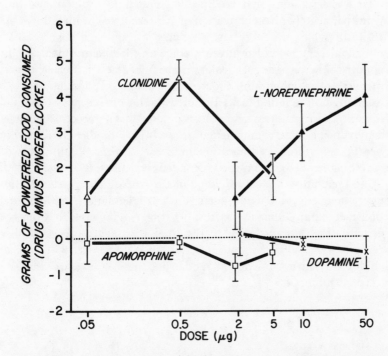

FIG. 13. Dose-response curves of feeding after intraventricular injections of clonidine, norepinephrine, apomorphine, and dopamine. Rats were allowed access to powdered Purina Lab Chow for one hour after drug treatments or control injections of Ringer-Locke solution. Data points indicate mean differences between drug and control intakes. Bars indicate standard errors. From Ritter Wise, & Stein, 1975.)

already occupied by exogenous NE, a direct activation of post-synaptic receptors could be ruled out as the mechanism of facilitation.

The second hypothesis asserts that NE systems influence self-stimulation and feeding by different mechanisms, in accordance with Skinner's (1938) operant-respondent distinction. This hypothesis simply assumes that feeding is under respondent rather than operant regulation, and that the feeding reflex is sensitized or dis-inhibited by NE receptor activation. According to this idea, exoge-nous NE obviously could (and should) facilitate feeding by a direct receptor action. Only the second interpretation was consistent with

Ritter's observations that feeding was enhanced by clonidine (an agent that acts by direct activation of NE receptors) or high doses of NE itself (which probably also produced a prolonged postsynaptic activation) (fig. 13). Also inconsistent with the operant idea and in support of the respondent idea are the results of earlier experiments with desmethylimipramine (Booth, 1968; Slangen & Miller, 1969). Desmethylimipramine blocks the presynaptic uptake of exogenous NE and thus increases its concentration at the receptor. Rather than reducing the feeding response to NE as predicted from the operant hypothesis, desmethylimipramine augments NE-induced feeding as predicted from the respondent hypothesis.

The facilitatory effects of clonidine on feeding contrast with the suppressive effects of this agent on self-stimulation (Ritter, unpublished data). Opposite effects on the two behaviors are also seen after high doses of NE (cf. figs. 8 and 13). These observations are consistent with the concept that NE systems may reinforce self-stimulation in an operant mode, but may regulate feeding in a respondent mode.

MEMORY CONSOLIDATION

Catecholamine theories of learning and long-term memory have been suggested by several investigators (Anlezark, Crow, & Greenway, 1973; Crow, 1968; Kety, 1970; Randt et al., 1971; Ritter & Stein, 1973; Roberts, Flexner, & Flexner, 1970). According to Kety (1970, 1972a), who has formulated the most detailed hypothesis, catecholamines released in affective states "may favor consolidation of learning by stimulating protein synthesis" or other "trophic processes occurring at recently activated synapses." A nice feature of Kety's theory is that it provides a mechanism for the selective consolidation of experiences that are significant for survival, since only these experiences are consistently accompanied by affective arousal and, hence, catecholamine release.

Although crucial evidence is still lacking, the idea that catecholamines are involved in memory fixation is compatible with many lines of indirect evidence (Gorelick, Bozewicz, & Bridger, in press; Kety, 1972a). Thus, while there is no evidence that the catecholamines themselves can favor memory consolidation when administered during or shortly after training, there are several reports that posttraining administration of the catecholamine-releasing agent amphetamine may facilitate discrimination learning (for review, see McGaugh, 1973), or counteract the amnesia produced by cycloheximide (Barondes & Cohen, 1968; Serota, Roberts, & Flexner, 1972). Conversely, several pharmacological (Berger et al., 1973; Dismukes & Rake, 1972; Hamburg & Cohen, 1973; Mason & Iversen, 1974; Osborne & Kerkut, 1972; Rake, 1973; Randt et al., 1971) and lesion (Anlezark, Crow, & Greenway, 1973; Kent & Grossman, 1973; McNew & Thompson, 1966) studies demonstrate learning or retention impairments after depletion or blockade of brain catecholamines.

An important role for NE, in particular, is suggested by the profound consequences of NE synthesis inhibition at the DBH stage in single-trial passive avoidance learning. DDC, an inhibitor of DBH which selectively depletes stores of NE in the brain, produced a permanent and nearly complete retention failure when administered 30 minutes before or immediately after the training trial, but not when the administration was delayed for two hours (Hamburg & Cohen, 1973; Randt et al., 1971). However, since DDC inhibits other enzymes (such as aldehyde dehydrogenase), the possibility remains that the amnesia was due to factors other than NE depletion.

Recently, Stein, Belluzzi, and Wise (1975) have tried to facilitate the consolidation of a passive avoidance response by injecting a single dose of NE into the lateral ventricle of the brain immediately after the training trial. Initial attempts were unsuccessful (see also Essman, 1973), but in these early experiments animals with normal levels of brain NE had been used. Facilitating effects of NE on self-stimulation behavior are also difficult to demonstrate in normal rats but are readily observed after depletion of central NE stores (Wise & Stein, 1969). Hence, it appeared reasonable to try the NE injections in animals that had been pretreated with DDC.

Rats were implanted with intraventricular cannulas, and, after a suitable recovery period, were given passive avoidance training in a small box with a shelf along one wall, three inches above a grid floor (Routtenberg & Holzman, 1973). Training consisted of four trials (see flow diagram in fig. 14). On each trial the rat was placed on the shelf and the step-down latency was recorded. Trials 1 and 2 were "habituation" trials and no shock was given after the

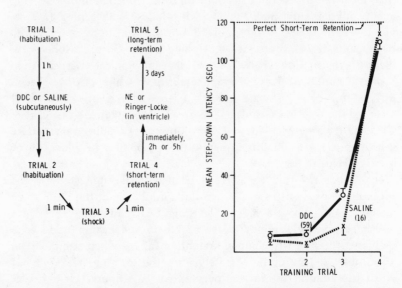

FIG. 14. (Left) Flow diagram of procedure in step-down avoidance test. (Right) Mean step-down latencies during training of groups treated with diethyldithiocarbamate (DDC) or saline. Number of rats shown in parentheses. * indicates significant group difference ($p < .05$). Bars indicate standard errors. (From Stein, Belluzzi, & Wise, 1975.)

step-down response. On trial 3, the rat received a scrambled foot shock (1 mA for 3 seconds) when it stepped off the shelf; 10 seconds after the shock had terminated, the rat was removed from the box. The same procedure was repeated on trial 4. On this trial, if the rat did not step down within 120 seconds (thus avoiding a second shock), it was returned to the home cage and a score of 120 seconds was recorded. The step-down latency on trial 4 was considered a measure of "short-term" memory, since the test was made only 1 minute after the presentation of shock on trial 3.

"Long-term" memory was evaluated in a retention test three days after training (trial 5). Each rat was placed on the shelf, exactly as before, and the step-down latency was recorded. If no response occurred within 180 seconds, the trial was terminated and a score of 180 seconds was recorded.

In the main experiment different groups of rats were injected subcutaneously, 1 hour before the shock-training trial, with DDC

(300 mg./kg.) or with an equal volume of saline (2 ml./kg.). This dose of DDC produces a significant reduction of brain NE in mice within 0.5 hour, with partial recovery at 8.5 hours. Observation of spontaneous activity indicated that the DDC-treated rats were sedated; nevertheless, the drugged rats consistently performed the step-down response on the trials prior to shock training. On trial 4, however, 1 minute after shock training, 50 of the 59 DDC-treated rats (and 14 of the 16 controls) remained on the shelf for the entire 120-second test period. The strong avoidance response displayed by the treated rats confirms previous reports (Hamburg & Cohen, 1973; Randt et al., 1971) that short-term memory is unimpaired by DDC.

Thirty-six cannulated rats in the DDC-treated group then received an intraventricular injection of NE (10 µg. of the hydrochloride salt, dissolved in 10 µl. of Ringer-Locke solution), which was administered slowly over a 1-minute period at the following intervals after the termination of trial 4: immediately (N = 17); 2h. (N = 10); 5h. (N = 9). A fourth group of 5 rats received an intraventricular injection of Ringer-Locke solution immediately after trial 4. Immediately treated rats received their injections in the experimental room near the apparatus, while the delayed treatments were administered on a table in the animal colony. All 41 animals previously had received two intraventricular injections of Ringer-Locke solution during the gentling period to ensure that the cannulas were patent, and to mitigate the initial traumatic effects of the injections.

The results of the long-term retention tests are summarized in figure 15 and table 3. Every rat in the saline-treated control group showed a substantial increase in response latency relative to that observed prior to shock training, and 11 of the 16 rats had perfect scores of 180 seconds. As found previously (Hamburg & Cohen, 1973; Randt et al., 1971), DDC-treated rats were clearly amnesic; 12 out of 18 had latencies shorter than 20 seconds and only 3 had scores of 180 seconds. Administration of NE within 1 minute after shock training seemed to restore the long-term memory capacity of DDC-treated rats to nearly normal levels (fig. 15); 10 of the 17 rats in this group had perfect avoidance scores of 180 seconds and only 4 rats had latencies shorter than 20 seconds. The restorative action of NE was greatly attenuated when administration was delayed by 2 hours, and it was totally abolished when delayed by 5 hours. A control injection of Ringer-Locke solution, injected immediately after training, also was ineffective.

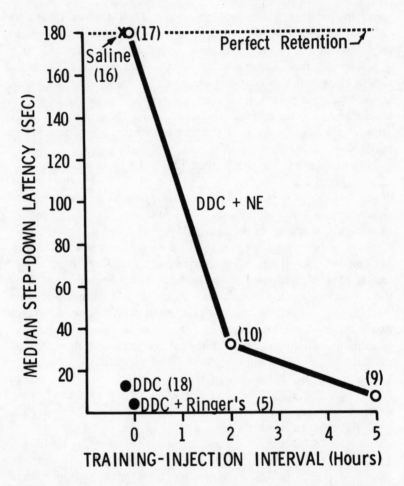

FIG. 15. Long-term retention of the passive avoidance response. Diethyl-dithiocarbamate (DDC)-treated rats are amnesic, but an intraventricular injection of norepinephrine (NE) immediately after shock training restores long-term memory. See flow diagram in fig. 13 and table 3 for procedure, identification of treatment groups, and significance tests. Number of rats shown in parentheses.

In a supplementary experiment, Stein, Belluzzi, and Wise examined the possibility that long-term retention failure caused by DDC was due merely to the change in drug state between training and test phases (i.e., state-dependent learning [Overton, 1968]), rather than to a disruption of memory consolidation by NE depletion. Although significant amnesia also occurs when DDC is administered immediately after training (Randt et al. 1971), recent work has opened the possibility of retrograde state-dependency effects (Chute & Wright, 1973). If the amnesia observed in our experiments were simply a state-dependent phenomenon, reinstatement of the drug state in the retention test would reinstate the passive avoidance response. Accordingly, 20 naive rats were given passive avoidance training under DDC, exactly as before; however, 1 hour prior to the long-term retention test, 10 of the rats received a second 300 mg./kg. drug dose (DDC:DDC) and 10 animals received saline (DDC: saline). An additional group of 10 rats received the same drug injections and training as the DDC:DDC animals, except that no shocks were administered.

Contrary to prediction from the state-dependency hypothesis, a significant retention deficit was obtained in the DDC:DDC treatment group (table 3); a similar result has already been reported (Hamburg & Cohen, 1973). Significant amnesia also was observed in the DDC:saline group, but the deficit was smaller than those obtained from similarly treated groups in the main experiment ("DDC" and "DDC + Ringer-Locke solution" treatments, table 3). Possibly, the saline injection prior to the retention test can enhance retrieval in the DDC:saline condition by serving as a "reminder" stimulus (Miller & Springer, 1973).

The results thus confirm previous reports that inhibition of NE biosynthesis during passive avoidance training prevents long-term (but not short-term) retention of the newly learned response. Furthermore, these experiments show that replenishment of NE stores by immediate posttraining administration of exogenous transmitter largely reinstates the capacity for long-term retention of the avoidance response. Since state-dependency explanations can be ruled out, these observations may be taken as evidence that NE neurons play a critical role in the consolidation of learning.

Nevertheless, even if physiologically released NE actually regulates the biochemical sequences that lead to long-term memory (Kety, 1970, 1972a), one still must explain how this presumably

**Table 3**

*Long-Term Retention in the Step-Down Avoidance Test*

| Treatment | Number of Rats | Step-Down Latency (sec.) | |
|---|---|---|---|
| | | Median | Mean ± S.E.M. |
| | Main experiment | | |
| Saline | 16 | 180.0 | 159.8 ± 10.0 |
| DDC | 18 | 13.4 | 48.2 ± 15.4*† |
| DDC + Ringer's | 5 | 5.7 | 34.6 ± 20.1*† |
| DDC + NE (immediately) | 17 | 180.0 | 121.1 ± 18.6 |
| DDC + NE (2 hours) | 10 | 33.6 | 58.3 ± 18.7*† |
| DDC + NE (5 hours) | 9 | 8.0 | 45.2 ± 25.5*† |
| | Supplementary experiment | | |
| DDC:Saline | 10 | 66.5 | 79.0 ± 18.8*† |
| DDC:DDC | 10 | 21.3 | 50.2 ± 21.7*† |
| DDC:DDC (no shock) | 10 | 5.0 | 7.7 ± 2.1*† |

*Note*: Central norepinephrine (NE) stores were depleted by subcutaneous administration of diethyldithiocarbamate (DDC, 300 mg./kg.) 1 hour before passive avoidance training (see flow diagram, fig. 14). In the main experiment, norepinephrine stores were replenished at the indicated times after training by an intraventricular injection of $l$-norepinephrine hydrochloride 10 µg.); in a control group, Ringer-Locke solution (Ringer's) was injected intraventricularly immediately after training. In the supplementary experiment, a second subcutaneous injection of diethyldithiocarbamate (or saline) was administered 1 hour before the retention test.

*Different from saline, $p < .01$.

† Different from DDC + NE (immediately), $p < .05$.

localized action at a specific network of synapses could be effectively mimicked by an intraventricular injection of NE, whose effects are both widely distributed and delayed for at least a few minutes after shock training. The required specificity could reasonably be conferred if the memory-fixation process depends on the continuing release of NE at the learning sites during a consolidation period of at least several minutes, and if the injected NE exerts its effects by replenishment of depleted presynaptic stores. In such a case, the normal consolidation process would simply be reinstated. On the other hand, the injected NE may exert its effects by a direct action on postsynaptic sites. Specificity in this case would require, as Kety suggests (1970, 1972a), that only recently activated cells be susceptible to the consolidating action of NE. To accommodate the present data, however, the susceptibility of these sites to exogenous NE must persist for at least a few minutes after shock training.

## SCHIZOPHRENIA

Sixty years ago, Bleuler (1911) coined the term *schizophrenia* (a splitting of the mind) to designate a disease in which integration of behavior and personality is fundamentally disturbed. The mental functions, he noted, "do not combine in a conglomeration of strivings with a unified resultant as they do in a healthy person"; rather, one group of ideas or drives "dominates the personality for a time, while other groups . . . are 'split-off' and seem either partly or completely impotent."

Purpose is the psychic glue, according to Bleuler's analysis, on which the coherence of behavior and personality depends. In schizophrenia, the association of ideas is not adequately "related and directed by any unifying concept of purpose or goal." As a result, schizophrenic "thinking becomes illogical and often bizarre," while "schizophrenic behavior is marked by a lack of interest, lack of initiative, lack of a definite goal, by inadequate adaptation to the environment."

In the related view of Rado (1962), the crucial defect in schizophrenia is based in the organizing action of pleasure or reward. According to Rado, "schizophrenic disorders may be viewed as so many experiments of Nature, showing what happens to central integration in the person whose pleasure resources are inherently deficient." In general, "absence of sufficient pleasure slows down and hinders psychodynamic integration, as the absence of an essential enzyme slows down or hinders a complex biochemical process."

A biological basis for these concepts of schizophrenia may perhaps be found in the work described above. If, as this work suggests, NE systems actually subserve reward and memory-consolidation functions, their involvement in associative thinking and goal-directed behavior would be obvious. It is equally obvious that malfunction of these systems would have serious consequences for normal behavior and logical thought. We will argue that schizophrenia is one such extreme consequence and, specifically, that a chronic dysfunction of the NE reward system is responsible for the characteristic derangement of thought and affect (Stein & Wise, 1971).

To evaluate the validity of this idea, Wise & Stein (1973) conducted postmortem studies of enzymes in human brain. Their finding that DBH activity is significantly reduced in schizophrenics' brains is consistent with the suggestion that disturbance or damage to NE (DBH-containing) neurons is etiologically related to the disease.

Damage to central NE neurons can be estimated by measuring the DBH in various regions of the brain. DBH is distributed in the brain with a regional pattern of activity that parallels levels of NE (Axelrod, 1972). Mechanical or chemical damage to central NE tracts causes similar reductions in the brain levels of NE and DBH (Reis & Molinoff, 1972). Indeed, the enzyme is used as a marker in immunofluorescence studies to visualize the NE pathways (Fuxe et al., 1970). As a first approach, we therefore assumed that measurements of DBH in postmortem samples of human brain could serve as an indicator of the integrity of NE systems *in vivo*.

Brain specimens were obtained from 8 male and 10 female patients with a diagnosis of chronic schizophrenia who died at Norristown State Hospital, Norristown, Pennsylvania, at a mean age of 71.2 years. The average duration of hospitalization of these patients was 34.4 years. Control material was obtained through the Medical Examiner's Office, New York City, from 6 male and 6 female subjects with no known psychiatric history, who died suddenly in accidents or from heart attacks at an average age of 57.2 years. Care was taken to exclude drug addicts, alcoholics, and suicides from the control group.

The pons-medulla, diencephalon, and hippocampus were dissected out at autopsy and frozen on dry ice. The brain parts were stored at $-15°$C. in plastic bags for several months prior to enzymatic analysis; periodic redeterminations of DBH in several cases revealed that the enzyme was stable under these storage conditions for almost one year. Autopsies generally were performed after postmortem intervals of several hours at room temperature and one to three days at $4°$C. To assess the effects of postmortem decomposition on brain DBH, we killed rats with ether or carbon dioxide and then exposed different groups prior to autopsy to roughly the same con-

**Table 4**

*Postmortem Deterioration of Dopamine-β-hydroxylase (DBH)*
*Activity in Whole Rat Brain (Minus Neocortex and Cerebellum)*

| Storage Time at 22° C. (hours) | Mean DBH Activity ± S.E.M. | % of 0-Hour Control |
|---|---|---|
| 0 | 24.2 ± 0.96 | — |
| 3 | 22.8 ± 0.80 | 94.1 ± 3.34 |
| 7 | 17.6 ± 0.59 | 72.6 ± 2.44 |
| 17 | 19.5 ± 1.72 | 80.4 ± 7.12 |
| 24 | 18.8 ± 1.06 | 77.6 ± 4.40 |

*Note*: Rats were killed by immersion in carbon dioxide and then stored at room temperature prior to autopsy for the indicated intervals. Enzyme activity is expressed as nanomoles of octopamine formed per gram of tissue per hour. Assay of Molinoff, Weinshilboum, & Axelrod (1971).

**Table 5**

*Dopamine-β-hydroxylase activity in Postmortem Specimens*
*of Brain from 18 Schizophrenic Patients and 12 Controls*

| Region | Control | Schizophrenic | |
|---|---|---|---|
| | Mean Activity ± S.E.M | Mean Activity ± S.E.M. | Percent. of Control |
| Pons-Medulla | 8.86 ± 0.86 | 6.09 ± 0.61* | 70.1 |
| Diencephalon | 5.83 ± 0.30 | 3.38 ± 0.39† | 57.9 |
| Hippocampus | 2.87 ± 0.52 | 1.42 ± 0.38‡ | 49.4 |

*Source*: Wise & Stein, 1973.

*Note*: Enzyme activity is expressed as nmoles/gm./20 min. The concentration of tyramine used in all assays was $9.6 \times 10^{-4}$ $M$; S.E.M., standard error of the mean.

* Differs from control, $p < .02$.

† Differs from control, $p < .001$.

‡ Differs from control, $p < .05$.

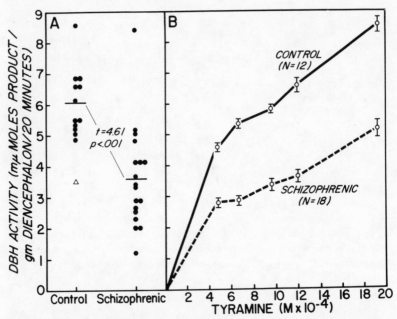

FIG 16. Dopamine-β-hydroxylase (DBH) activity in postmortem specimens of diencephalon from 18 schizophrenic patients and 12 normal controls. (A) Distributions of individual values of diencephalic DBH. Each point is the average of 30 assays (six determinations at each of five different tyramine concentrations); these values are used for all analyses of diencephalic DBH reported in the text. Horizontal lines indicate mean of distributions. Triangle shows DBH activity from a control case which was excluded from statistical analysis because of anoxic necrosis of the brain. The highest value in the schizophrenic group represents a case that had been autopsied eight days after death. (B) DBH activity as a function of substrate concentration. Activity in schizophrenic group is significantly reduced ($p < .001$) as compared to control group at every concentration of tyramine. Bars indicate standard errors. (From Wise & Stein, 1973.)

ditions of time and temperature as those encountered in our human studies. DBH activity was reduced by only 23 percent after 24 hours at room temperature, and storage at 4°C. for an additional one to three days led to only small further decreases (table 4).

There was a significant reduction in DBH activity in the schizophrenic group in all brain regions examined (table 5). The deficits were somewhat larger in rostral regions (diencephalon and hippocampus) where the nerve terminals are localized than in caudal

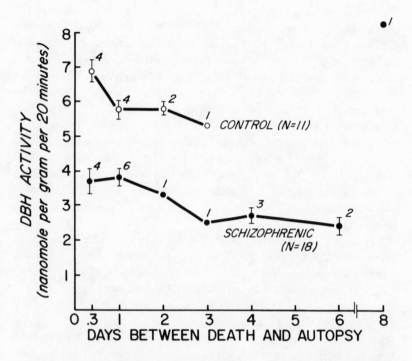

FIG. 17. Dopamine-β-hydroxylase activity as a function of the time between death and autopsy. Parallel curves for schizophrenic patients and
normal controls suggest similar rates of postmortem deterioration in
the two groups. The number of cases at each time point is indicated.
Note that the highest value in the schizophrenic group is the case autopsied eight days after death. Bars indicate standard errors. (From Wise,
Baden, & Stein, 1974.)

regions (pons-medulla) where the cell bodies are localized. Individual
values of diencephalic DBH in the two groups were distributed with
little overlap; values for only three schizophrenics fell in the normal
range (fig. 16). Significant deficits in diencephalic DBH were found
over a wide range of substrate (tyramine) concentrations.

Control experiments were conducted to rule out the possibility
that the DBH deficiency resulted from postmortem changes. We
matched control and schizophrenic cases for morgue-to-autopsy time
and still found a significant group difference ($p < .001$). Furthermore, we observed that two other enzymes, lactate dehydrogenase
and monoamine oxidase, exhibited undiminished activities (table 6).

This negative result makes it unlikely that gross deterioration of the schizophrenic brain specimens could have been responsible for the DBH deficits. Finally, it is possible that, as a result of unknown factors, the DBH in the schizophrenics' brains deteriorated at a more rapid rate after death than the DBH in normal brain. We therefore plotted the course of deterioration of the enzyme for the two groups (fig. 17). A difference in the rate of postmortem deterioration would have produced divergent curves. Instead, the two curves followed roughly parallel courses and were well separated at all time points, which suggests that the deterioration of DBH was similar in the two groups. Indeed, a significant deficit in schizophrenic DBH activity was obtained in a test involving only the eight cases that had received autopsies on the day of death $(p < .02)$.

We next examined the possibility that antipsychotic medications caused the DBH deficiency. Since various phenothiazines had been administered at one time or another to nearly all of our patients, we could not use our human material to determine whether these drugs might inhibit DBH in the brain. We therefore gave rats daily doses (20 mg./kg.) of chlorpromazine for prolonged periods. The drug did not inhibit brain DBH, even at this high dosage; in fact, after 12 weeks of treatment, a small but statistically reliable increase in enzyme activity was found $(p < .02)$.

Our analyses also convinced us that the schizophrenic deficits could not be attributed to age, sex, or cause of death (tables 7-9). No relationship was found between DBH and duration of hospitalization, although in our sample of chronic schizophrenics, institutionalization ranged from 5 to 60 years. Furthermore, the mean DBH of 12 patients hospitalized for more than 30 years did not differ significantly from that of 6 patients hospitalized for less than 30 years. These results do not support the idea that institutionalization causes the schizophrenics' DBH deficit, but final evaluation requires further study of nonhospitalized schizophrenics and hospitalized controls.

The foregoing results suggest that the DBH deficiency in schizophrenic patients cannot be attributed to extraneous factors such as postmortem deterioration, drugs, age differences, sex, cause of death, or duration of hospitalization. The deficit might therefore be associated with the disease itself. Whether this enzyme deficiency is specific to schizophrenia remains to be demonstrated.

**Table 6**

*Monoamine Oxidase Activity in Postmortem Specimens of Brain from 18 Schizophrenic Patients and 12 Controls*

| Group | Mean Activity ± S.E.M. | | |
|---|---|---|---|
| | Pons-Medulla | Diencephalon | Hippocampus |
| Control | $1.75 \pm 0.102$ | $1.80 \pm 0.081$* | $1.95 \pm 0.096$ |
| Schizophrenic | $1.99 \pm 0.081$ | $1.93 \pm 0.089$ | $1.98 \pm 0.121$ |

*Source:* Wise, Baden, & Stein, 1974.

*Note:* Enzyme activity is expressed as $\mu$moles/gm./hr. Assay of Wurtman & Axelrod (1963). S.E.M., standard error of mean.

* Number of cases = 11.

**Table 7**

*Control for Age*

| Group | Number of Cases | Age (Years) | Diencephalic DBH (nmoles/g./20min.) |
|---|---|---|---|
| | *Total Sample* | | |
| Control | 12 | 57.2 | $6.08 \pm 0.32$ |
| Schizophrenic | 18 | 71.2 | $3.61 \pm 0.39$* |
| | *Age-Matched Sample* | | |
| Control | 9 | 64.1 | $5.89 \pm 0.25$ |
| Schizophrenic | 14 | 66.8 | $3.96 \pm 0.42$† |

*Note:* The age-matched sample includes all schizophrenic and control subjects who died between the ages of 45 and 80 years. Although the mean age at death for the matched groups is nearly identical, the schizophrenics' dopamine-$\beta$-hydroxylase (DBH) activity is still significantly reduced.

* Differs from control, $p < .001$.

† Differs from control, $p < .005$.

Table 8
*Control for Sex*

| Group | Sex | Number of Cases | Diencephalic DBH (nmole/g./20 min.) |
|---|---|---|---|
| Control | Male | 6 | 5.80 ± 0.33 |
| | Female | 6 | 6.38 ± 0.58 |
| Schizophrenic | Male | 8 | 3.23 ± 0.48* |
| | Female | 10 | 3.90 ± 0.62* |

*Note*: Similar dopamine-$\beta$-hydroxylase (DBH) deficiencies are found for male and female schizophrenics, consistent with the similar incidence of the disease in the two sexes.
* Differs from same-sex control, $p < .01$.

The concept that schizophrenia may involve a deficit in DBH function is supported by the frequent observation of psychosis in alcoholics after overdoses of the DBH inhibitor disulfiram. According to Angst (1956), disulfiram psychosis can be symptomatically indistinguishable from schizophrenia. Furthermore, Heath et al. (1965) report that disulfiram produces extreme mental and physical changes, including an increase in psychotic symptoms, in schizophrenic patients, but at comparable doses only minimal changes in a prisoner control group.

The DBH deficits in the schizophrenic group may be explained in several ways. For example, it is possible that schizophrenics' DBH is different from and, hence, intrinsically less active than normal enzyme; however, similarities in the physiochemical properties and assay parameters of the two enzymes do not support this idea (Wise & Stein, 1973). It is also unlikely that the schizophrenics' DBH deficit was due to an excess of endogenous inhibitors. These would have been inactivated in the assay, and dialysis of homogenates did not affect the activity of the enzyme. The deficits could be the result of a defect in the synthesis or utilization of DBH, or they could reflect a more general pathological condition of NE neurons. As has already been suggested (Stein & Wise, 1971; Kety, 1972b), a defect in DA hydroxylation could lead to both an insufficiency of NE and an excess of DA at noradrenergic synapses. It is also possible that the NE neurons themselves are disturbed, or damaged, or fail to develop normally in schizophrenia. Fur-

**Table 9**
*Control for Cause of Death*

| Group | Number of Cases | Diencephalic DBH (nmole/g./20 min.) | |
|---|---|---|---|
| Control, Accident | 7 | 6.45 ± 0.50 | n.s. |
| Control, Heart Attack | 5 | 5.59 ± 0.30 | $p < .01$ |
| Schizophrenic, Heart Attack | 9 | 3.48 ± 0.42 | |

*Note*: When only heart attack victims are compared, the schizophrenics still exhibit a significant dopamine-$\beta$-hydroxylase (DBH) deficiency. Furthermore, within the control group, the heart attack and accident cases do not exhibit a significant difference in enzyme activity.

thermore, because regions rich in nerve terminals exhibited larger reductions in DBH than regions rich in cell bodies, it seems possible that the NE nerve terminal may be particularly susceptible to the schizophrenic disease process. Such vulnerability of terminals would be consistent with a suggestion that the schizophrenic process involves the formation of a toxic metabolite of DA, such as 6-hydroxydopamine (Stein & Wise, 1971) or dopamine $o$-quinone (Stein, Wise, & Berger, 1972; Adams, 1972). As already noted, 6-hydroxydopamine has been shown in studies on animals to cause selective damage to central catecholamine nerve endings.

Needless to say, in view of the many false hopes and disappointments that biochemical studies of schizophrenia have produced, our findings must be viewed with skepticism until other researchers provide confirmation (Wyatt et al., 1975; Wise & Stein, 1975). Still, it may be useful to note briefly some therapeutic implications of our experiments. The general aim would be to correct or compensate for the presumed pathology of NE systems. One could try to increase the formation of DBH, or to promote supersensitivity of NE receptors (Stein, Wise, & Berger, 1972) or even, ideally, to stimulate the regeneration of damaged NE terminals, as for example, by suitable central administration of nerve growth factor (Björklund & Stenevi, 1972; Berger, Wise, & Stein, 1973). Alternatively, in analogy to the use of $l$-DOPA to elevate the central levels of DA in Parkinson's disease (Hornykiewicz, 1972), one could try to increase the concentration of NE in the brains of schizophrenic patients by administration of a precursor.

REFERENCES

Adams, R. N. Stein and Wise theory of schizophrenia: A possible mechanism for 6-hydroxydopamine formation *in vivo*. *Behavioral Biology*, 1972, **7**, 861-866.

Anand, B. K., & Brobeck, J. R. Hypothalamic control of food intake in rats and cats. *Yale Journal of Biology and Medicine*, 1951, **24**, 123-140.

Angst, A. Zur Frage der Psychosen bei Behandlung mit Disulfiram (Antabus). *Schweizerische Medizinische Wochenschrift*, 1956, 46, 1304-1306.

Anlezark, G. M., Arbuthnott, G. W., Christie, J. E., Crow, T. J., & Spear, P. J. Electrical self-stimulation in relation to cells of origin of catecholamine-containing neural systems ascending from the brain stem. *Journal of Physiology*, 1974, **237**, 31p-32p.

Anlezark, G. M., Crow, T. J., & Greenway, A. P. Impaired learning and decreased cortical norepinephrine after bilateral locus coeruleus lesions. *Science*, 1973, **181**, 682-684.

Arbuthnott, G., Fuxe, K., & Ungerstedt, U. Central catecholamine turnover and self-stimulation behavior. *Brain Research*, 1971, **27**, 406-413.

Axelrod, J. Dopamine-$\beta$-hydroxylase: Regulation of its synthesis and release from nerve terminals. *Pharmacological Reviews*, 1972, **24**, 233-243.

Barondes, S. H., & Cohen, H. D. Arousal and the conversion of "short-term" to "long-term" memory. *Proceedings of the National Academy of Science*, 1968, **61**, 923-929.

Baxter, B. L., Gluckman, M. I., Stein, L., & Scerni, R. A. Self-injection of apomorphine in the rat: Positive reinforcement by a dopamine receptor stimulant. *Pharmacology Biochemistry and Behavior*, 1974, **2**, 387-392.

Belluzzi, J. D., Ritter, S., Wise, C. D., & Stein, L. Substantia nigra self-stimulation: Dependence on noradrenergic reward pathways. *Behavioral Biology*, 1975, **13**, 103–111.

Berger, B. D., Ritter, S., Wise, C. D., & Stein, L. Learning and memory after 6-hydroxydopamine (6OH-DA). *Federation Proceedings*, 1973, **32**, 3038.

Berger, B. D., Wise, C. D., & Stein, L. Norepinephrine: Reversal of anorexia in rats with lateral hypothalamic damage. *Science*, 1971, **172**, 281-284.

Berger, B. D., Wise, C. D., & Stein, L. Nerve growth factor: Enhanced recovery of feeding after hypothalamic damage. *Science*, 1973, **180**, 506-508.

Björklund, A., & Stenevi, U. Nerve growth factor: Stimulation of regenerative growth of central noradrenergic neurons. *Science*, 1972, **175**, 1251-1252.

Bleuler, E. *Dementia Praecox or the Group of Schizophrenias*, 1911. Translated by J. Zinkin. New York: International Universities Press, 1950.

Booth, D. A. Localization of the adrenergic feeding system in the rat diencephalon. *Science*, 1967, **158**, 515-516.

Booth, D. A. Mechanism of action of norepinephrine in eliciting an eating response on injection into the rat hypothalamus. *Journal of Pharmacology and Experimental Therapeutics*, 1968, **160**, 336-348.

Broekkamp, C. & Van Rossum, J. M. Clonidine induced intrahypothalamic stimulation of eating in rats. *Psychopharmacologia* (Berlin), 1972, **25**, 162-168.

Chute, D. L., & Wright, D. C. Retrograde state dependent learning. *Science*, 1973, **180**, 878-880.

Clavier, R. M., & Routtenberg, A. Ascending monoamine-containing fiber pathways related to intracranial self-stimulation: Histochemical fluorescence study. *Brain Research*, 1974, **72**, 25-40.

Crow, T. J. Cortical synapses and reinforcement: A hypothesis. *Nature*, 1968, **219**, 736-737.

Crow, T. J. Catecholamine-containing neurones and electrical self-stimulation: 1. A review of some data. *Psychological Medicine*, 1972, **2**, 414-421. (a)

Crow, T. J. A map of the rat mesencephalon for electrical self-stimulation. *Brain Research*, 1972, **36**, 265-273. (b)

Crow, T. J., Spear, P. J., & Arbuthnott, G. W. Intracranial self-stimulation with electrodes in the region of the locus coeruleus. *Brain Research*, 1972, **36**, 275-287.

Dahlström, A., & Fuxe, K. Evidence for the existence of monoamine-containing neurons in the central nervous system. I. Demonstration of monoamines in the cell bodies of brain stem neurons. *Acta Physiologica Scandinavica*, 1964, **62** (Suppl. 232), 1-55.

Deutsch, J. A. *The structural basis of behavior*. Chicago: University of Chicago Press, 1960.

Dismukes, R. K., & Rake, A. V. Involvement of biogenic amines in memory formation. *Psychopharmacologia* (Berlin), 1972, **23**, 17-25.

Essman, W. B. Neuromolecular modulation of experimentally-induced retrograde amnesia. *Confinia Neurologica*, 1973, **35**, 1-22.

Fuxe, K., Goldstein, M., Hökfelt, M., & Joh, T. H. Immunohistochemical localization of dopamine-$\beta$-hydroxylase in the peripheral and central nervous system. *Research Communications in Chemical Pathology and Pharmacology*, 1970, **1**, 627-636.

Fuxe, K., Hökfelt, T., & Ungerstedt, U. Morphological and functional aspects of central monoamine neurons. *International Review of Neurobiology*, 1970, **13**, 93-126.

Gallistel, C. R. Self-stimulation: The neurophysiology of reward and motivation. In J. A. Deutsch (Ed.), *The physiological basis of memory.* New York: Academic Press, 1973. Pp. 176-267.

German, D. C., & Bowden, D. M. Catecholamine systems as the neural substrate for intracranial self-stimulation: a hypothesis. *Brain Research,* 1974, **73,** 381-419.

Glowinski, J., & Axelrod, J. Effect of drugs on the uptake, release, and metabolism of $H^3$-norepinephrine in the rat brain. *Journal of Pharmacology and Experimental Therapeutics,* 1965, **149,** 43-49.

Gold, R. M., Kapatos, G., & Carey, R. J. A retracting wire knife for stereotaxic brain surgery made from a microliter syringe. *Physiology and Behavior,* 1973, **10,** 813-815.

Goldstein, M., & Nakajima, K. The effect of disulfiram on catecholamine levels in the brain. *Journal of Pharmacology and Experimental Therapeutics,* 1967, **157,** 96-102.

Gorelick, D. A., Bozewicz, T. R., & Bridger, W. H. The role of catecholamines in animal learning and memory. In A. J. Friedhoff (Ed.), *Catecholamines and behavior.* New York: Plenum Press, in press.

Grossman, S. P. Eating or drinking elicited by direct adrenergic or cholinergic stimulation of hypothalamus. *Science,* 1960, **132,** 301-302.

Grossman, S. P. Hypothalamic and limbic influences on food intake. *Federation Proceedings,* 1968, **27,** 1349.

Hamburg, M. D. & Cohen, R. P. Memory access pathway: Role of adrenergic versus cholinergic neurons. *Pharmacology, Biochemistry and Behavior,* 1973, **1,** 295-300.

Heath, R. G., Nesselhof, W., Bishop, M. P., & Byers, L. W. Behavioral and metabolic changes associated with administration of tetraethylthiuram disulfide (Antabus). *Diseases of the Nervous System,* 1965, **26,** 99-105.

Hillarp, N. A., Fuxe, K., & Dahlström, A. C. Demonstration and mapping of central neurons containing dopamine, noradrenaline, 5-hydroxytryptamine and their reactions to psychopharmaca. *Pharmacological Reviews,* 1966, **18, 727-741.**

Hornykiewicz, O. Dopamine and extrapyramidal motor function and dysfunction. In I. J. Kopin (Ed.), *Neurotransmitters.* Baltimore: Williams & Wilkins, 1972. Pp. 390-415.

Jacobowitz, D. M. Effects of 6-hydroxydopa. In E. Usdin & H. S. Snyder (Eds.), *Frontiers in Catecholamine Research.* New York: Pergamon Press, 1973. Pp. 729-739.

Kent, E. W., & Grossman, S. P. Elimination of learned behaviors after transection of fibers crossing the lateral border of the hypothalamus. *Physiology and Behavior,* 1973, **10,** 953-963.

Kety, S. S. The biogenic amines in the central nervous system: Their possible roles in arousal, emotion and learning. In F. O. Schmitt (Ed.), *The neurosciences: Second study program.* New York: Rockefeller University Press, 1970. Pp. 324-336.

Kety, S. S. The possible role of the adrenergic systems of the cortex in learning. In I. J. Kopin (Ed.), *Neurotransmitters.* Baltimore: Williams & Wilkins, 1972. Pp. 376-389. (a)

Kety, S. S. Toward hypotheses for a biochemical component in the vulnerability to schizophrenia. *Seminars in Psychiatry,* 1972, **4**, 233-238. (b)

Klüver, H., & Barrera, E. Method for combined staining of cells and fibers in the nervous system. *Journal of Neuropathology and Experimental Neurology,* 1953, **12**, 400-403.

Kojima, H., Ritter, S., Wise, C. D., & Stein, L. Unpublished data (cited in Stein & Wise, 1973).

König, J. F. R., & Klippel, R. A. *The rat brain: A stereotaxic atlas of the forebrain and lower parts of the brain stem.* Baltimore: Williams & Wilkins, 1963.

Leibowitz, S. F. Central adrenergic receptors and the regulation of hunger and thirst. In I. J. Kopin (Ed.), *Neurotransmitters.* Baltimore: Williams & Wilkins, 1972. Pp. 327-358.

Liebman, J. M., & Butcher, L. L. Effects on self-stimulation behavior of drugs influencing dopaminergic neurotransmission mechanisms. *Naunyn-Schmeidelberg's Archiv für Experimentelle Pathologie und Pharmakologie,* 1973, **277**, 305-318.

Liebman, J. M., Mayer, D. J., & Liebeskind, J. C. Self-stimulation in the midbrain central gray matter of the rat. *Behavioral Biology,* 1973, **9**, 299-306.

Lindvall, O., & Björklund, A. The organization of the ascending catecholamine neuron systems in the rat brain as revealed by the glyoxylic acid fluorescence method. *Acta Physiologica Scandinavica,* 1974, (Suppl. 412), 1-48.

Lippa, A. S., Antelman, S. M. Fisher, A. E., & Canfield, D. R. Neurochemical mediation of reward: A significant role for dopamine. *Pharmacology Biochemistry and Behavior,* 1973, **1**, 23-25.

Margules, D. L. Noradrenergic rather than serotonergic basis of reward in dorsal tegmentum. *Journal of Comparative and Physiological Psychology,* 1969, **67**, 32-35.

Mason, S. T., & Iversen, S. D. Learning impairment in rats after 6-hydroxydopamine induced depletion of brain catecholamines. *Nature,* 1974, **248**, 697-698.

Mayer, D. J., & Liebeskind, J. C. Pain reduction by focal electrical stimulation of the brain: An anatomical and behavioral analysis. *Brain Research,* 1974, **68**, 73-93.

McGaugh, J. L. Drug facilitation of learning and memory 6563. In H. W. Elliott, R. Okun, & R. George (Eds.), *Annual review of pharmacology*. Vol. 13. Palo Alto, Calif.: Annual Reviews, Inc., 1973. Pp. 229-241.

McNew, J. J., & Thompson, R. Role of the limbic system in active and passive avoidance conditioning in the rat. *Journal of Comparative and Physiological Psychology*, 1966, **61**, 173-180.

Miller, R. R., & Springer, A. D. Amnesia, consolidation, and retrieval. *Psychological Reviews*, 1973, **80**, 69-79.

Molinoff, P. B., Weinshilboum, R., & Axelrod, J. A. sensitive enzymatic assay for dopamine-$\beta$-hydroxylase. *Journal of Pharmacology and Experimental Therapeutics*, 1971, **178**, 425-431.

Olds, J. Hypothalamic substrates of reward. *Physiological Reviews*, 1962, **42**, 554-604.

Olds, J., & Milner, P. Positive reinforcement produced by electrical stimulation of septal area and other regions. *Journal of Comparative and Physiological Psychology*, 1954, **47**, 419-427.

Olson, L., & Fuxe, K. Further mapping out of central noradrenaline neuron systems: Projections of the "subcoeruleus" area. *Brain Research*, 1972, **43**, 289-295.

Osborne, R. H., & Kerkut, G. A. Inhibition of noradrenaline biosynthesis and its effects on learning in rats. *Comparative and General Pharmacology*, 1972, **3**, 359-362.

Overton, D. A. Dissociated learning in drug states (state dependent learning). In D. H. Efron (Ed.), *Psychopharmacology; a review of progress, 1957-1967*. Washington, D.C.: U.S. Government Printing Office, 1968. Pp. 918-930.

Phillips, A. G., & Fibiger, H. C. Dopaminergic and noradrenergic substrates of positive reinforcement: Differential effects of d- and l-amphetamine. *Science*, 1973, **179**, 575-576.

Poschel, B.P.H., & Ninteman, F. W. Norepinephrine: A possible excitatory neurohormone of the reward system. *Life Science*, 1963, **2**, 782-788.

Rado, S. *Psychoanalysis of behavior*. Vol. 2. New York: Grune & Stratton, 1962.

Rake, A. V. Involvement of biogenic amines in memory formation: The central nervous system indole amine involvement. *Psychopharmacologia* (Berlin), 1973, **29**, 91-100.

Randrup, A., & Munkvad, I. Stereotyped activities produced by amphetamine in several animal species and man. *Psychopharmacologia* (Berlin), 1967, **1**, 300-310.

Randrup, A., & Munkvad, I. Biochemical, anatomical and psychological investigations of stereotyped behavior induced by amphetamines. In E. Costa & S. Garattini (Eds.), *Amphetamines and related compounds* New York: Raven Press, 1970. Pp. 695-713.

Randt, C. T., Quartermain, D., Goldstein, M., & Anagnoste, B. Norepinephrine biosynthesis inhibition: Effects on memory in mice. *Science*, 1971, **172**, 498-499.

Reis, D. J., & Molinoff P. B. Brain dopamine-$\beta$-hydroxylase: Regional distribution and effects of lesions and 6-hydroxydopamine on activity. *Journal of Neurochemistry*, 1972, **19**, 195-204.

Ritter, S., Belluzzi, J. D., Wise, C. D., & Stein, L. Unpublished data (cited in Belluzzi et al., in press).

Ritter, S., & Stein, L. Self-stimulation of noradrenergic cell group (A6) in the locus coeruleus of rats. *Journal of Comparative and Physiological Psychology*, 1973, **85**, 443-452.

Ritter, S., & Stein, L. 'Self-stimulation in the mesencephalic trajectory of the ventral noradrenergic bundle. *Brain Research*, 1974, **81**, 145-157.

Ritter, S., Wise, C. D., & Stein, L. Neurochemical regulation of feeding in the rat: Facilitation by $\alpha$-noradrenergic, but not dopaminergic, receptor stimulants. *Journal of Comparative and Physiological Psychology*, 1975, **88**, 778-784.

Roberts, R. B., Flexner, J. B., & Flexner, L. B. Some evidence for the involvement of adrenergic sites in the memory trace. *Proceedings of the National Academy of Science*, 1970, **66**, 310-313.

Routtenberg, A., & Holzman, N. Memory disruption by electrical stimulation of substantia nigra, pars compacta. *Science*, 1973, **181**, 83-86.

Routtenberg, A., & Malsbury, C. Brainstem pathways of reward. *Journal of Comparative and Physiological Psychology*, 1969, **68**, 22-30.

Sclafani, A., & Grossman, S. P. Hyperphagia produced by knife cuts between the medial and lateral hypothalamus in the rat. *Physiology and Behavior*, 1969, **4**, 533-537.

Serota, R. G., Roberts, R. B., & Flexner, L. B. Acetoxycycloheximide-induced amnesia: Protective effects of adrenergic stimulants. *Proceedings of the National Academy of Science*, 1972, **69**, 340-342.

Skinner, B. F. *The behavior of organisms.* New York: Appleton-Century-Crofts, 1938.

Slangen, J. L., & Miller, N. E. Pharmacological tests for the function of hypothalamic norepinephrine in eating behavior. *Physiology and Behavior*, 1969, **4**, 543-552.

Stein, L. Effects and interactions of imipramine, chlorpromazine, reserpine and amphetamine on self-stimulation: Possible neurophysiological basis of depression. In J. Wortis (Ed.), *Recent advances in biological psychiatry*. Vol. 4. New York: Plenum Press, 1962. Pp. 288-308.

Stein, L. Reciprocal action of reward and punishment mechanisms. In R. G. Heath (Ed.), *The role of pleasure in behavior*. New York: Hoeber Medical Division, Harper & Row, 1964. Pp. 113-139 (a)

Stein, L. Self-stimulation of the brain and the central stimulant action of amphetamine. *Federation Proceedings*, 1964, **23**, 836-850. (b)

Stein, L. Chemistry of reward and punishment. In D. H. Efron (Ed.), *Psychopharmacology: A Review of Progress, 1957-1967.* Washington, D.C.: U.S. Government Printing Office, 1968. Pp. 105-123.

Stein, L., Belluzzi, J. D., & Wise, C. D. Memory enhancement by central administration of norepinephrine. *Brain Research*, 1975, **84**, 329–335.

Stein, L., & Seifter, J. Possible mode of antidepressive action of imipramine. *Science*, 1961, **134**, 286-287.

Stein, L., & Wise, C. D. Release of norepinephrine from hypothalamus and amygdala by rewarding forebrain bundle stimulation and amphetamine. *Journal of Comparative and Physiological Psychology*, 1969, **67**, 189-198.

Stein, L., & Wise, C. D. Behavioral pharmacology of central stimulants. In W. G. Clark (Ed.), *Principles of psychopharmacology.* New York: Academic Press, 1970. Pp. 313-325.

Stein, L., & Wise, C. D. Possible etiology of schizophrenia: Progressive damage to the noradrenergic reward system by 6-hydroxydopamine. *Science*, 1971, **171**, 1032-1036.

Stein, L., & Wise, C. D. Amphetamine and noradrenergic reward pathways. In E. Usdin & H. S. Snyder (Eds.), *Frontiers in catecholamine research.* New York: Pergamon Press, 1973. Pp. 963-968.

Stein, L., Wise, C. D., & Berger, B. D. Noradrenergic reward mechanisms, recovery of function, and schizophrenia. In J. L. McGaugh (Ed.), *The chemistry of mood, motivation, and memory.* New York: Plenum Press, 1972. Pp. 81-103.

Stein, L., Wise, C. D., & Berger, B. D. Antianxiety action of benzodiazepines: Decrease in activity of serotonin neurons in the punishment system. In S. Garattini, E. Mussine, & L. Randall (Eds.), *The benzodiazepines.* New York: Raven Press, 1973. Pp. 299-326.

Stenevi, U., Bjerre, B., Björklund, A., & Mobley, W. Effects of localized intracerebral injections of nerve growth factor on the regenerative growth of lesioned central noradrenergic neurons. *Brain Research*, 1974, **69**, 217-234.

Stinus, L., & Thierry, A-M. Self-stimulation and catecholamines. II Blockade of self-stimulation by treatment with alpha-methylparatyrosine and reinstatement by catecholamine precursor administration. *Brain Research*, 1973, **64**, 189-198.

Stinus, L., Thierry, A-M., Blanc, G., Glowinski, J., & Cardo, B. Self stimulation and catecholamines. III. Effect of imposed or self stimulation in the area ventralis tegmenti on catecholamine utilization in the rat brain. *Brain Research*, 1973, **64**, 199-210.

St.-Laurent, J., Leclerc, R. R., Mitchell, M. L., & Milliaressis, T. E. Effects of apomorphine on self-stimulation. *Pharmacology, Biochemistry and Behavior*, 1973, 1, 581-585.

Ungerstedt, U. Histochemical studies of the effect of intracerebral and intraventricular injections of 6-hydroxydopamine on monoamine neurons in the rat brain. In T. Malmfors & H. Thoenen (Eds.), *6-Hydroxydopamine and catecholamine neurons*. New York: American Elsevier Pub. Co. 1971. Pp. 101-27. (a)

Ungerstedt, U. Stereotaxic mapping of the monoamine pathways in the rat brain. *Acta Physiologica Scandinavica*, 1971, 82 (Suppl. 367), 1-48. (b)

Von Brügger, M. Fresstrieb als hypothalamisches symptom. *Helvetica Physiologica et Pharmacologica Acta*, 1943, 1, 183-198.

Wauquier, A., & Niemegeers, C.J.E. Intracranial self-stimulation in rats as a function of various stimulus parameters. II. Influence of haloperidol, pimozide and pipampherone on medial forebrain bundle stimulation with monopolar electrodes. *Psychopharmacologia* (Berlin), 1972, 27, 191-202.

Wauquier, A., & Niemegeers, C.J.E. Intracranial self-stimulation in rats as a function of various stimulus parameters. III. Influence of apomorphine on medial forebrain bundle stimulation with monopolar electrodes. *Psychopharmacologia* (Berlin), 1973, 23, 163-172.

Wise, C. D., Baden, M. M. and Stein, L. Postmortem measurement of enzymes in human brain: Evidence of a central noradenergic deficit in schizophrenia. *Journal of Psychiatric Research*, 1974, 11, 185-198.

Wise, C. D., Berger, B. D., & Stein, L. Evidence of $\alpha$-noradrenergic reward receptors and serotonergic punishment receptors in the rat brain. *Biological Psychiatry*, 1973, 6, 3-21.

Wise, C. D., & Stein, L. Facilitation of brain self-stimulation by central administration of norepinephrine. *Science*, 1969, 163, 299-301.

Wise, C. D., & Stein, L. Amphetamine: Facilitation of behavior by augmented release of norepinephrine from the medial forebrain bundle. In E. Costa & S. Garattini (Eds.), *Amphetamines and related compounds*. New York: Raven Press, 1970. Pp. 463-485.

Wise, C. D., & Stein, L. Dopamine-$\beta$-hydroxylase deficits in the brains of schizophrenic patients. *Science*, 1973, 181, 344-347.

Wise, C. D., & Stein, L. "Dopamine-β-hydroxylase activity in the brains of chronic schizophrenic patients": Reply to Wyatt, Schwartz, Erdelyi and Barchas, *Science*, 1975, 187, 370.

Wurtman, R. J., & Axelrod, J. A sensitive and specific assay for the estimation of monoamine oxidase. *Biochemical Pharmacology*, 1963, 12, 1439-1441.

Wyatt, R. J., Schwartz, M. A., Erdelyi, E., & Barchas, J. D. Dopamine-$\beta$-hydroxylase activity in the brains of chronic schizophrenic patients. *Science*, 1975, 187, 368–370.

# Intracranial Self-Stimulation Pathways as Substrate for Memory Consolidation

## Aryeh Routtenberg[1]

*Northwestern University*

## INTRODUCTION

*I*t is twenty years since the discovery by Olds and Milner (1954) of brain regions which appear to represent the physical substrate for reward and pleasure. It may be of value to review the contributions that this discovery has provided and to assess the progress which has been made toward its understanding. One can readily observe this progress in the nature of the contributions in the present symposium. I shall review the work on the anatomy of self-stimulation performed in my laboratory and attempt to show how such data may aid in understanding some of the general problems that have been raised by the other contributors.

I shall begin with the theory of schizophrenia proposed by Stein and Wise (1971) and discussed in detail by Stein in this symposium. In this connection, I will briefly go over the recently gained monoamine anatomy which relates also to Dr. Hoebel's work. Certain theoretical problems raised by our work relate to the motivational plasticity described by Dr. Valenstein and to the theoretical significance of self-stimulation described by Dr. Gallistel. Finally, I shall propose a model of the brain systems which support intracranial self-stimulation that points to the behavioral importance of these mechanisms in memory consolidation.

1. With the assistance of Drs. Rebecca Santos-Anderson and Ronald Clavier.

I. NOREPINEPHRINE HYPOTHESIS
INTRACRANIAL SELF-STIMULATION,
AND SCHIZOPHRENIA

Quite early after the discovery of self-stimulation, Olds (1959) demonstrated that intracranial self-stimulation (ICSS) could be manipulated by psychoactive drugs, such as tranquilizers, stimulants, and depressants. This led him to advance the notion that disorders of mood and aberrations of personality were corrected through the use of various drugs by virtue of the drug action on the ICSS fiber systems. This hypothesis has to this day been an acceptable one with no evidence of detractors.

In the early 1960s Larry Stein and his group at Wyeth demonstrated that those drugs which manipulated brain levels of norepinephrine had a profound effect on ICSS. Through the 1960s the hypothesized relationship between norepinephrine and ICSS received support from a wide variety of experiments which are well reviewed in this symposium by Dr. Stein. In light of the earlier suggestion that behavior abnormalities were related to the ICSS fiber systems, Stein and Wise (1971) proposed that schizophrenic behavior results from a malfunction of the norepinephrine-mediated "reward" system. The evidence supporting this theory is marshaled by Stein in this symposium, and at this juncture it can be said that it is still a viable theory that relates to the theory of affective disorders (Schildkraut & Kety, 1967), which also postulates a critical role for norepinephrine in emotional states.

If the ICSS effect and motivational-emotional states share a common anatomical and pharmacological substrate, it would then be predicted that those neural systems which support self-stimulation have norepinephrine as their mediating neurotransmitter. Data obtained in my laboratory over the past few years do indeed indicate an intimate association between norepinephrine fiber systems and ICSS, but it must be emphasized that much of the evidence clearly shows that this close relationship may be correlational and that ICSS may in some cases be derived from systems other than those specifically containing norepinephrine. Thus, the norepinephrine pathways and ICSS loci relationship documented most recently by German and Bowden (1974) may, in fact, prove to be coincidental with other as yet unidentified fiber systems providing the critical substrate.

## II. ON THE PROBLEMS OF INTERPRETING LOCALIZATION OF BRAIN STIMULATION EFFECTS

One of the advances made over the past twenty years has been the gradual shift away from the unchallenged acceptance of the location of the electrode tip as conclusive evidence for the brain localization of the ICSS effect. What should have been obvious is now abundantly clear: that several fiber systems are stimulated by an electrode, and that the nuclear group surrounding its tip may not be the best indicator of the system important in supporting ICSS behavior.

An example of the complexity of the situation may be drawn from what has come to be known as "lateral hypothalamic" ICSS. This refers to the self-stimulation observed when electrodes are situated in the area of the lateral hypothalamic nucleus. Specifically, ICSS was most consistently obtained when electrodes were within the medial forebrain bundle (MFB). For this reason, the MFB-lateral hypothalamic area has come to be considered the "focus" of ICSS. Whether this ICSS depended upon systems which either terminated or originated in the lateral hypothalamic area, however, has yet to be determined. Then, too, it is incorrect to think of the MFB as a functionally or anatomically homogeneous structure. Rather, it is a composite of ascending and descending fiber systems which link forebrain structures with midbrain structures. Considering the multiplicity of neurotransmitters which characterize these various fiber systems, it becomes clear that a complex array of neuropharmacological synaptic events, some at several millimeters away from the electrode tip, must accompany MFB ICSS. Even focusing our attention on catecholamine systems, norepinephrine, and dopamine, we are faced with the fact that at some points in its trajectory, the "MFB region" contains two separate norepinephrine systems and two separate dopamine systems (Ungerstedt, 1971). Thus, it is necessary, as a beginning, to assess the relative individual contribution of each of these systems to the final product of MFB ICSS. Toward this goal, we have already shown that in the lateral aspect of the MFB, self-stimulation may depend on efferents from the substantia nigra, pars compacta (Huang & Routtenberg, 1971) Routtenberg & Malsbury, 1969), the frontal cortex (Routtenberg, 1971; Routtenberg & Sloan, 1972), or the ventral tegmental area of Tsai

(Clavier & Routtenberg, 1974; Routtenberg & Kane, 1966; Routtenberg & Malsbury, 1969).

What has been said above has come to be realized over the past five years as a result of an evolution of experiments in my laboratory which made it clear that our initial attitudes toward localizing brain stimulation effects were far too optimistic.

### III. PERSONAL HISTORY OF BRAINSTEM MAPPING FOR INTRACRANIAL SELF-STIMULATION

I became interested in the anatomy of brainstem ICSS as a result of the question of whether or not it was related to the brainstem reticular formation, the classical arousal mechanism of the brain. Glickman (1960) had related ICSS to arousal, but Olds and Peretz (1960) were able to dissociate the two phenomena. Such a dissociation implied separate anatomical systems, and indeed many placements along the reticular core, from the medulla to the midbrain, were subsequently shown not to support ICSS (Routtenberg & Malsbury, 1969).

If not the reticular formation, what brainstem system or systems were important to ICSS? Some initial clues were contained in the results of a midbrain stimulation and lesion study (Routtenberg & Kane, 1966). In that experiment lesions made at ICSS sites in the ventral midbrain tegmental area resulted in reduction of body weight, while lesions in the dorsal or central tegmentum, where little ICSS was observed, caused no weight reduction. Thus, both ICSS and body weight maintenance seemed related to fibers in the ventral tegmentum, and not to those of the dorsal or central tegmuntum.

Just when things seemed to be promising with respect to localizing the ICSS effect to ventral midbrain, Sugar and I (1968) discovered several cases of ICSS in *dorsal* midbrain and *dorsal* pontine tegmentum. It is of special interest to note that Margules (1969) also described dorsal tegmental ICSS, which he suggested had a noradrenergic basis. Since relatively little was known about the cellular origins or terminations of these systems, more data were required to answer the simple question, Where can one obtain self-stimulation in the brainstem? I was concerned not just with the ICSS in the anterior midbrain regions, which at that time was considered a dramatic demonstration of the posterior extent of self-stimulation, but also with the pons and medulla. I thus began a map of the brainstem using a somewhat rigid behavioral testing procedure (Routtenberg, 1973) in order to discern the sites of self-stimulation that were most important. Such could be achieved, in my view, by using minimum amounts of current and no behavioral shaping (Routtenberg & Malsbury, 1969).

In this experiment, then, we showed that self-stimulation could be obtained from a variety of sites, in anterior medulla–posterior pons at the level of the genu of the facial nerve and anteriorly along the pathway of the brachium conjunctivum. Such findings along with our discovery of the sites of self-stimulation in the ventral tegmental area and the substantia nigra suggested that the extrapyramidal system was involved with ICSS. Thus, two *brainstem* motor structures, the brachium conjunctivum and the substantia nigra, were implicated in ICSS.

We were puzzled by the fact that ICSS was obtained from the brachium conjunctivum and we suspected that there were fiber systems in this region that would project to the "focus" of ICSS, the medial forebrain bundle–lateral hypothalamic region. In an effort to determine whether this was true, we made lesions at self-stimulation sites and followed the trajectory of the degenerating fibers with the Nauta (1957) method. No degeneration was observed in the lateral hypothalamus. Although a negative statement with these silver impregnation methods must be viewed cautiously, the lateral hypothalamic region did not seem to be implicated in brachium conjunctivum ICSS. Since we could observe degeneration quite clearly along the brachium conjunctivum as it ascends into the midbrain following a pathway to the red nucleus and also to thalamus, it seemed to us that the brachium conjunctivum was indeed involved in ICSS.

Our satisfaction in discovering that this major efferent of the cerebellum had importance for ICSS was rapidly tempered by a series of dramatic new anatomical findings which helped place the catecholamines (CA) of the brain into specific brainstem fiber systems. This opened the door to investigations aimed at relating ICSS pathways to these individual CA systems.

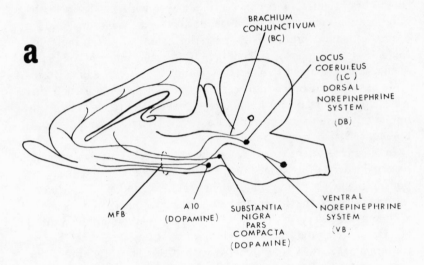

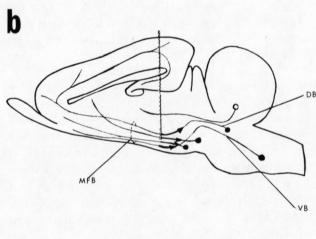

FIG. 1. Diagram to show the major catecholamine systems (a) and consequences of lesions at ICSS sites in medial forebrain bundle (b),

**c**

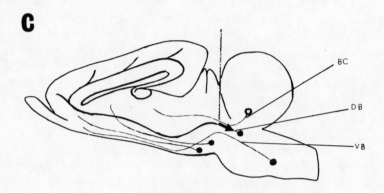

"BRACHIUM CONJUNCTIVUM"
POSITIVE
SS

**d**

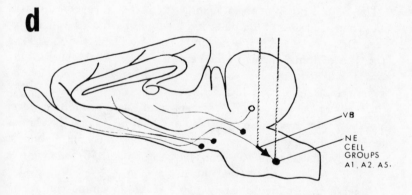

VENTRAL NOREPINEPHRINE SYSTEM
NEGATIVE
SS

"brachium conjunctivum" (c), and the ventral norepinephrine bundle (d). See text for further details.

In order to understand the work to be discussed, it will be necessary to review briefly certain aspects of the CA pathways. A recent description of the anatomy of the ascending adrenergic systems is that by Ungerstedt (1971), who has suggested that there are two separate ascending norepinephrine fiber bundles. Each bundle is bilaterally represented and for the most part there is very little contralateral innervation by either system. Figure 1a schematically shows the relative locations of the various bundles. The dorsal bundle originates in the locus coeruleus, a compact nucleus of cell bodies which lies just below the fourth ventricle at the posterior pontine level of the brainstem. The axons of these neurons project forward through the pontine tegmentum, where they intermingle with the axons of the brachium conjunctivum. Rostral to this, the dorsal bundle is separated from the brachium and occupies a position ventrolateral to the mesencephalic central gray. At the hypothalamic level, the dorsal fibers are within the MFB at its dorsal aspect. Some of the dorsal bundle axons terminate in the hypothalamus, but the majority ascend anteriorly to innervate the amygdala, hippocampus, and the cerebral cortex.

The ventral norepinephrine bundle originates in several different cell groups situated in the pons and medulla. Each of these groups, labeled simply as "A1," "A2," and "A5" by Dahlström and Fuxe (1964), contributes axons to the ventral bundle. At the level of the pons, the ventral bundle axons are situated just below those of the dorsal bundle. There is, in fact, no certain way to discern visibly which fibers belong to which system. Only at the midbrain level does the ventral system separate and dip down to occupy the ventral mesencephalic tegmental area. Rostral to this, the ventral bundle axons are situated along the ventral aspect of the MFB, the majority of which terminate in hypothalamic nuclei.

Ungerstedt also described two ascending dopamine containing systems (see fig. 1a). The nigro-neostriate fiber bundle originates in the substantia nigra, pars compacta; this nucleus was labeled "A9" by Dahlström and Fuxe (1964). Axons from these cells join the lateral aspect of the MFB at its posterior level. Further anteriorly, these fibers enter the medial edge of the internal capsule, and project to the neostriatum or caudate-putamen complex. The mesolimbic dopamine bundle has its origin in the "A10" group of cell bodies situated in the ventral mesencephalic tegmentum, overlapping Tsai's area. These cells presumably lie below the region of passage of the ventral norepinephrine bundle; however, our observations indicate that the latter fibers course through the region of the A10 cells. Axons of the mesolimbic system ascend in the ventrolateral portion of the MFB, and terminate in the olfactory tubercle and nucleus accumbens.

These descriptions of CA histochemistry will assist in understanding our recent experimental results with regard to the involvement in ICSS of the CA systems. Fuxe and Lidbrink (1970) suggested that certain of our brachium conjunctivum placements were quite close to the norepinephrine system which originates in the locus coeruleus, and that the reported ICSS resulted from the activation of these norepinephrine fibers. As can be readily appreciated, such a view is coherent with the arguments made by Olds, quite early on, and subsequently by Stein, that ICSS is exclusively a derivative of norepinephrine fiber pathways.

This involvement of norepinephrine pathways in ICSS has gained especially strong support from Crow, Spear, and Arbuthnott (1972) and Ritter and Stein (1973), who demonstrated that ICSS could be obtained by stimulation of the locus coeruleus. In the context of our prior discussion, that statement should read that self-stimulation was obtained with electrodes whose tip was in proximity to the locus coeruleus. In this area of research it is particularly discouraging to point out that in both the Crow and the Ritter and Stein papers the figures presented are of sufficiently poor quality as to preclude identification of many of the electrode tip locations. This is the case in the Crow paper, where many of the electrodes are difficult to discern; and in the Ritter and Stein paper, the locus coeruleus is not shown, since they have chosen a myelin (Weil) stain to demonstrate their histology. It is, therefore, not possible to make a statement concerning the presence of the locus coeruleus with respect to the electrode tip. Having made that critical statement, nonetheless, we can accept the fact that self-stimulation can be obtained from a region in close proximity to, if not associated with, the locus coeruleus. It is indeed possible that the locus coeruleus itself supports self-stimulation. This is certainly the weight of evidence which both papers provide.

If brachium conjunctivum self-stimulation did involve locus coeruleus pathways, then several predicted results should support this idea. First, there should be no self-stimulation in the cell bodies of origin of the brachium conjunctivum. This was shown by Huang and Routtenberg (1971) and by Crow et al. (1972). Second, lesions at self-stimulation sites in the brachium conjunctivum should affect only the dorsal norepinephrine bundle. This effect should be seen in the fluorescence microscope, since lesions cause a pile-up of transmitter back along the axon bundle toward the cells or origin. This buildup can then be visualized through the fluorescence microscope following special histochemical treatment of the tissue. Only those systems close enough to the electrode to be damaged by the lesion may be involved in the self-stimulation observed. Thus, for example, only the dorsal norepinephrine system should be observed in the flourescence microscope following brachium conjunctivum lesions at ICSS sites. Finally, lesions of the locus coeruleus should eliminate self-stimulation from the brachium conjunctivum. We have recently performed the latter two experiments and I wish to discuss them now in some detail.

Clavier and I (1974) took advantage of the lesion and buildup technique and made lesions at self-stimulation sites and observed the catecholamine buildup.[2] Most relevant to the present discussion was our finding that lesions at ICSS sites in the brachium conjunctivum always led to buildup in the dorsal bundle (fig. 1c). In one case of self-stimulation, the buildup was observed only in the dorsal bundle, while in other cases of self-stimulation, the buildup appeared to be in the dorsal and the ventral bundle. As shown in figure 1d, the ventral bundle did not appear to be involved in ICSS, however, since caudal pontine stimulation of the ventral fiber bundle itself, as revealed by buildup in that bundle, did not support self-stimulation. In addition, stimulation of three cell groupings that contribute to the ventral bundle, the A1, A3, and A5 cells (Dahlström & Fuxe, 1964), did not yield ICSS. We showed that at such ventral bundle non-ICSS sites, lesions gave rise to buildup in the ventral bundle. Although the association between the site of stimulation and the site of lesion may not be perfect, on the basis of lack of self-stimulation effects (a) from the cell bodies of origin and (b) in the region of the ventral bundle as demonstrated by histochemical fluorescence of buildup in the ventral bundle, it seems justified to conclude that the ventral bundle was not likely associated with

2. We found (Clavier & Routtenberg, 1974) that the MFB is not the best place to test this experimental paradigm. As figure 1b shows, the four CA systems were too closely aligned, and buildup was usually seen in all bundles. Thus, individual contributions could not be assessed.

self-stimulation.[3] The dorsal bundle, on the other hand, as it passed through the brachium conjunctivum, did appear to be associated with self-stimulation, since it was shown that ICSS was always associated with dorsal bundle buildup.

We realized, however, that this was not sufficient to prove the involvement of the locus coeruleus in brachium conjunctivum self-stimulation. In a second study (Clavier & Routtenberg, 1975) we again placed stimulating electrodes at brachium conjunctivum points where we obtained a steady rate (200-600 responses/15 min.) of bar pressing for brain stimulation. Then, lesions were made in the ipsilateral locus coeruleus. After we had completed this experiment, we performed another experiment in which we made ipsilateral lesions and then followed a few weeks later by contralateral lesions to eliminate the locus coeruleus totally. Much to our surprise we found that ipsilateral and bilateral locus coeruleus lesions had no consistent effect on brachium conjunctivum ICSS. There were some cases in which ICSS was attenuated slightly, and there were cases in which ICSS was augmented slightly following unilateral and bilateral lesions. These results were analyzed in a variety of ways. We found that electrode placements which were most closely associated with the dorsal bundle were actually more likely to be augmented by lesions of the locus coeruleus than were stimulating electrodes that seemed more closely associated with the brachium conjunctivum. The major point of this study was the clear indication that ICSS obtained in the region of the brachium conjunctivum was not dependent upon the integrity of the locus coeruleus.

If my argument has been followed up to this point, it will be seen that the two major norepinephrine systems which have been implicated in ICSS, the dorsal bundle–locus coeruleus system (Crow et al., 1972; Ritter & Stein, 1973) and the ventral bundle (A1, A2, and A5 system (Arbuthnott, Fuxe, & Ungerstedt, 1971), are suspect as candidates for supporting ICSS. Is it possible, then, that norepinephrine is not involved in ICSS? We have presented evidence that the two major norepinephrine systems presumed to contribute to

---

3. The work of Hoebel showing that lesions of the ventral bundle either by electrocoagulation or presumably selective chemical technique leads to hyperphagia is of considerable interest in this regard, since according to Hoebel, it would be predicted that destruction of the ventral norepinephrine bundle should augment ICSS. This result again would argue against the role of the ventral norepinephrine system in ICSS.

ICSS may not be involved, i.e., the dorsal bundle can be eliminated and not affect ICSS (Clavier & Routtenberg, 1975), and the ventral bundle can be shown not to be associated with self-stimulation (Clavier & Routtenberg, 1974). At this juncture it is not unwise to consider some of the disclaimers that have been made with regard to the norepinephrine hypothesis, which has been strongly supported by data from Dr. Stein's laboratory. One such report (Roll, 1970) indicated that disulfiram, the agent which blocks the enzymatic conversion of dopamine to norepinephrine, and which Stein had shown decreases ICSS rates, actually did not affect ICSS but affected the animal's overall behavior: the animal would fall asleep. While this experiment is hardly definitive, it does call attention to a serious criticism of the norepinephrine hypothesis.

While there is a considerable amount of "interlocking" evidence for the involvement of norepinephrine in ICSS, the evidence has been for the most part of a correlative nature. Thus, the demonstration has not been forthcoming of a specific norepinephrine fiber pathway presumably related to ICSS being specifically manipulated by this particular drug, and that the manipulation of this fiber pathway by the drug whether it be a stimulant, such as d-amphetamine, or a depressant, such as disulfiram, is specifically responsible for altering that ICSS. In sum, while evidence that norepinephrine is involved in ICSS exists, it is by no means conclusive.

Nor, it should be noted, is it definitive that norepinephrine is not involved in ICSS. I would like at this juncture to point out some possible experiments that would be useful to do in order to determine whether ICSS is dependent upon norepinephrine fiber pathways. We have shown that the ventral bundle does not support self-stimulation. It is conceivable that the suspected aversive effects of stimulation in this region masked the rewarding effects of stimulation of the ventral bundle. That aversive brain stimulation could mask rewarding brain stimulation has been demonstrated, using two brain probes in each animal. It was shown that self-stimulation in the hypothalamus was attentuated both by electrical and by chemical activation of an aversive brain locus in the dorsal midbrain tegmentum (Routtenberg & Olds, 1966). Therefore, our conclusion that self-stimulation is not supported by the ventral bundle may be erroneous, since other competing aversive effects could have been recruited which masked the reward effects of brain stimulation in that area. In order to evaluate this possibility, it may be necessary to determine what aversive systems are involved. One possibility is that nucleus reticularis gigantocellularis could play a role since Keene and Casey (1970) demonstrated that it was activated by MFB ICSS sites, responded to aversive stimuli, and yielded aversive effects when stimulated directly. It may be possible that lesions of the ventral bundle may have an effect on brachium conjunctivum self-stimulation, since many of the placements are close to the ventral bundle and there is a ventral bundle buildup following lesions of brachium conjunctivum in the majority of our ICSS placements.[4] With regard to the lack of effect of locus coeruleus lesions on brachium conjunctivum self-stimulation, it is possible that the dorsal bundle is involved in ICSS but that because the electrode size was too great or the current level too high, several other fiber pathways, not only the dorsal bundle, were activated. Lesions of the locus coeruleus, while eliminating an important fiber pathway related to ICSS, failed to abolish the animal's responding since the other fiber pathways activated by this intense stimulation were sufficient to maintain ICSS. Although this possibility must be seriously considered, it also must be admitted that the current levels employed are lower than those used by other workers.

Irrespective of the role of dorsal bundle fiber system, what then are the other fiber pathways that are involved? Clearly the conclusion must be that there are at least several pathways as yet unknown which support "brachium conjunctivum" ICSS. This may be viewed as somewhat discouraging in the sense that one would have expected that in twenty years it would be possible to describe, in a definitive way, the anatomy of self-stimulation. That clearly cannot be said to be the accomplishment of the first twenty years, although should we pursue the approach that is presently being taken it is conceivable that these pathways will be defined. It remains, then, an exciting direction for future exploration to specify the fiber pathways which support ICSS. In addition, it must be reiterated that the association between norepinephrine and ICSS can be questioned on anatomical and histochemical grounds as we presently understand them.[5] Further approaches to this problem are clearly desirable before the norepinephrine hypothesis can be accepted.

4. This experiment has recently been performed, and no effects on ICSS were observed. This finding is consistent with a lack of involvement of the ventral bundle in dorsal tegmental ICSS (Clavier & Routtenberg, 1975).

5. The periventricular norepinephrine bundle, however, represents a newly described pathway (Lindvall & Björklund, 1974).

IV. FUNCTION OF THE FIBERS WHICH SUPPORT
INTRACRANIAL SELF-STIMULATION

In the preceding sections I have pointed out that we have yet to specify the particular *fiber pathways* which are involved in ICSS. However, we have achieved a map of the *specific regions* where ICSS is most easily demonstrated. In this section I wish to show that these regions which support ICSS overlap with those regions which lead to memory-disruptive effects following electrical stimulation. I have interpreted such findings to indicate that the fiber systems which support ICSS are those fiber systems which are active during memory-consolidation processes. Hence, electrical stimulation during or immediately after learning disrupts the normal physiological activity in the systems necessary for establishing a permanent memory trace.

Before introducing the data relevant to this proposed relationship between self-stimulation and memory disruption, I would like to discuss the pitfalls of an apparently obvious test of this theory.

An obvious test of the hypothesized association between ICSS and memory disruption is to observe the effect of localized brain stimulation on memory and then to test if the same stimulation supports self-stimulation. One would predict that memory disruption would be associated with ICSS and the absence of memory disruption would be accompanied by lack of ICSS. This apparently simple test is actually insufficient for arriving at any definite conclusion regarding the relationship between memory mechanisms and ICSS substrates. Consider two possible results which appear to disconfirm the theory. First, when brain stimulation does not produce memory disruption but supports ICSS, one could argue that the stimulation causes alterations in performance, by virtue of its rewarding characteristics, which preclude the demonstration of the memory-disruptive effects. Such an explanation is particularly relevant to the passive-avoidance situation used in our laboratory in which brain stimulation is applied when the animal ascends onto a platform following grid foot shock. Since the animal receives brain stimulation while on the platform, it is possible that if the brain stimulation were rewarding, the animal would prefer to remain on the platform. On the retention test 24 hrs. later, although the brain stimulation may have disrupted memory for the foot shock, it might also have increased the probability that the animal would stay on the platform in order to obtain more brain stimulation.

The second apparently damaging observation is the case in which stimulation of the brain results in memory impairment but no ICSS is demonstrated. Such a situation could occur if memory-disruption effects had a lower threshold than the reward effect. In fact, we have obtained disruptive effects at 5μA (Bresnahan & Routtenberg, 1972), but at this low current level we did not demonstrate ICSS.

It should be clear, then, that all four possible combinations of the absence and presence of ICSS and memory disruption can exist without actually weakening the theory that self-stimulation pathways are indeed the pathways of memory consolidation. The simple, straightforward test of the theory, therefore, may not be the most appropriate, although one might expect to observe a trend or statistically significant correlation were a sufficient number of cases used.

A first and necessary step toward establishing an association between memory and self-stimulation pathways is to demonstrate that sites which have been shown to support ICSS are similar to those sites which produce memory disruption. Some of these data have been reviewed (Routtenberg, 1975).

Wurtz and Olds (1963) demonstrated self-stimulation in the medial, but not the lateral, portions of the amygdala. Bresnahan and Routtenberg (1972) obtained memory disruption with stimulation of the medial, but not the lateral, portions of the amygdala. Routtenberg and Malsbury (1969) and Huang and Routtenberg 1971) demonstrated ICSS primarily in the substantia nigra, pars compacta; Routtenberg and Holzman (1973) demonstrated memory-disruptive effects primarily from the substantia nigra, pars compacta. Routtenberg (1971) and Routtenberg and Sloan (1972) demonstrated self-stimulation in the frontal cortex; Santos-Anderson and Routtenberg (1975) demonstrated disruptive effects following stimulation of those frontal cortex areas associated with ICSS. Ursin, Ursin, and Olds (1966) have demonstrated ICSS in the dorsal hippocampus; numerous investigators (Barcik, 1969; Brunner, Rossi, Stutz, & Roth, 1970; Hirano, 1965; Kesner & Conner, 1972; Kesner & Doty, 1968; Lidsky & Slotnick, 1971; Vardaris & Schwartz, 1971) have demonstrated memory-disruptive effects from dorsal hippocampus stimulation. Olds, Travis, and Schwing (1960) and Routtenberg (1971) have demonstrated self-stimulation in the caudate nucleus; Wyers and his associates (Wyers, Peeke, Williston, & Herz, 1968; Wyers & Deadwyler, 1971; Wyers, Deadwyler, Hirasuna, & Montgomery, 1973) demonstrated memory disruption following caudate stimulation. Cooper and Taylor (1967) demonstrated ICSS in the nonspecific midline thalamic nuclei; Wilburn and Kesner (1972) demonstrated memory-disruptive effects from stimulation of midline thalamic nuclei. Valenstein and Meyers (1964) demonstrated self-stimulation in the septal region; Brunner, Rossi, Stutz, and Roth (1970) and Kasper (1964) demonstrated memory disruption from septal area stimulation. It is interesting that we have begun to study the disruptive effects of locus coeruleus stimulation (Santos-Anderson & Routtenberg (1975) and we have not succeeded in obtaining disruptive effects. This finding relates closely to our data indicating no disruptive intracranial self-stimulation effects resulting from destruction of the locus coeruleus system. In addition, Amaral and Routtenberg (1975) have not obtained ICSS with electrode placements in locus coeruleus using the rigid behavioral testing procedure in our laboratory.

Finally, in a recently completed study Bresnahan and Routtenberg (1975) using similar methods, investigated the memory-disruptive effects of MFB stimulation. Since this is the "focus" of ICSS, it was shown, as would be expected, that memory impairment occurred. It is particularly interesting to note that MFB sites which were associated with memory disruption were in the lateral portion of the MFB, along the medial edge of the internal capsule. This region contains axons ascending from the substantia nigra (Moore, Bhatnagar, & Heller, 1971), afferent and efferent fibers associated with the amygdala (Cowan, Raisman, & Powell, 1965), and descending fibers from the frontal cortex (Routtenberg, 1971). It is possible, therefore, that MFB stimulation results in memory disruption by producing interference with the activity of the fiber systems whose cell bodies of origin have already been implicated in memory-disruptive effects.

It can be concluded, then, that some association exists between brain sites which support ICSS behavior and those which give rise to memory disruption when stimulated during or after learning. I wish to emphasize that the fiber pathways which are involved have not been specified, although we feel that we are quite close to demonstrating the involvement of several fiber pathways, to wit, the nigro-neostriatal system, the descending frontal system, and a system intermingled with the brachium conjunctivum and dorsal norepinephrine bundle.

Two ideas related to the contributions of the other participants in the symposium may be worth mentioning. First, Dr. Valenstein has suggested a somewhat controversial view of motivational circuits in which neural components have the capacity for switching to various behaviors; in particular, switching between eating and drinking has been demonstrated (Valenstein, Cox, & Kakolewski, 1968). The idea that neural plasticity is a property of these motivational circuits is certainly compatible with the view that these circuits are important in memory consolidation. Indeed, it is not inconceivable that synaptic junctions in these circuits have sufficiently unique properties to provide for this motivational switching. Such plasticity may be a reflection of the capability of this system for adjustment on the basis of the current external environment; and this may be an appropriate mechanism for information storage. It is interesting, in this regard, that lesions of the substantia nigra lead to degeneration and removal of synaptic terminals in the caudate nucleus 24 hrs. after lesions (Routtenberg & Tarrant, unpublished observations). This is a most rapid alteration which is perhaps an indication of certain unique properties of synaptic junctions in the caudate nucleus.

Dr. Gallistel has expanded upon the Deutsch interpretation of ICSS; one phenomenon which has occupied his attention has been the priming effect, the need to prime the animals in order to provide drive motivation. It is interesting that the interpretation of the priming effect has, according to them, been in terms of lack of drive, and that priming engages the drive system. However, it is also possible that the priming effect is related to the fact that the reinforcing stimulation — that which is obtained at the end of the runway — manipulates memory. My interpretation is that the brain stimulation possesses a memory-disruptive component at the end of the runway and that the animal receives essentially a "reminder" (Miller & Springer, 1972) when it receives the priming stimulation just before runway performance. As in our experiments, the reinforcing brain stimulation does not *eliminate* memory; rather it disrupts it to some extent. This disruption is attenuated, then, by the "reminder" priming brain stimulation.

Finally, the general question may be raised as to the relation between motivation and memory. In current behavioral science these systems are quite often divorced one from the other. For example, cognitive psychology, learning, and memory typically exist as quite separate from personality and abnormal psychology. The two approaches to the problem of behavior seem to be quite different. It is interesting that the father of physiological psychology, Sigmund Freud, clearly saw an important relationship between the motivational system and the memory storage system. This was seen in his extensive analysis of dream material in which the memory retrieval concepts of supression and repression were employed. Thus, forgetting occurred as a consequence of the activation of motivational emotional circuits. It is interesting and relevant that the treatment procedures for the emotional disorder manic-depression also have profound effects on memory-consolidation processes. It is also important to note that the major antipsychotic agents manipulate those systems which are closely associated with the pathways of intracranial self-stimulation and memory disruption. Also, children with learning disabilities are often difficult to treat because of the complication of emotional disorder which intertwines with the learning disability. Finally, it is pertinent to note that schizophrenia, associated with ICSS systems (Stein & Wise, 1971), is often considered to have loss of contact with reality as a major symptom and cognitive slippage as the major factor contributing to this symptom. It seems to me that we have made an unnecessary distinction between emotional states and cognitive states and that the two are, indeed, closely related. One could envisage, for example, a neural mechanism which, when active in one state, engages memory-consolidation mechanisms and, when active in the other state, forms a substrate of an emotional condition. The two would interact, so that an optimal level of activity could be achieved which was compatible with both memory consolidation and an appropriate level of affect.

REFERENCES

Amaral, D. G., & Routtenberg, A. Locus coeruleus and intracranial self-stimulation: A cautionary note. *Behavioral Biology*, 1975, **13**, 331-338.
Arbuthnott, G., Fuxe, K., & Ungerstedt, U. Central catecholamine turnover and self-stimulation behavior. *Brain research*, 1971, **27**, 406-413.

Barcik, J. D. Hippocampal afterdischarges and memory disruption. *Preceedings of the 77th Annual Convention, A.P.A., 1969,* 185-186.

Bresnahan, E., & Routtenberg, A. Memory disruption by unilateral low-level subseizure stimulation of the medial amygdaloid nucleus. *Physiology and Behavior,* 1972, **9,** 513-525.

Bresnahan, E., & Routtenberg, A. Passive avoidance retention deficits as a function of unilateral, low-level medial forebrain bundle stimulation during learning. 1975, submitted.

Brunner, R. L., Rossi, R. R., Stutz, R. M., & Roth, T. G. Memory loss following posttrial electrical stimulation of the hippocampus. *Psychonomic Science,* 1970, **18,** 159-60.

Clavier, R. M., & Routtenberg, A. Ascending monoamine-containing fiber pathways related to intracranial self-stimulation: Histochemical fluorescence study. *Brain Research,* 1974, **72,** 25-40.

Clavier, R. M., & Routtenberg, A. Brainstem self-stimulation attenuated by lesions of medial forebrain bundle but not by lesions of locus coeruleus or the caudal ventral norepinephrine bundle. 1975, submitted.

Cooper, R. M., & Taylor, L. H. Thalamic reticular system and central grey: Self-stimulation. *Science,* 1967, **156,** 102-103.

Cowan, W. M., Raisman, G., & Powell, T.P.S. The connexions of the amygdala. *Journal of Neurology, Neurosurgery and Psychiatry,* 1965, **28,** 137-151.

Crow, T. J., Spear, P. J., & Arbuthnott, G. W. Intracranial self-stimulation with electrodes in the region of the locus coeruleus. *Brain Research,* 1972, **36,** 275-287.

Dahlström, A., & Fuxe, K. Evidence for the existence of monoamine-containing neurons in the central nervous system. I. Demonstration of monoamines in the cell bodies of brainstem neurons. *Acta Physiologica Scandinavica,* 1964, **62,** Suppl. 232, 1-55.

Fuxe, K., & Lidbrink, P. On the function of central catecholamine neurons: Their role in cardiovascular and arousal mechanisms. Paper read at the Congress on the Pharmacology and Physiology of Monoamines in the Central Nervous System, Palo Alto, California, 1970.

German, D. C., & Bowden, D. M. Catecholamine systems as the neural substrate for intracranial self-stimulation: An hypothesis. *Brain Research,* 1974, **73,** 381-419.

Glickman, S. E. Reinforcing properties of arousal. *Journal of Comparative and Physiological Psychology,* 1960, **53,** 68-71.

Hirano, T. Effects of functional disturbances of the limbic system on the memory consolidation. *Japanese Psychological Research,* 1965, **7,** 171-182.

Huang, Y. H., & Routtenberg, A. Lateral hypothalamic self-stimulation pathways in Rattus Norvigicus. *Physiology and Behavior*, 1971, 7, 419-432.

Kasper, P. Attenuation of passive avoidance by continuous septal stimulation. *Psychonomic Science*, 1964, 1, 219-220.

Keene, J. J., & Casey, K. L. Excitatory connection from lateral hypothalamic self-stimulation sites to escape sites in medullary reticular formation. *Experimental Neurology*, 1970, 28, 155-156.

Kesner, R. P., & Conner, H. S. Effects of electrical stimulation of rat limbic system and midbrain reticular formation upon short- and long-term memory. *Physiology and Behavior*, 1972, 12, 5-12.

Kesner, R. P., & Doty, R. W. Amnesia produced in cats by local seizure activity initiated from the amygdala. *Experimental Neurology*, 1968, 21, 58-68.

Lidsky, A., & Slotnick, B. M. Effects of posttrial limbic stimulation on retention of a one-trial passive avoidance response. *Journal of Comparative and Physiological Psychology*, 1971, 76, 337-348.

Lindvall, O., & Björklund, A. The organization of ascending catecholamine neuron systems in the rat brain as revealed by the glyoxylic acid fluorescence method. *Acta Physiologica Scandinavica*, 1974, suppl. 412, 1-48.

Margules, D. Noradrenergic rather than serotonergic basis of reward in the dorsal tegmentum. *Journal of Comparative and Physiological Psychology*, 1969, 67, 32-35.

Miller, R. R., & Springer, A. D. Induced recovery of memory in rats following electroconvulsive shock. *Physiology and Behavior*, 1972, 8, 645-651.

Moore, R. Y., Bhatnagar, R. K., & Heller, L. Anatomical and chemical studies of the nigro-neostriatal projection in the cat. *Brain Research*, 1971, 30, 119-136.

Nauta, W.J.H. Silver impregnation of degenerating axons. In W. F. Windle (Ed.), *New Research Techniques of Neuroanatomy*. Springfield, Ill.: Thomas, 1975. Pp. 17-26.

Olds, J. Studies of neuropharmacologicals by electrical and chemical manipulation of the brain in animals with chronically implanted electrodes. In P. B. Bradley, P. Deniker, & C. Redsuco (Eds.), *Neuropsychopharmacology*. Amsterdam: Elsevier, 1959. Pp. 20-32.

Olds, J., & Milner, P. Positive reinforcement produced by electrical stimulation of septal area and other regions of rat brain. *Journal of Comparative and Physiological Psychology*, 1954, 47, 419-427.

Olds, J., & Peretz, B. A motivational analysis of the reticular activating system. *Electroencephalography and Clinical Neurophysiology*, 1960, 12, 445-454.

Olds, J., Travis, R. P. & Schwing, R. C. Topographic organization of hypothalamic self-stimulation functions. *Journal of Comparative and Physiological Psychology*, 1960, **53**, 23-32.

Ritter, S., & Stein, L. Self-stimulation of noradrenergic cell group (A6) in locus coeruleus of rats. *Journal of Comparative and Physiological Psychology*, 1973, **85**, 443-452.

Roll, S. K. Intracranial self-stimulation and wakefulness: Effect of manipulating ambient brain catecholamines. *Science*, 1970, **168**, 1370-1372.

Routtenberg, A. Forebrain pathways of reward in Rattus Norvegicus. *Journal of Comparative and Physiological Psychology*, 1971, **75**, 269-276.

Routtenberg, A. Intracranial self-stimulation pathways as substrate for stimulus-response integration. In J. Maser (Ed.), *Efferent Organization for Integrative Behavior*. New York: Academic Press, 1973. Pp. 263-318.

Routtenberg, A. Significance of intracranial self-stimulation. In: P. B. Bradley (Ed.), *Methods in Brain Research*. New York: Wiley, 1974, in press.

Routtenberg, A., & Holzman, N. Memory disruption by electrical stimulation of substantia nigra, pars compacta. *Science*, 1973, **181**, 83-86.

Routtenberg, A., & Kane, R. S. Weight loss following lesions at the self-stimulation point: Ventral midbrain tegmentum. *Canadian Journal of Psychology/Revue Canadienne de Psychologie*, 1966, **20**, 343-351.

Routtenberg, A. & Malsbury, C. Brainstem pathways of reward. *Journal of Comparative and Physiological Psychology*, 1969, **68**, 22-30.

Routtenberg, A., & Olds, J. The effect of dorsal midbrain stimulation on septal and hypothalamic self-stimulation. *Journal of Comparative and Physiological Psychology*, 1966, **62**, 250-255.

Routtenberg, A., & Sloan, M. Self-stimulation in the frontal cortex at Rattus Norvegicus. *Behavioral Biology*, 1972, **7**, 567-572.

Routtenberg, A., & Sugar, R. Runway performance following lesions at the self-stimulation point in midbrain tegmentum. Unpublished MS, Northwestern University, 1968.

Santos-Anderson, R. M., & Routtenberg, A. Stimulation of rat medial or sulcal prefrontal cortex during passive avoidance learning differentially influences retention performance. 1975, submitted.

Schildkraut, J. J., & Kety, S. S. Biogenic amines and emotion. *Science*, 1967, **156**, 21-30.

Stein, L., & Wise, C. D. Possible etiology of schizophrenia: Progressive damage to the noradrenergic reward system by 6-hydroxydopamine. *Science*, 1971, **171**, 1032-1036.

Ungerstedt, U. Stereotaxic mapping of the monoamine pathways in the rat brain. *Acta Physiologica Scandinavica*, 1971, Suppl. 367, 1-48.

Ursin, R., Ursin, H., & Olds, J. Self-stimulation of hippocampus in rats. *Journal of Comparative and Physiological Psychology*, 1966, **61**, 353-359.

Valenstein, F. S., Cox, V. C., & Kakolewski, J. W. Modification of motivated behavior elicited by electrical stimulation of the hypothalamus. *Science*, 1968, **159**, 1119-1121.

Valenstein, E. S., & Meyers, W. J. Rate-independent test of reinforcing consequences of brain stimulation. *Journal of Comparative and Physiological Psychology*, 1964, **57**, 52-60.

Vardaris, R. M., & Schwartz, K. E. Retrograde amnesia for passive avoidance produced by stimulation of dorsal hippocampus. *Physiology and Behavior*, 1971, **6**, 131-135.

Wilburn, M. W., & Kesner, R. P. Differential amnestic effects produced by electrical stimulation of the caudate nucleus and nonspecific thalamic system. *Experimental Neurology*, 1972, **34**, 45-50.

Wurtz, R. H., & Olds, J. Amygdaloid stimulation and operant reinforcement in the rat. *Journal of Comparative and Physiological Psychology*, 1963, **56**, 941-949.

Wyers, E. J., & Deadwyler, S. A. Duration and nature of retrograde amnesia produced by stimulation of the caudate nucleus. *Physiology and Behavior*, 1971, **6**, 97-103.

Wyers, E. J., Deadwyler, S. A., Hirasuna, N., & Montgomery, D. Passive avoidance retention and caudate stimulation. *Physiology and Behavior*, 1973, **6**, 809-819.

Wyers, E. J., Peeke, H.V.S, Williston, J. S., & Herz, M. J. Retroactive impairment of passive avoidance learning by stimulation of the caudate nucleus. *Experimental Neurology*, 1968, **22**, 350-366.

# Motivation as Central Organizing Process: The Psychophysical Approach to Its Functional and Neurophysiological Analysis[1]

## C. R. Gallistel[2]

*University of Pennsylvania*

## INTRODUCTION

*E*xtreme behaviorists have occasionally attacked the *raison d'etre* of this famous and durable series of symposia. They have suggested that motivation is a vague concept, incapable of operational definition — a concept that has no place in the scientific analysis of behavior. Many neurophysiologists are inclined to believe that motivation is the kind of psychological concept that is unlikely to have any interesting neurophysiological implications. Since I am trying to determine the neurophysiological bases for motivational processes, I begin by discussing the reasons why these processes may be assumed to exist and to play a fundamental role in an analysis of the neurophysiological bases of behavior.

The first section of the Introduction argues that motivational processes constitute the capstones in the hierarchical structuring of the functional units of sensorimotor coordination. The second section suggests that the effect of reinforcement is to restructure the hierarchy, rather than to create new sensorimotor coordinations. To-

1. The research by the author and his students reviewed in this paper was supported by NIMH Grant No. 13628, by a Summer Research Grant from the University of Pennsylvania and by NIH Physiological Training Grant No. GM OI 036.

2. I am grateful to Rochel Gelman, Duncan Luce, and George Mandler for critical readings of an early draft. Their cogent criticisms helped clarify several issues addressed in this paper.

gether, the first two sections advance a hypothesis about the nature of the motivation and reinforcement processes activated by electrical stimulation of upper brain stem loci (particularly areas in or near the medial forebrain bundle). The third section describes what was gained from the classical neurophysiological work that used a psychophysical approach to behavioral phenomena produced by electrical stimulation of peripheral neural tissue. The Introduction concludes with a discussion of the evidence that *both* motivation *and* reinforcement processes contribute to the self-stimulation phenomenon.

The remainder of the paper reviews the literature on the psychophysical approach to the motivating and reinforcing effects of electrical stimulation of the rat brain. Much of this literature deals with the self-stimulation phenomenon, since this phenomenon appears to involve both effects. The review emphasizes the parallels between modern psychophysical experiments on the effects of brain stimulation and the classical experiments that used psychophysical techniques to analyze the substrate for the effects produced by electrical stimulation of peripheral nerves and muscle.

The Concept of Motivation

*Functional units.* In the 1930s, Paul Weiss carried out an analysis of the temporal patterns of contraction and relaxation among the approximately 30 muscles that play an important role in a simple behavior (locomotion) of the salamander. His work demonstrates in detail something that is obvious even from casual observation, namely, that the behavior of most organisms is composed of complex yet *selectively organized or integrated* temporal-spatial sequences.

From an evolutionary standpoint, it could hardly be otherwise. If the low-level, e.g., reflex, mechanisms of behavior were not integrated by higher-level mechanisms, then the organism's behavior would be a spastic display. Each reflex would be activated whenever its proper stimulus came along, without regard to how the movement produced by that reflex fitted in with the movements being produced by other reflexes at or about the same time. As convulsive disorders demonstrate, such a situation produces spectacular but nonfunctional behavior. If there were ever an organism whose reflexes were not coordinated by higher processes, that organism could neither maintain itself nor participate in the propagation of a species. In the course of evolution, such organisms are bound to be supplanted by those whose low-level behavioral mechanisms are given coherent direction (integrated) by higher mechanisms. The fact that the highly organized nature of behavior is obvious and the fact that it could hardly be otherwise for evolutionary reasons should not deceive us into believing that the general nature of the mechanisms underlying this organization is obvious.

For years many physiologists and psychologists assumed that the Sherringtonian (and Sechenovian-Pavlovian) analysis of complex behaviors into chained reflexes revealed the general nature of the processes underlying the overall organization of behavior. I suspect that some such view underlies the skepticism of modern motivational "agnostics." This view maintains that organisms do not consist of just any set of reflexes. Rather, the reflexes are such that the stimulus consequences of one reflex are just those that are required to trigger an *appropriate* next reflex. This complementarity in the set of reflexes is assumed to be largely the product of evolution, in lower organisms, and learning, in higher organisms. Analytic decompositions of complex behavior sequences into a chain of reflexes (or stimulus-response events) are given in detail in Sherrington's (1906) famous analysis of locomotion and in a number of treatises on learning (e.g., Hull, 1943; Skinner, 1938).

The observations of Weiss (1938) mentioned above reveal the degree to which such analyses are incomplete. Weiss found that a number of different temporal sequences can occur if one studies locomotion under varying circumstances. Sequence 1 below indicates the approximate temporal pattern of muscular activation in the six major muscles of the salamander's forelimb when the salamander is walking forward (Weiss, 1938, p. 35). Sequence 2 indicates the pattern of muscular activation when the salamander is retreating (Weiss, 1938, p. 49). The groups of muscles that are active at approximately the same time are enclosed in parentheses. The muscles involved are the elevator (El), flexor (Fl), abductor (Ab), depressor (De), extensor (Ex), and the adductor (Ad).

|  | Stepping the foot forward | Foot planted, body advancing | Stepping the foot forward |
|---|---|---|---|
| (1) | &#124; (El, Fl, Ab)* | (De, Ex, Ad) | &#124; (El, Fl, Ab) ... |

|  | Stepping the<br>foot backward | Foot planted,<br>body retreating | Stepping the<br>foot backward |
|---|---|---|---|
| (2) | \| (El, Fl, Ad) | (De, Ex, Ab)* \| | (El, Fl, Ad) ... |

In sequences 1 and 2 above, the asterisks mark the point in each sequence at which the leg is extended diagonally forward and planted on the ground. In sequence 1 the muscle activity that immediately follows this point is De, Ex, Ad, whereas in sequence 2 the immediately following activity is El, Fl, Ad. Note, also, that in sequence 1 the abductor is active at the same time as the elevator and flexor, while the adductor is active at the same time as the depressor and extensor. In sequence 2, the reverse is true.

These simple observations of different temporal patterns in the same musculature forces the chained reflex analysis to posit two different *sets* of reflexes, one set active when the animal advances, another set active when the animal retreats. This in turn requires one to posit a higher influence that inhibits one set of reflexes and potentiates the other, so that during any given period only one set of reflexes has control of the musculature.

Actually, tendon-crossing and limb-reversal experiments showed that the same fixed patterns of muscular activity appeared even when one radically altered the mechanical consequences of those patterns. This led Weiss (1938) to reject the chained-reflex analysis in favor of a central programming scheme of some kind. Lashley's classic paper "The Problem of Serial Order in Behavior" (1951) advanced a number of further reasons for believing that many muscular sequences are governed by central programming mechanisms.

Weiss mentioned in passing the kind of observation that led von Holst to develop an alternative model of what the patterning mechanism in locomotion might be. Weiss (1938, p. 36) noted that although the front and hind legs of the salamander generally step in a fixed temporal sequence, instances in which the legs step out of sequence are by no means uncommon. Von Holst studied these instances in detail. His attention was first drawn to them by his studies on the coordination of the movement of the swimming fins in decerebrate fish. He subsequently studied this class of phenomena in a variety of species, from millipeds to humans. Sequence 3 below is an excerpt from an analysis of the hindleg-foreleg coordination in a freely walking sheep dog (von Holst, 1939, fig. 6). The sequence indicates the order in which the movements of the right foreleg and right hindleg were *initiated* (the movements themselves overlapped each other). The stepping forward movements of the fore- and hindlimb are symbolized F, and R, respectively. The movements of planting one or the other foot and using it as a pivot to propel the body forward are symbolized by Ḟ and Ṙ.

(3)  FṘFR  FṘFR  *FḞRFḞR*

Note that the temporal order in which the movements are initiated breaks down over the italicized interval. The front leg makes two complete steps during a period when the hindleg makes only one. In fact, the excerpt shown in 3 was taken from a sequence in which the foreleg made 25 steps while the hindleg was making only 20 steps.

A detailed analysis of such instances led von Holst (1939) to suggest that in locomotion the "functional units of behavior" (Sherrington's term for the reflex) were endogenously active central oscillators. In von Holst's model, the coordination between muscle groups is mediated by variable couplings between the central oscillators that control muscles or groups of muscles. Differing sequences are generated by varying the coupling between the oscillators, thereby varying the phase relations between their outputs. Thus, one and the same set of oscillators can mediate sequence 1 and sequence 2. The coupling between these oscillators is all that need be adjusted. In order to explain sequences such as 3, one need only assume that the two legs are being driven by oscillators with different fundamental frequencies and that the coupling between the oscillators is sufficiently weak to allow phase drift (or "relative coordination," as von Holst termed it).

In recent years, von Holst's ideas have been taken up by neurophysiologists working on the problem of motor coordination in invertebrates. Sequential problems of the kind highlighted by Weiss and von Holst are particularly prominent in insects, which have six legs that are stepped in a variety of organized sequences. Wilson (1966) gives an elegant and detailed coupled oscillator analysis of locomotion in the cockroach. Considerable recent electrophysiological data testify to the neurophysiological reality of the coupled-oscillator concept (e.g., Davis, Siegler, & Mpitsos, 1973).

*The organizing role of motivational processes.* The introduction of a new functional unit of behavior does not, however, remove the need to consider higher processes involved in the direction (overall organization) of behavior. If one persisted in a careful analysis of basic motor coordination, one would probably want to introduce still further functional units, for example, Fraenkel and Gunn's (1961) taxes. Even with a store of functional units richer than Sherrington left us with, we would still need to consider higher-level organizing processes. These higher-level processes are not themselves functional units. They serve instead to organize the multifarious functional units of basic coordination, determining which functionally integrated groups of such units shall be active and when.

The influence of these higher processes is seen in the sexual behavior of the praying mantis (see Roeder, 1967, chap. 10, for review). In the praying mantis, the final stages of the male's copulatory behavior sometimes involves a peculiar coordination of its leg movements, by which he rotates himself alongside of the female and mounts her. During the latter stages of the mounting maneuver, the male's abdomen begins a rhythmic arching that becomes more pronounced as the male's mount becomes more secure. An analysis of the sensorimotor coordinations involved in this behavior would almost certainly involve varying combinations of the three functional units I have already mentioned — reflexes, coupled oscillators, and taxes — as well as (I suspect) several functional units that have not yet been clearly characterized.

We know — for reasons that become clear shortly — that the machinery whereby the activities of the various functional units are coordinated so as to carry out the final stages of a successful mount and fertilization is contained in a lower part of the male mantis's nervous system, a part located in his abdomen. One might be tempted to assume, therefore, that this sensorimotor apparatus is all that there is to the story of the final stages of the male mantis's sexual escapades. One might assume that the machinery is ready and waiting and requires only the appropriate stimulus input to set it in motion. This is not the case, however. Particularly in some hybrid species, the mechanism underlying this complex behavioral sequence is held in check by an inhibitory influence from a higher part of the male's nervous system — the part located in his head. Thus, the male may get into an appropriate situation vis-à-vis the female, yet fail to go into the final stages or enter into them so weakly as to be ineffective. Luckily, the female seems to realize the source of the difficulty. She frequently cures the male's impotence by biting off his head. When thus freed from his inhibitions, the

male becomes a more vigorous copulator! And this is the only condition under which the peculiar body-rotating coordination appears.

Clearly, there is a process that regulates the appearance and
nonappearance of this final stage in the male's copulatory behavior.
This process acts upon, but does not form part of, the mechanism
that generates the coordinated sequence of muscular contractions
required for a functional mount and fertilization.

Wine and Krasne (1972) reached a similar conclusion after a
detailed analysis of escape reflexes in the crayfish. That is, they
concluded that the excitability of the various escape reflexes was
extensively and selectively modified by higher-level influences.
Dethier (1966; Dethier & Bodenstein, 1958) was led to a similar
conclusion by his study of the way in which hunger controls the
proboscis-extension reflex in the blowfly.

The necessity for higher-level controlling processes arises from
the fact that the same musculature is also utilized by other mechanisms of coordination. It is virtually a truism that all the muscles
are involved in any action of the organism. Thus, there must be
processes that maintain a coherent direction to behavior by keeping
the differing mechanisms of sensorimotor coordination from competing with each other for control of the musculature. *Processes that
potentiate and inhibit the lower-level mechanisms of sensorimotor
coordination in order to ensure an overall coherence and direction
to behavior are what I refer to as motivational processes.* The existence of such processes, regardless of what one chooses to call them,
seems beyond dispute.

In visualizing the relation between motivational processes and
the mechanism of sensorimotor coordination, I follow von Holst
and von St. Paul (1963), Tinbergen (1951), and Weiss (1938) in
imagining the mechanisms of coordination as being arranged in
the latticelike hierarchy shown in figure 1. At the bottom of the
hierarchy are the reflexes, endogenous oscillators, taxes, and other
functional units (building blocks) of behavior. The nodes at each
higher level of the hierarchy integrate certain combinations of the
coordinations represented by the next lower level. I assume that
for the most part this integration is achieved by sending appropriately timed inhibitory and disinhibitory signals to the lower
nodes. The motivational processes may then be thought of as con-
stituting the apexes of such a lattice hierarchy. When the motivational process represented by a particular apex is in the as-

MOTIVATIONAL STATES

BEHAVIOR SEQUENCES

SIMPLE ACTS}
*e.g.,* LOCOMOTION

FUNCTIONAL UNITS}
*e.g.,* REFLEXES, TAXES,
OSCILLATORS, ETC.

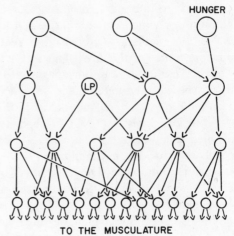

HUNGER

TO THE MUSCULATURE

FIG. 1. Schematic representation of the structure that organizes an animal's behavioral output. The nodes at each level of the hierarchy receive sensory inputs (not shown) that enable them to time the flow of potentiating (facilitating) and inhibitory signals to the subordinate nodes under their control.

cendancy, a signal descends through the lattice hierarchy, as shown in figure 2. This motivational signal potentiates the lower-level units that can be reached from the apex by following the arrows. The nodes in the middle levels temporally pattern this potentiation. All other lower units are inhibited by this same motivational signal. Thus, a motivational signal specifies a coordinated set of behavior patterns that will tend, either individually or in their entirety, to serve a single purpose (e.g., restoration of the animal's water balance or the fertilization of a female). At the same time, the motivational signal inhibits competing responses.

It should be noted that the motivational signals descending from various apexes play the role of Stellar's "central excitatory states," that is, they serve to determine which stimuli will be effective (Stellar, 1960, p. 1502). As Stellar points out in this same article, the motivational signals ("central excitatory states") are themselves functions of a variety of variables — internally monitored variables, such as water balance and nutritional balance, hormones, and certain types of external stimuli or stimulus complexes. Thus, stimulus

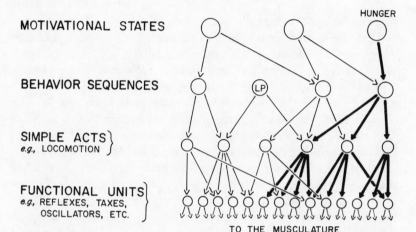

MOTIVATIONAL STATES

BEHAVIOR SEQUENCES

SIMPLE ACTS}
*e.g.,* LOCOMOTION

FUNCTIONAL UNITS}
*e.g.,* REFLEXES, TAXES,
OSCILLATORS, ETC.

HUNGER

LP

TO THE MUSCULATURE

FIG. 2. Schematic representation of the downward distribution of a motivational signal in the sensorimotor hierarchy.

inputs are received by the highest levels of the sensorimotor hierarchy as well as the lowest. At the lowest level of the hierarchy, external stimuli directly elicit (reflexes), or guide (taxes), the action of a functional unit. At higher levels of the hierarchy, stimuli serve to specify which subsets of functional units should be potentiated or inhibited at any given time. Thus, the role that a stimulus plays in determining the sequence of actions depends on which level of the hierarchy processes the stimulus.

The likelihood that the anatomical locus of the motivational apexes was in the upper brain stem (the diencephalon and immediately adjacent areas) was first suggested by the lesioning experiments reviewed by Stellar (1960). (See also Teitelbaum & Epstein, 1962.) This suggestion was greatly reinforced by the pioneering brain-stimulation work of Hess (1957), von Holst and von St. Paul (1963), and Miller and his coworkers (Miller, 1961), which showed that electrical stimulation delivered to sites in the diencephalon could elicit the integrated purposive behavior one would expect upon stimulating one of the motivational apexes shown in figure 1. These pioneering studies on the cat, the chicken, and the rat have been followed by the comparative work of Roberts (1970), which has shown that stimulation in the hypothalamus elicits a variety of complex species-specific behaviors. One is clearly dealing with areas that impose on an animal's behavior the integrated patterns characteristic of the animal's species.

That the motivational effects of diencephalic stimulation can be interpreted by the scheme I have sketched is shown by the work of Flynn (1972). Flynn has analyzed the cat's predatory behavior into its functional units. He has then studied the way in which these units are affected by naturally occurring motivation and by the motivation elicited through stimulation of the diencephalon. MacDonnell and Flynn (1966) provide a simple illustration of lower-level functional units being selectively potentiated or inhibited by a motivational state. In this case, the functional units were the reflexes that may be elicited by touching the cat's muzzle. When one touches the muzzle of a quiet but alert cat, the cat turns its head *away* from the touch. When one has induced predatory stalking behavior in a cat by introducing a mouse into its cage, a touch to the muzzle elicits a turn of the head *toward* the touch. A touch near the lips elicits biting. The role of these last two reflexes during the final stages of a predatory attack is obvious. The point to be emphasized is that they cannot be demonstrated in the unaroused cat. They are masked by an opposing reflex! A suitable motivational state, however, inhibits the opposing reflex and potentiates the reflexes that subserve attack. MacDonnell and Flynn demonstrated that the same effect is produced by electrical stimulation of the brain at a site that elicits predatory attack. The more intense the centrally delivered electrical stimulation, the wider the sensory field in which the peripheral touch stimulus will elicit the biting reflexes. Central stimulation does not *produce* the biting reflexes; rather, it potentiates them so that they are elicited by peripheral stimuli that would be ineffective in the absence of the central stimulation.

The extensive work on the sexual behavior of female rodents provides another illustration of the potentiating effect that motivational variables (female sex hormones) exert on a spinal reflex (the lordosis reflex — see Adler, 1973, for review). The work of Lisk (1962) and Stumpf (1968) further suggests that the effect of the female sex hormones on the lordosis reflex in female rats is mediated *in part* through a central effect of the hormones on receptor sites in the basal diencephalon. The work of Bard (1940) and Hart (1969) suggests that the potentiating effect of the diencephalon operates through disinhibition of the spinal reflex.

Thus, a variety of work leads to the view that sites in or near the diencephalon serve as a source of motivational signals. These signals may be imagined to descend through a lattice hierarchy, as indicated in figure 2, giving coherence to an animal's behavior by potentiating sensorimotor coordinations that serve a common purpose and inhibiting competing sensorimotor coordinations. Motivation in this view does not energize behavior. The energy expended in behavior is contained in the functional units (indeed, it is contained in the individual muscle fibers). Motivation is an internally patterned *signal* that potentiates (permits, facilitates) or inhibits (does not permit) the activity of lower-level sensorimotor units. A consequence of this view is that no firm line can be drawn between sensorimotor coordinating processes and motivating processes. The one grades into the other as one moves up the sensorimotor hierarchy. *The study of motivation is the study of the processes near the top of the action hierarchy.*


The Concept of Reinforcement

*Restructuring the hierarchy.* The description of motivation as central organizing process has so far failed to mention another central organizing process — a process that might better be termed a central reorganizing process. I am referring to the process whereby an animal's behavior is reorganized as a result of the outcomes it has produced. The work of Thorndike served to focus psychologists' attention on a fact about the behavior of higher organisms that had been intuited by a great many observers of behavior (starting at least as far back as Aristotle), namely, that behavior is to some extent governed by its consequences. Unfortunately, Thorndike's "law of effect," stated as I have just stated it, appears to require that time run backwards. Restating the law so as to assert that the consequences of earlier behavior govern the course of subsequent behavior straightens out the chain of cause and effect, allowing time to run in its usual direction. Such a restatement does not, however, make it clear how we should represent the process by which the consequences of earlier behavior govern subsequent behavior. I wish to suggest that we can think of this central reorganizing process as consisting of a quasi-permanent alteration in one or more of the paths (arrows) by which the motivational signal is distributed through the lattice hierarchy. I assume that certain kinds of experiences restructure the lattice hierarchy. As a result of the restructuring, one or more motivational signals will be distributed to parts of the hierarchy they did not previously reach. Since the distribution of a motivational signal within the sensorimotor hierarchy determines the pattern of an animal's behavior, an altered distribution will result in an altered pattern of behavior. Provided, of course, that the motivational signal in question is in the ascendancy and the environment is providing the stimulus inputs required by the newly favored (potentiated) sensorimotor patterns. If either of these last two provisos fails to hold, the new distribution network for the motivational signal will not be apparent from the animal's behavior.

This representation of what would normally be called reinforcement is shown in figure 3. The node labeled LP in figure 3 controls the coordination required to press a lever. In the naive animal this node is not potentiated by hunger. If, however, the animal finds that pressing the lever produces food, this experience produces the new pathway indicated by the dashed arrow in figure 3. Thenceforth this new pathway will convey the hunger signal to the LP node. Lever pressing will now appear whenever the animal is hungry and in the appropriate environment.

*New sensory-motor coordinations.* The view of reinforcement I am suggesting differs from more traditional views in that reinforcement has little to do with the creation of new sensorimotor coordinations ("habits," in Hullian terminology). Reinforcement simply leads to the appearance of preexisting coordinations in motivational contexts in which they did not previously appear. This does not mean that animals do not develop new sensorimotor coordinations. Most higher animals clearly do. However, I believe that this learning has little to do with traditional reinforcers — food, water, sexual gratification, etc. Anyone who brings a household pet into a new environment will observe that the animal makes it his business to learn his way around the new environment. This systematic exploration of the environment and manipulation of objects in it appears to have little to do with any immediate nutritional, sexual, or social need. Kavanau's (1969) experiments provide striking instances of "unmotivated" exploration and spatial learning in captive white-footed mice. Menzel (1973) provides similar "map-making" evidence for spatial learning in the chimpanzee.

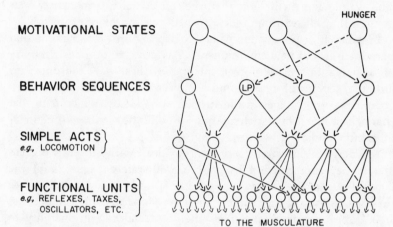

MOTIVATIONAL STATES

BEHAVIOR SEQUENCES

SIMPLE ACTS}
*e.g.,* LOCOMOTION

FUNCTIONAL UNITS}
*e.g,* REFLEXES, TAXES,
OSCILLATORS, ETC.

HUNGER

LP

TO THE MUSCULATURE

FIG. 3. Schematic representation of the restructuring effect of a reinforce-ment variable. Food reinforcement has restructured the hierarchy so as to bring the node that controls a lever-pressing sequence (the LP node) under the control of the hunger signal.

Deutsch's (1960) cognitive map model for maze learning in rats provides a model for the type of learning that enables an animal to generate learned but novel (i.e., never previously generated) locomotory sequences that bring it from one point in its environment to another via the shortest available route. Deutsch's model uses the teleotaxis as its functional response unit. The sensorimotor coordination between this response unit and the environment is mediated by a cognitive map. The learning of new sensorimotor sequences lies almost entirely in the construction of the cognitive map, which proceeds independently of motivation and reinforcement. Reinforcers such as food and water serve only to channel appropriate motivational signals into appropriate points on the cognitive map. The motivational signals in turn serve only to specify the to-be-approached points on the map. Thus, in terms of the scheme portray-ed in figures 1-3, some of the behavior-sequencing nodes in the lat-tice hierarchy may take the form of cognitive maps.

Deutsch (1960) spelled out his cognitive map model for maze learn-ing in considerable detail and built an electromechanical embodiment of it. The construction of a working embodiment of the model should dispel any lingering belief that cognitive map models are inherently more vague and mentalistic than the traditional S-R models, which assume that all learning depends on the action of reinforcers.

In summary, the creation of new sensorimotor coordinations that permit control of new environments is assumed to be a basic activity of higher animals. Reinforcement presses these new coordinations into the service of one or more motivational states. This is accomplished by changes in the structure of the lattice hierarchy that channels motivational potentiation or inhibition to the functional units of behavior.

My description of reinforcement has dealt with how this process should be represented. I have been deliberately vague about the class of events that act as reinforcers. Although we generally agree that certain events, for example, obtaining food, belong to this class, it is quite unclear what defines the class. Indeed, the inability to define the class of reinforcers has been an Achilles' heel of traditional learning theory.

As in the case of motivation, part of the difficulty that confronts an attempt to establish the neurophysiological basis of a reinforcement process has been the inability to specify or control the stimuli for the process. Olds and Milner's (1954) discovery that electrical stimulation of the brain can serve as a stimulus for the reinforcement process goes a long way toward overcoming this difficulty. *The fact that we now know how to activate motivation and reinforcement processes with an easily controllable stimulus makes it possible to adopt a psychophysical approach to the neurophysiology of these processes.*

Psychophysical Methods in Neurophysiology

Modern neurophysiology may be said to have begun with Galvani's discovery (at the end of the 18th century) that nerves and muscles can be excited by electrical currents, and with the subsequent development, during the 19th century, of techniques for precisely controlling the parameters of the electric stimulus.

In 1852, DuBois Reymond established that there was an endogenous electric potential in nerve and muscle and that this potential decreased momentarily when "excitation" passed down a nerve or along a muscle. From that time forth it was widely assumed that the momentary change in electric potential (i.e., the whole nerve action potential) was an intrinsic part of the "conducting process" in nerve and muscle. However, as late as 1936 some of the leading workers in the field (e.g., Hill, 1936) regarded the "electric wave theory" as little more than a plausible hypothesis for which there was as yet no really compelling evidence. Meanwhile, a succession of German, French, and English researchers established, by what we would now term psychophysical techniques, an extensive qualitative and quantitative characterization of the process of neural (and muscular) excitation and conduction.

The psychophysical approach to the physiology of the excitation and conduction process was pioneered by Helmholtz (1850, 1852), who showed that it was possible to measure the conduction velocity of neural excitation. Shortly thereafter (1854), he explored the parameters of temporal summation in neural excitation. Helmholtz, who set the pattern for much of the work that followed, worked with a motor nerve and its attached muscle, using the magnitude of the twitch in the muscle as an index of excitation in the nerve. He then manipulated the temporal and spatial parameters of the electric stimulus to the nerve and studied the effect that these parametric manipulations had on his behavioral index of neural excitation — the muscle twitch.

By 1920, work on the Helmholtz nerve-muscle preparation had established that individual neurons and muscle fibers conducted excitation in an all-or-nothing fashion; that the excitatory effect of a constant current stimulus approached asymptote exponentially (suggesting to Lapicque, in 1907, that the nerve membrane might behave as a resistance and a capacitance in parallel); that the conducting tissue was absolutely refractory to further excitation for a brief period following the passage of a conducted excitation; that this period of absolute refractoriness was followed by a period of relative refractoriness, which in turn was followed (in some nerves) by a period of heightened excitability; that weak electric stimuli produced a nonconducted subthreshold excitation; that the temporal summation of the excitatory effects of successive stimulus pulses more than a millisecond or two apart occurred at the neuromuscular junction or in the contractile apparatus of the muscle fiber but not in the nerve being stimulated; and so on. In addition, they had accumulated a substantial body of data on parametric differences between tissues with differing functions, for example, nerve and muscle, and between tissues with similar functions in differing species, for example, motor nerve in vertebrates and invertebrates.

(For reviews, see Adrian, 1932; Bernstein, 1912; Lapicque, 1926; Lucas, 1917a; Hermann, 1879; Howell, 1905, chaps. 3, 4, & 5).

All of this knowledge about the qualitative and quantitative properties of neural excitation and conduction processes was obtained without observing the actual electrical impulse in an individual neuron. Direct observation of the conducted impulse in a single neuron was impossible before the development of the vacuum tube amplifier and the cathode ray tube during the 1920s. The psychophysical approach to the process of neural excitation and conduction yielded an accurate characterization of the process despite the fact that the index of excitation — the muscular contraction — was an indirect and complex reflection of neural excitation. The muscle twitch reflected the activity in a population of neurons, not the activity of an individual neuron. And a number of poorly understood processes with quite different properties — most notably junctional transmission at the nerve-muscle interface and the activation of the contractile apparatus of the muscle fibers — intervened between the neural excitation and the observed twitch of the innervated muscle.

For the purpose of the argument I wish to develop in this paper, it is more important to note that psychophysical work on the conduction process played an important role in establishing the likelihood that the electrical waves observed by DuBois Reymond were, in fact, the basis of the conducted disturbance in nerve. This point can be illustrated by two examples. Bernstein (1871, chap. 1) measured the conduction velocity of DuBois Reymond's electrical wave (i.e., the whole nerve action potential) to see whether it agreed with the velocity of the "excitation process" (Erregungsvorgang), as measured by Helmholtz's psychophysical procedure. Bernstein found the conduction velocities to be the same. He argued that the sameness of the conduction velocities strengthened the hypothesis that the wave of variation in electrical potential observed by DuBois Reymond was in fact the basis of the conducted excitation in the nerve. Later, Gotch and Burch (1899), in doing further work on the whole nerve action potential, thought they found instances in which two stimulus pulses in rapid succession produced two conducted disturbances but only one action potential. This finding led many workers to doubt that the electrical wave was the true basis of neural conduction. Later work, however, showed Gotch and Burch's recording system was simply too insensitive to reveal the attenuated action potential characteristic of nerves whose neurons are in a state of relative refractoriness. Thus, Gotch and Burch failed to see the small action potential produced by the second of the two stimulus pulses.

In essence, then, the psychophysical characterization of the process of neural excitation and conduction provided criteria against which one could evaluate the reductionist hypothesis that the electrical action potential (or any other hypothesized process) was the basis of neural conduction. It is this aspect of the psychophysical approach that makes it a valuable tool in the study of the neurophysiology of behavior. If one is interested in purely neurophysiological questions, modern advances in recording techniques provide more direct access to the phenomena one wants to study. If, however, one wants to study the neurophysiological events underlying a behavioral phenomenon, then one must have criteria for deciding whether the neurophysiological events one observes in direct recordings are in fact the basis of the behavioral phenomenon one is interested in. Psychophysical data provide such criteria.

I believe that the excitement of modern sensory-system electrophysiology derives in part from the interplay between the extensive psychophysical data characterizing the components of certain sensory systems, for example, the color vision system, and the electrophysiological data on the behavior of individual neurons within those systems (see DeValois, 1965). Part of the interest in lateral inhibition in the visual system surely derives from the fact that Mach inferred it in 1865 from psychophysical data (see Ratliff, 1965). My thesis is that the discovery of motivating and reinforcing processes that can be activated by electrical stimulation of the central nervous system opens up similar possibilities for the study of the neurophysiological basis of motivation (organizing) and reinforcement (reorganizing) processes. By adopting a psychophysical approach to the study of the behavioral phenomena elicited by brain stimulation we can construct a qualitative and quantitative characterization of the neural substrate, which will permit us to recognize this substrate and analyze it by more direct techniques.

Secondly, I believe that the psychophysical approach is a valuable tool in the *functional* analysis of brain stimulation effects. It can help decide whether two or more behavioral effects are mediated by the same or different substrates. And when the same effect is produced by stimulation at two different loci, the psychophysical approach can help determine the extent to which a common substrate is involved.

Finally, a knowledge of the parametric properties of the substrates for the various behavioral effects elicited by brain stimulation may enable us to adjust the parameters of our electrical stimulus so as to produce a relatively selective activation of one or another substrate. Thus, brain stimulation will become a more refined tool for the analysis of the functional relation between the various behaviorally significant processes elicited by the stimulation.

Brain-stimulation experiments designed to characterize the neural substrate(s) underlying the behavioral effects of the stimulation are relatively few and recent. Firm conclusions must wait for replication and extension of the findings so far reported. In the review that follows I focus on the logic of the experiments and their potential for answering important questions.

Motivation and Reinforcement in Self-Stimulation

The self-stimulation phenomenon is particularly appropriate for the application of the psychophysical approach in that the phenomenon involves two different stimulation-induced processes, one of which has the character of a motivational variable, the other of which has the character of a reinforcement (learning) variable.

A recent experiment by Gallistel, Stellar, and Bubis (1974) was designed to highlight the differing characters of these two variables. Rats ran an alley for a brain-stimulation reward. Just before each trial they received additional brain stimulation in a waiting box outside the runway. The experiment consisted of two series of conditions. In one series the amount of pretrial stimulation in the waiting box was held constant (at 10 trains; 1 train/sec.; 64 pulses/train; 100 pps; 0.1 msec. pulse duration), while the amount of stimulation received as a reward for running was varied. The rats ran for 20 trials to a reward of 10 trains, then for 20 trials to a reward of 1 train (other parameters the same), then to 1 train with only 8 pulses, then to no stimulation (i.e., an extinction condition), then again to 1 train (64 pulses), and finally back to 10 trains. In the other series, the amount of stimulation the rats received as a reward for running was held constant (at 10 trains) and the amount of pretrial stimulation in the waiting box was varied every 20 trials, through the same sequence used in the first series of conditions.

Our first finding was that, when the stimulation received as a reward for running is held constant, running speed is a function of the amount of stimulation received noncontingently just before each trial. When this pretrial stimulation is in turn held constant, running speed is also a function of the amount of stimulation received contingently, that is, as a reward for running. Thus (rewarding) brain stimulation affects behavior partly by virtue of its being contingent on the instrumental response, that is, by virtue of its being a reward. However, it also affects behavior, by virtue of its simple occurrence (whether contingently or noncontingently) just before the behavior is to be performed. (See Deutsch & Howarth, 1963, and Gallistel, 1973, for a review of other experiments making this same point.)

The findings so far leave open the question of whether one and the same process underlies both effects of the stimulation. Further findings, however, suggest that two different processes are involved. First, the two effects of the stimulation have different critical ranges. In general, we found that pretrial stimulation had no effect on running speed until the amount of stimulation was increased to more than one train, whereas the effect of response-contingent (reward) stimulation on running speed was already maximal at 1 train. Reducing the amount of response-contingent stimulation did not, in general, reduce running speed until the amount reached either 1 train with only 8 pulses or no stimulation at all. (See Gallistel, 1969b, for another demonstration of this difference in critical ranges.)

Second, the course of the change in performance following a change in the stimulation suggests that the processes underlying the two effects of stimulation have different functional properties. The trial-by-trial adjustments in running speed following behaviorally significant increases or decreases in the amount of either pretrial stimulation or response-contingent stimulation are plotted in figure 4. When we changed the amount of pretrial ("priming") stimulation, there was an immediate and very nearly complete change in running speed on the first trial (solid lines, fig. 4). In other words, the data did not suggest that the adjustment in running speed following a change in pretrial stimulation depended on learning to any appreciable extent. On the other hand, the change in running speed following a change in the response-contingent stimulation developed gradually

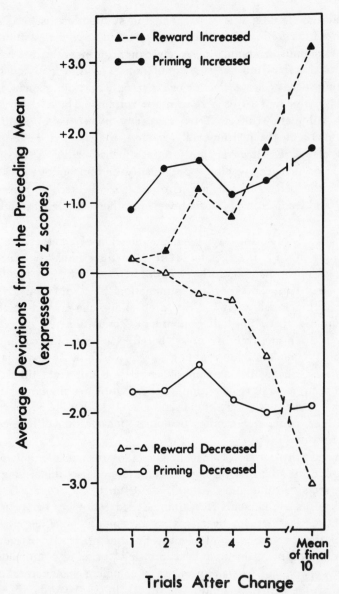

FIG. 4. The change in running speed as a function of the number of trials since a change in the amount of stimulation. The trial-by-trial deviations from the prechange means were normalized and then averaged. From Gallistel et al. (1974). Reproduced by permission of the American Psychological Association.

over several trials. It was not complete even after 5 trials (dashed lines, fig. 4). In other words, the adjustment in running speed following a change in response-contingent stimulation appeared to depend on the rats' learning over several trials that the level of reward had changed.

The immediate adjustment in running speed following a change in the pretrial stimulation suggests that, under the conditions of this experiment (10 minute interval between trials), the rats' running speed was influenced only by the pretrial stimulation received just before a given trial, and not by any memory (or record, or persisting effect) of the pretrial stimulation received on earlier trials. This in turn suggests that the effect of pretrial stimulation derives from a time-dependent process, which dissipates in a matter of minutes after it is activated by the stimulation. Thus, one should be able to vary the effect of pretrial stimulation on running speed simply by varying the time between the termination of pretrial stimulation and the beginning of the next trial. And, indeed, it has repeatedly been shown that increasing this interval, by the simple expedient of increasing the intertrial interval in a runway experiment, decreases running speed (e.g., Reid, Hunsicker, Kent, Lindsay, & Gallistel, 1973). The effect of a change in the intertrial interval is complete, or nearly complete, on the first trial (Gallistel, 1967, 1969a; Panksepp, Gandelman, & Trowill, 1968), suggesting again that the effect does not depend on learning.

The effect of time on the efficacy of pretrial stimulation has also been shown in an experiment by Deutsch, Adams, & Metzner (1964), in which rats were offered a choice between water and brain-stimulation reward. Deutsch et al. studied the rats' preference as a function of hours of water deprivation and recency of pretrial priming stimulation. The more thirsty the rats and the longer the time elapsed since pretrial priming, the more likely the rats were to choose water reward in preference to brain-stimulation reward. Conversely, the more recent the priming and the less the thirst, the more likely rats were to choose brain-stimulation reward in preference to water. Clearly, then, *rewarding brain stimulation activates a time-dependent process that transiently and selectively motivates the instrumental behaviors that produce more brain-stimulation reward.*

When brain stimulation is contingent on an instrumental response, however, another process comes into play. This process involves learning. The brain stimulation leaves behind a memory (or record, or persisting effect) of some kind. This memory reflects the amount of stimulation produced by a response. And this memory constitutes another variable that influences the rats' instrumental behavior — a variable that is event dependent rather than time dependent. Its effect on the instrumental behavior of the rat is altered only when the rat repeats the instrumental behavior and receives an amount of stimulation different from the amount previously received. Several such discrepant outcomes are necessary to effect a complete adjustment of the memory variable!

This brief review of certain aspects of the self-stimulation literature has advanced reasons for believing that (rewarding) brain stimulation activates two different processes, one having the character of a motivational variable, such as hunger, the other having the character of a reinforcement variable, such as food. This characterization of the two variables rests on the following analogy: The change in instrumental behavior produced by making an animal hungry appears immediately and can be reversed simply by satiating the animal, whereas the change in instrumental behavior produced by giving an animal food contingent upon an instrumental response develops over several trials and can be reversed only by re-creating the context in which the animal received the food and failing to provide further food. Similarly, the change in instrumental behavior produced by pretrial stimulation appears immediately and can be reversed simply by waiting a few minutes for the motivating aftereffect of the stimulation to dissipate, whereas the change in behavior produced by giving rewarding brain stimulation contingent on an instrumental response develops over several trials and can be reversed only by re-creating the context in which the stimulation was obtained and failing to provide renewed stimulation.

In terms of the conceptualization of motivation and reinforcement outlined in the first two sections, the motivating aftereffect of rewarding brain stimulation behaves as a transient motivational signal in the lattice hierarchy. The reinforcing effect behaves as a variable that restructures the lattice hierarchy, so that the transient motivating signal potentiates the instrumental behavior that has produced the stimulation.

For present purposes one can think of the "memory" left behind by response-contingent stimulation as nothing more than a restructuring of the lattice hierarchy. I suspect that the situation is actually more complex; that the memory produced by response-contingent stimulation includes a representation of the response that produced the stimulation, together with a representation of the magnitude of the resulting stimulation. However, at present we do not have any data upon which to base a theory of what this complex representation might look like; nor have we any immediate need to formulate such a theory. Within the limits of our present experimental paradigms, the reinforcing effect of brain stimulation is equivalent to a restructuring effect on the distribution network for a motivating signal. The other effect of rewarding brain stimulation — the transient aftereffect, commonly known as the priming effect — is equivalent to a transient motivating signal, which, because of the restructuring of the lattice hierarchy, selectively potentiates the stimulation-producing instrumental behavior. Thus the self-stimulation phenomenon affords us the opportunity to study a stimulation-elicited motivating process *and* a stimulation-elicited reinforcing process. It is not surprising that this phenomenon has played a central role in experimental attempts to construct a psychophysical characterization of the substrate(s) underlying the motivating and reinforcing effects that can be produced by electrical stimulation of the central nervous system.

PSYCHOPHYSICAL CHARACTERISTICS

The Recovery from Refractoriness

*Early work.* Helmholtz (1854) studied the summated muscle contraction produced by delivering two electric pulses to the motor nerve in rapid succession. He found that when the second pulse followed the first pulse at a very short interval (1.6 msec. or less) there was no summation; the resulting muscular contraction was no greater than that produced by the first pulse alone. Lengthening the interval between pulses slightly led to the abrupt reappearance of a summated muscular contraction. This was the first indication that nerve tissue was refractory to further excitation for a brief period following an initial excitation. A second stimulus falling during this refractory period fails to initiate a second volley of impulses. This effect was not studied very thoroughly until Gotch and Burch (1899) demonstrated the same effect, using the whole nerve action potential, rather than the summated muscle twitch, as their index of neural excitation.

A decade later Lucas and his student, Adrian, returned to the nerve-muscle preparation and began a systematic study of the effect (see Lucas, 1917a, chap. 6, for review). Lucas (1917b) was the first to use the refractory property of excitable tissue for the psychophysical separation and characterization of neural substrates with differing functions. Lucas was studying the motor innervation of the claw-closing muscle in the crayfish. In his initial work on this nerve-muscle preparation, he observed that the muscle exhibited two different types of contractions in response to motor nerve stimulation at different intensities and frequencies. At high intensities the muscle showed a twitchlike contraction that rapidly fatigued. At lower intensities and with repeated pulses the muscle showed a slow contraction that built up over several pulses. Lucas asked whether the two different behaviors of the muscle were produced by one and the same set of motor neurons or whether the nerve he was stimulating contained two distinct motor neuron populations, one for each behavior of the muscle.

One approach Lucas took to this question was to study the refractory period. His refractory-period experiments fell into two different categories. In both categories, he first stimulated the nerve until the neuromuscular junction (or some subsequent point in the linkage between nerve impulses and muscular contraction) was fatigued to the point that the volley of nerve impulses produced by a single shock to the nerve would not produce a contraction in the muscle. The volleys produced by two shocks in succession would produce a contraction — provided the interval between the pulses was neither too long nor too short. Thus, the occurrence of a contraction indicated that the second stimulus shock had initiated a second volley of impulses, which, in summating with the subthreshold effects of the first volley, was able to produce a contraction. The failure of a contraction to occur in response to two shocks indicated that the second shock had failed to initiate a second volley.

In his Category I refractory-period experiments Lucas measured refractory period(s) in the motor nerve by stimulating the nerve with two stimulus shocks of constant intensity, varying the interval between these two stimuli, and plotting the height of the muscular contraction as a function of the interval between the two stimuli.

In his Category II experiments he used an initial stimulus of con-

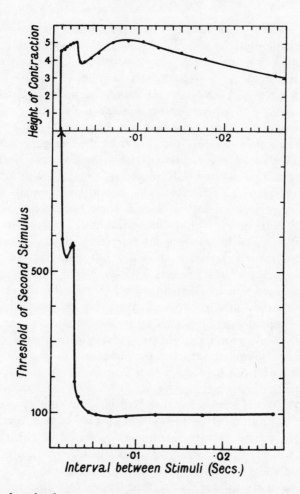

FIG. 5. Results of refractory-period experiments on the nerve innervating the claw-closing muscle of the crayfish. In the upper graph, the height of the muscular contraction is plotted as a function of the interval between the two stimulus pulses. In the lower graph, the threshold current intensity of the second pulse (i.e., the minimum intensity required to produce a contraction) is plotted as a function of the interval between the first and second pulse. Reproduced from Lucas (1917b).

stant intensity and varied both the delay and the intensity of the second stimulus. At each delay (i.e., at each interstimulus interval), he determined the current intensity required to produce a muscle contraction, that is, to initiate a second volley of impulses.

In some cases Lucas was able to perform both the Category I and the Category II experiment on one and the same preparation. His data from one such preparation are shown in figure 5. The upper part of figure 5 presents the data from the Category I experiment; the lower part presents the data from the Category II experiment.

Lucas noted that the Category I data suggest the presence of two different recovery processes. The second shock produced no contraction when it came less than 1 msec. (.001 sec.) after the first shock. This indicates that during the first 1 msec. after an initial excitation all of the neurons are refractory. Beyond 1 msec. a contraction abruptly appears at nearly full strength, indicating that at least some of the neurons have recovered from refractoriness. As the interval is lengthened beyond 3 msec. the magnitude of the contraction begins to drop off abruptly. However, this drop-off is interrupted by a rise back up to a second maximum. Lucas attributed this second rise to the recovery of a second innervation that was also contributing to the contraction.

The data from the Category II experiment (lower part of fig. 5) present the same picture. As the interval between the stimuli was shortened, the current intensity required by the second pulse in order to produce a contraction shows a rapid rise toward infinity at about 3 msec. However, at intensities above 500 this rise is interrupted by a second curve, of similar character, whose asymptote is slightly less than 1 msec.

Lucas correctly concluded from these data that there were at least two excitatory motor innervations of the closing muscle in the claw and that the innervation requiring a higher stimulus intensity also exhibited a shorter refractory period.

All of the work on refractory periods in the behavioral effects of brain stimulation utilizes one or the other of Lucas's experimental paradigms. The Category I paradigm plots variations in the behavioral output as a function of variations in the interval between the stimulus pulses. The Category II paradigm maintains a constant behavioral output by plotting the change in one stimulus parameter (e.g., the intensity of the pulses) required to compensate for a change in another parameter (e.g., the interval between pulses).

These two paradigms have arisen whenever there has been extensive psychophysical work, regardless of the problem area. Lucas's Category II belongs to what Brindley (1970, chap. 5) calls Class A observations, and Category I belongs to what Brindley calls Class B observations. Neither of these terminologies (Category I–II, Class A–B) helps the reader to remember what the distinction is. Since the distinction is fundamental (see Brindley, 1970), it seems worthwhile to devise a more transparent terminology. In what follows I will refer to experiments or data that fit Lucas's Category I paradigm as *output-vs.-input* paradigms. In an output-vs.-input paradigm, the output is plotted as a function of some experimentally varied parameter of the input (the stimulus). Thus, in a magnitude estimation experiment (on, say, loudness) the numerical loudness estimates that the subject outputs are plotted as a function of the stimulus intensity. Similarly, the latter part of this review refers frequently to experiments that plot running speed (output) as a function of varied parameters of the electrical stimulus (current intensity, pulse duration, number of pulses, etc.)

By contrast, Category II paradigms will be referred to as *equivalent-stimuli* paradigms. In an equivalent-stimuli paradigm one determines which combinations of values for the various parameters of the stimulus are equivalent from the standpoint of the output. Put another way, one determines equivalence classes for the stimulus vectors. (A stimulus vector is a set of numerical values — one value for each relevant dimension, i.e., parameter, of the stimulus.) In Lucas's Category II experiment the stimulus vector (100, .012) was equivalent to the vector (530, .002). The first number in each of these vectors refers to the current strength of the second pulse; the second number refers to the interval between pulses. These stimulus vectors were equivalent in that each of them was just sufficient to produce a contraction. The lower graph in figure 5 is a plot of *all* the current-vs.-interpulse-interval vectors that just sufficed to produce a contraction. In audition, equal-loudness curves belong to the equivalent-stimuli paradigm.[3] They specify the combinations of frequency and sound pressure that yield equivalent judgments of loudness. Not uncommonly, equivalent-stimuli functions are de-

3. However, Brindley (1970) would not regard them as belonging to his Class A, because, although the pitch-vs.-sound-pressure vectors specified by an equal loudness curve are equivalent with respect to one output (loudness judgments), they are not equivalent with respect to other outputs (e.g., pitch judgments).

rived from a family of output-vs.-input functions (see Strength–Duration and Temporal Summation below; also, Brindley, 1970). Generally speaking, an equivalent-stimuli function permits stronger conclusions about underlying variables than does an output-vs.-input function (see Methodological Critique below, and Brindley, 1970).

Before reviewing studies on the refractory periods for centrally elicited behaviors, I wish to deal with a question which frequently arises with psychophysical studies of the recovery from refractoriness in electrically stimulated neural systems. Lucas interpreted his data in terms of the recovery from refractoriness in the nerve tissue being directly stimulated. What reasons are there for believing that his effects could not equally as well reflect the time course of recovery processes "downstream," that is, processes at the neuromuscular junction or in the muscle fiber. The basic answer is that at the junctions between electrically conducting tissues, that is, at synapses or neuromuscular junctions, there is usually a considerable degree of temporal averaging, or "smoothing," of the input. Thus, the postjunctional processes generally reflect the average number of prejunctional pulses ("spikes") over some appreciable time frame (5 msec.–several seconds). Except in some special cases (e.g., the auditory system), the postjunctional spike train does not reflect fine temporal structure in the succession of input spikes.

Because of the temporal smoothing at the junctions, the results of refractory-period experiments are usually surprisingly independent of the properties of the subsequent links in the chain. Bazett (1908) found, for example, that the nerve-muscle preparation (sciatic-grastrocnemius of the frog) yields the refractory period of the nerve even when the refractory period of the muscle used as the index of nerve excitation is twice as long as the refractory period of the nerve. Sherrington and Sowton (1915) used the reflex contraction of the muscles in the leg of a spinal cat as a behavioral index in determining the refractory period of sensory nerves. Despite the fact that a set of synaptic connections of unknown complexity intervened between the stimulated nerve and the reflex index of

Brindley's criterion for admission to Class A is that the vectors be equivalent with regard to all possible outputs. Although metameric color-matching data would appear to satisfy this criterion, it is not clear how, in principle, one could ever be certain that the criterion was satisfied. Nor is it clear why this is an appropriate criterion in a reductionist analysis of systems that process inputs in a variety of ways.

sensory nerve excitation, Sherrington and Sowton obtained refractory-period values for sensory nerve that were similar to the values for motor nerve. Adrian and Olmstead (1922) replicated this finding and went on to show that *narcotizing the spinal cord had no effect on the value obtained for the refractory period of the (unnarcotized) sensory nerve up to the point where the narcotic blocked reflex conduction altogether!* Clearly, profound changes in the characteristics of the intervening links had little effect on the psychophysically determined refractory period.

*Self-stimulation.* Deutsch (1964) was the first to study the recovery from refractoriness in the substrate for a behavioral phenomenon (self-stimulation) produced by electrical stimulation of the central nervous system. He conducted two experiments, one designed to measure the recovery from refractoriness in the substrate for the reinforcing effect, the other designed to measure the recovery from refractoriness in the substrate for the motivating aftereffect. The reward-effect experiment used an equivalent-stimuli paradigm. That is, Deutsch used the threshold for the reward effect as his constant output level and plotted the threshold current intensity for the pulse pairs against the interval between the pulses. Because a single pair of pulses was not sufficient to produce a threshold effect, Deutsch used trains consisting of several pairs of pulses, with the spacing between pairs being much greater than the spacing within pairs.

Deutsch's priming-effect experiment used the output-vs.-input paradigm. Under conditions where the priming effect was assumed to be controlling response rate, he plotted the response rate as a function of the intrapair interval. Pulse intensity was held constant.

The recovery-from-refractoriness curves for the two effects of rewarding brain stimulation are shown in figure 6. From the fact that the recovery curve for the reward effect rises sooner (at about 0.5–0.6 msec.) than the recovery curve for the priming effect (0.8–1.1 msec.), Deutsch concluded that the two effects derived from the stimulation of two different neural substrates having different characteristic refractory periods.

We have replicated Deutsch's experiment (Gallistel, Rolls, & Green, 1969), using a different technique for separating the reinforcing effect from the priming effect. We used the runway and waiting box paradigm described in the Introduction. In order to study the recovery from refractoriness in the substrate for the priming effect, we held the reward received for running the alley constant

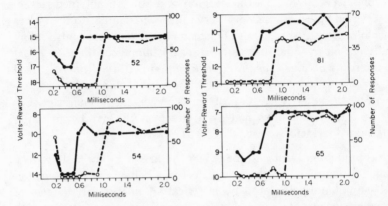

FIG. 6. The recovery from refractoriness in the reward effect (solid lines, right-hand ordinates) and the priming effect (dashed lines, left-hand ordinates). The rise in some curves at very short intervals (< .3 msec.) was probably due to latent addition in a fringe population of neurons subliminally excited by the first pulse (see Gallistel, 1973, p. 220). Redrawn from Deutsch (1964). Used by permission of the American Psychological Association.

and varied the parameters of the pretrial priming stimulation. In order to study the recovery from refractoriness in the substrate for the reinforcing effect, we held the pretrial stimulation constant and varied the parameters of the reward received for running. In both experiments we used an output-vs.-input paradigm, that is, we kept pulse intensity fixed and plotted running speed as a function of the intrapair interval. Like Deutsch, we used trains consisting of several pairs, because a single pair of pulses would not produce a threshold effect.

Our data are shown in figure 7. They agree with Deutsch's findings. The recovery from refractoriness in the substrate for the reinforcing effect occurred in the neighborhood of 0.5–0.6 msec.; the recovery from refractoriness in the substrate for the priming effect occurred in the neighborhood of 0.9–1.1 msec.

Subsequently, Smith and Coons (1970) and Ungerleider and Coons (1970) have published recovery from refractoriness curves for self-stimulation. The experiments of Coons and his collaborators were not aimed primarily at the determination of refractoriness. They did not separate the reinforcing effect from the priming effect,

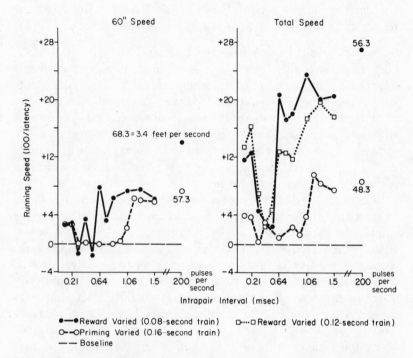

FIG. 7 The recovery from refractoriness in the reward effect (solid lines and filled circles, or dotted line with squares) and in the priming effect (dashed line with open circles). The running speeds are deviations from the baseline speed (O on the ordinate), which was the speed when the second pulse in each pair was omitted altogether. The left-hand graph is for true *running* speed, that is, the reciprocal of the running latency. The right-hand graph is for the speed of overall performance, that is, the reciprocal of the running latency plus the start latency. The reward curve was determined twice, with two different train durations. During the first determination (dotted line with squares on right-hand graph) only the overall latency was recorded. Each point on the graphs is the mean of 40 observations. This graph is from Gallistel (1973). The data were originally published in Gallistel et al. (1969). Reproduced by permission of Academic Press.

nor did they measure either period with precision. Rolls (1971a) replicated Deutsch's determination for the priming effect.

*Stimulation-elicited consummatory behavior.* Halboth and Coons (1973) demonstrated a refractory period in stimulation-elicited eating, using both an output-vs.-input paradigm and an equivalent-stimuli paradigm. They did not, however, test a sufficient number of intrapair intervals to define the recovery from refractoriness with any precision. Their data show that the recovery occurs somewhere between 0.5 and 1.2 msec. Rolls (1973), using an output-vs.-input paradigm, found that the recovery from refractoriness occurred in the interval .5–.7 msec.

Rolls (1973) and Hu (1973) both used output-vs.-input paradigms to measure the recovery from refractoriness in the substrate for stimulation-elicited drinking. Unfortunately, they obtained somewhat different recovery curves. Hu's data show an abrupt and nearly complete recovery occurring at about .9 msec., whereas Rolls's data show a more gradual recovery which begins at around .5-.7 msec. In my laboratory, Beagley (1973) obtained data similar to those of Rolls. The first statistically significant evidence of recovery from refractoriness occurred at .7 msec. (1 rat) or .8 msec. (2 rats). The slight conflict in these findings may derive from the fact that the output-vs.-input paradigm was used in all three studies (see Methodological Critique below). Or the "conflict" may simply reflect fine differences between the rats in the different studies. In all the studies, the number of rats was small (3–4).

Rolls and Kelly (1972) and Beagley (1973) both used output-vs.-input paradigms to determine the recovery from refractoriness in the substrate for stimulation-elicited locomotion. Again the findings are slightly discrepant. Rolls and Kelly found the first detectable recovery from refractoriness in the range .73–1.1 msec., whereas Beagley found values of .6 msec. and .9msec.

*Other motivational aftereffects of medial forebrain bundle stimulation.* Beagley's (1973) work was prompted by his discovery that the same medial forebrain bundle (MFB) stimulation that produces eating, drinking, or locomotion and sustains self-stimulation behavior also produces a grooming aftereffect. Thus, for example, when stimulation that elicits drinking is turned off, the drinking ceases within a few seconds, but shortly thereafter the rat begins a bout of intense grooming, lasting from 20 seconds to several minutes.

In some rats, for certain parameters of stimulation, grooming appears during rather than after the brain stimulation.

Beagley (1973) used an output-vs.-input paradigm to measure the recovery from refractoriness in the substrate controlling the grooming effect. In all six of the rats for which determinations were made, the first statistically significant recovery from refractoriness occurred at 1.1 msec. These experiments were carried out with the same rats that were used in determining the recovery from refractoriness in eating, drinking, or locomotion effects. Recall that those determinations all showed significant recovery from refractoriness at intrapair intervals at least as short as .8 msec. Beagley concluded that grooming derived from the excitation of a substrate different from that underlying the other behaviors elicited by stimulation. Since the eating, drinking, and locomotion typically appear during stimulation whereas the grooming typically appears after stimulation, Beagley suggested that excitation rises and decays rapidly in one substrate and slowly in the other. He further suggested that the substrates mutually inhibit each other's output. Thus, the rapidly rising output prevails during stimulation and the slowly decaying output prevails after stimulation. The fact that the recovery from refractoriness in the substrate for the grooming aftereffect and in the substrate for the priming aftereffect in self-stimulation are nearly coincident suggests that the effects may have a common substrate (or related substrates).

Rose (1974) has reported refractory-period determinations on what may be another behavioral manifestation of activity in this substrate (or family of substrates). His work was prompted by Reynolds's (1969, 1971) discovery that focal brain stimulation could produce a powerful analgesic effect, an effect so powerful that one could perform abdominal surgery on rats rendered indifferent to pain by the brain stimulation. Rose — like Mayer, Wolfe, Akil, Carder, and Liebeskind (1971) — noted that many — though not all — of the sites producing this effect would also produce self-stimulation and, also, that the analgesic effect of stimulation outlasted the stimulation by several seconds to several minutes. These observations led Rose to ask whether the rewarding effect of brain stimulation derived from its analgesic effect, as had been suggested by Ball (1967). Thus, Rose's determinations of the recovery from the refractoriness of the substrate were aimed primarily at deciding whether this recovery began before or after 0.7 msec. (This intrapair interval was critical for the decision because the data of Deutsch [1964] and Gallistel et al. [1969] indicated that recovery in the reward substrate always began at shorter intervals, whereas recovery in the priming substrate always began at longer intervals.) Using an output-vs.-input paradigm, Rose found that the recovery from refractoriness in the substrate for the analgesic effect began *after* 0.7 msec. Rose did not test enough intrapair intervals in most of his rats to fully delineate the recovery from refractoriness, but it appeared to occur at about 1.0 msec. This finding suggested that the substrate for analgesia was the same as, or related to, the substrate for the priming effect rather than the substrate for the rewarding effect.

In his dissertation, Rose (1972) also showed that noncontingent stimulation delivered to a rat before placing it in the experimental apparatus suppressed the rat's running speed when it was running to escape foot shock (the analgesic effect) and heightened the rat's running speed when it was running to obtain more rewarding brain stimulation (the priming effect). Thus, the effect of priming on the running response depended on the environment in which the response was performed and the goal or end to which the response was directed.

Rose interpreted his findings in terms of the conceptualization of motivation that I outlined in the Introduction. He argued that the analgesic effect of brain stimulation derives from the excitation of a strong appetitive motivational state of some kind. This state potentiates certain appetitive behaviors, for example, instrumental responses directed toward obtaining brain stimulation reward, and inhibits competing behaviors, for example, aversive responses to noxious stimuli.

*Summary.* Recent psychophysical studies on the recovery from refractoriness in the substrates underlying the behavioral effects of electrical stimulation of the MFB suggest the presence of at least two, and possibly three, psychophysically and functionally distinct substrates or types of substrates. The one that exhibits the earliest recovery from refractoriness mediates the reinforcing effect of MFB stimulation. The one that exhibits the longest refractory period mediates the priming effect in self-stimulation and, possibly, other slowly decaying aftereffects of the stimulation, viz., the grooming aftereffect and the inhibition of responses to noxious stimuli.[4]

All three of the aftereffects may be manifestations of a decaying appetitive motivational state. This appetitive motivational state potentiates behavior directed toward brain-stimulation reward while inhibiting behavior directed toward a food reward (Cox, Kakolewski & Valenstein 1969; Stellar & Gallistel, 1975, in press) as well as inhibiting responses to noxious stimuli. The grooming aftereffect of MFB stimulation may be a displacement behavior, brought on by the frustration of this intense appetitive motivational state.

There also appears to be a substrate that recovers from refractoriness at intermediate intrapair intervals and that mediates stimulation-elicited consummatory behavior such as eating, drinking, and locomotion.

Of course, subsequent research on other psychophysical properties of these three tentatively identified substrates may indicate that the substrates should be further subdivided. Even the tentative identification of three substrates strains the inherently limited resolving power of refractory-period analysis (see below).

*Methodological critique.* When determination of the recovery-from-refractoriness curves for differing behavioral effects of stimulation are performed on different rats one must be cautious in concluding that different refractory-period values indicate different substrates. All of the studies so far reported on any given effect show individual differences on the order of $\pm 0.1$ to $\pm 0.2$ msec. These individual differences, together with the limited range of possible refractory periods (.4–2.5 msec., judging by studies of refractory periods in peripheral nerve — Grundfest, 1940), place inherent limits on the resolving power of this technique.

Second, the output-vs.-input paradigm, used in nearly all of the studies to date, has a possible source of artifactual differences that could be avoided by the use of an equivalent-stimuli paradigm. This artifact arises from the possibility that two behavioral effects deriving from the stimulation of one and the same substrate may be differentially sensitive to initial increases in the effect of the second pulse.[5]

4. For an alternative interpretation of the refractory-period experiments in self-stimulation, see Szabo (1973a, b).

5. For an extensive and cogent discussion of this problem, see Yeomans (1974).

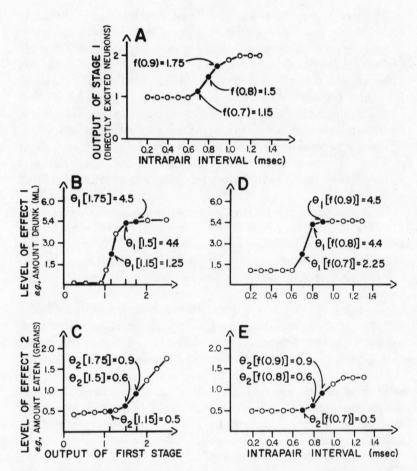

FIG. 8. Schematic illustration of possible performance-function artifacts in the output-vs.-input paradigm.

This possible artifact in the output-vs.-input paradigm is illustrated in figure 8. Figure 8a plots the amount of excitation in the directly stimulated (Stage 1) neurons, as a function of the interval between two stimulus pulses. The output produced by the first pulse alone is taken as unity. At short intrapair intervals the second pulse finds the entire substrate refractory, hence it has no effect on the output. At longer intervals, the second pulse finds some of the substrate no longer refractory, hence the second pulse produces some increment in the output. When the substrate is entirely recovered from refractoriness, two pulses produce twice the output of one pulse alone. In figure 8, the recovery-from-refractoriness function (Graph A) is called the $f(\ )$ function.

We do not, however, experimentally observe the output of Stage 1; we observe some behavioral consequence of this output. The only thing we usually feel safe in assuming about the relation (i.e. function) between the output of Stage 1 and the level of behavior we actually observe is that this function is a monotonic one. The details of such monotonic functions between the output of Stage 1 and its behavioral consequences are likely to vary from behavior to behavior. These functions, which I term the performance functions, are also likely to depend a good deal on the details of the behavioral testing procedure, for example, whether the dependent variable is latency to eat or amount eaten, etc.

In figure 8, I have *assumed* that the performance function (symbolized $\theta_1$) for one behavioral effect (drinking) has the form shown in Graph B, while the performance function ($\theta_2$) for another behavioral effect (eating) has the form shown in Graph C. The resulting, behaviorally determined, recovery-from-refractoriness curve for drinking (Graph D) shows most of its rise over the interval from 0.6 to 0.8 msec., whereas that for eating (Graph E) hardly rises over this same interval. The eating curve shows most of its rise over the interval from 0.8 to 1.1 msec. Thus, although the two effects were derived (by assumption) from the same substrate, the use of output-vs.-input paradigms would lead to the erroneous conclusion that there were two substrates with differing refractory periods.

This possible artifact would be eliminated by using equivalent-stimuli paradigms. In an equivalent-stimuli paradigm the output (level of behavioral effect) is held constant by determing how much of an adjustment in the level of one stimulus parameter, for example, the current intensity, is required to compensate for a change in another parameter, for example, the interval between the first and second pulse (the intrapair interval). In figure 8, reducing the intrapair interval from 0.8 to 0.6 msec. produces only a small reduction in the amount eaten (from .6 to .5 grams) but greatly reduces the amount drunk (from 4.4 to 2.25 ml.). Nonetheless, the increase in the current intensity necessary to return eating to the .6-gram level would be the same as the increase in current intensity necessary to return drinking to the 4.4-ml. level. Thus, equivalent-stimuli paradigms will in most cases eliminate performance-function arti-facts from the psychophysical data. This is particularly important when one uses psychophysical data to distinguish substrates for different behavioral effects.

## The Strength-Duration Curve

*Early work.* Early work on the effect of varying either the duration or the intensity of the electrical pulses used to stimulate the Helm-holtz nerve-muscle preparation commonly employed output-vs.-input paradigms. Since the quantitative aspects of these data depended greatly on the performance function (the state of the muscle), the data were of limited use (see Lapicque, 1926, p. 48, and, in general, for an excellent, albeit prejudiced, review of early work on the strength-duration curve). By the time of Hoorweg's (1892) classical work, however, investigators had switched to the use of the equivalent-stimuli paradigm. They determined the trade-off between current intensity and pulse duration in pulses that produced a fixed level of muscular contraction (usually, a just noticeable contraction). The use of this paradigm gave rise to the strength-duration curve — the curve that plots the relation between pulse strength (current intensity) and pulse duration in pulses of equal efficacy.

Lucas (1917b) used this curve, as well as the recovery-from-re-fractoriness curve, as evidence for the existence of two distinct neural substrates, one for the twitchlike closure of the crab's claw and one for the slow contraction. Lucas found that he could elicit a twitch with a single strong shock, and also that he could elicit a slow contraction, without any twitch, if he used three or four weak shocks, spaced about ½ second apart. When he determined the strength-duration curve for twitch-eliciting shocks, he obtained the upper curve in figure 9. When he determined the strength-duration function for the weak, widely spaced pulses that elicited only the summated slow contraction, he obtained the lower curve in figure 9. He adduced the evident difference between these two strength-duration curves as further proof that there were two distinct neural substrates for the two effects.

Lucas (1906; 1906-1907a, 1906-1907b, 1907-1908) had pioneered the use of the strength-duration curve to identify different "excitable substances," that is, different neural substrates. In working on

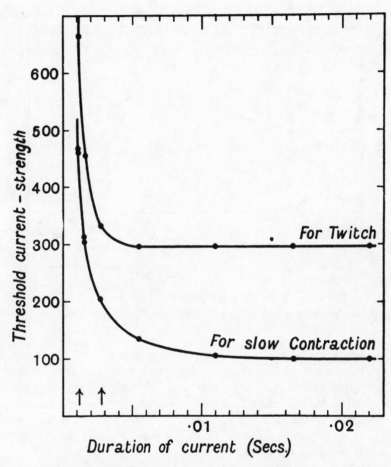

FIG. 9. The strength-duration curves for the twitch contraction and the slow contraction produced by stimulating the motor nerve to the claw-closing (adductor) muscle of the crayfish. Reproduced from Lucas (1917b).

the strength-duration curve of the toad sartorius, Lucas (1906-1907b) obtained the data shown in figure 10. He argued that the discontinuity in slope of the strength-duration curve of figure 10 indicated the presence of two excitatory substrates, one having the strength-duration curve AB (and its dashed extension), the other having the strength-duration curve BC (and its dashed extension). He adduced evidence that the curve AB derived from the direct electrical excitation of the muscle fibers; whereas the curve BC reflected

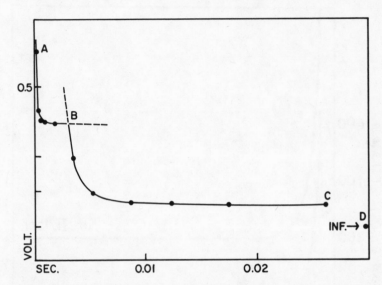

FIG 10. The strength-duration curve for the innervated region of the toad sartorius. Reproduced from Lucas (1906-1907a).

the excitation of motor nerves, which in turn excited the muscle. In other words, Lucas suggested that nerve fibers and muscle fibers had different strength-duration curves. When electrical stimuli were applied to the innervated regions of muscle, there would be a discontinuity in the slope of the strength-duration curve at the point where the strength-duration curve for nerve crossed the strength-duration curve for muscle.

After considerable controversy, Lucas's findings were confirmed by Rushton (1931), who showed that they applied to a wide range of nerve-muscle preparations. Adrian (1916) applied Lucas's approach to human patients recovering the voluntary use of muscle following nerve injury. He found that the strength-duration curve for the recovering muscle began to exhibit a Lucas-type discontinuity at about the same time as the patient regained voluntary control of the muscle. Adrian argued that the return of voluntary control of the muscle must, therefore, reflect reinnervation of the muscle rather than a recovery process in the muscle itself.

*Self-stimulation.* We have recently determined several strength-duration curves in self-stimulating rats, with electrodes in the MFB

(Barry, Walters, & Gallistel, 1974). In order to separate the rein-forcing effect from the priming effect, we employed the runway and waiting box paradigm. To determine the strength-duration function for the reinforcing effect, we held the parameters of pretrial priming stimulation constant and we varied the duration and current intensity of the pulses in the reward the rat received for pressing the lever at the goal end of the runway. To determine the strength-duration relation for the priming effect, we reversed this procedure: We varied the parameters of the pretrial priming stimulation while holding the lever-produced stimulation constant.

Our strength-duration curves were derived from families of out-put-vs.-input curves. Each member of the family was generated by plotting mean running speed as a function of current intensity at a fixed pulse duration. The current values used to generate each curve were sufficient to produce mean running speeds that ranged from minimal to maximal. Different curves (different members of the family) were generated by using different pulse durations. Figure 11a shows one such family of curves for the priming effect. Each curve in figure 11a is a plot of mean running speed as a function of the current intensity in the pulses, with pulse duration fixed at the value indicated near the top of the curve.

We have used this procedure to determine the strength-duration function for the reinforcing effect in 4 rats, and for the priming effect in one of these rats (Barry et al., 1974). The 5 families of output-vs.-input curves so far obtained are highly similar. All of the curves have approximately the same steep slope. They rise from the minimum mean running speed to the maximum mean running speed over an increment in current intensity of about 0.1 log unit (1 db). The 95% confidence intervals in figure 11a (vertical bars) are also typical.

A strength-duration function is derived from these curves by choos-ing an intermediate running speed (say, 30) and drawing a horizontal line across the curves at this level (the dashed line in fig. 11a). Each intersection between this line and one of the curves specifies a point on the strength-duration function. The abscissa of the intersection gives the current intensity. The pulse duration for the intersected curve gives the duration. The strength-duration curve derived from the data in figure 11a is plotted in figure 11b in log-log coordinates. (The advantages of log-log coordinates are discussed by Rushton, 1931.)

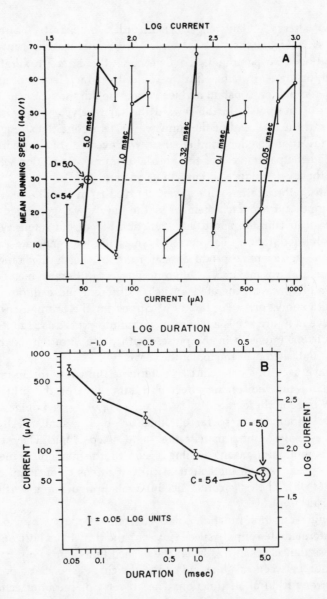

FIG 11. A: A family of running-speed-vs.-current-intensity curves at various pulse durations (indicated along each curve). The vertical bars indicate the 95% confidence intervals about the means. B: The strength-duration curve derived from the output-vs.-input curves in A, using an output level of 30. An intersection in A and its corresponding point on B are circled.

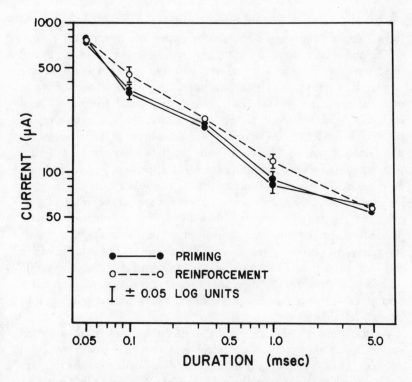

FIG 12. Strength-duration curves for the priming effect (both replications shown) and the reinforcing effect (replication not shown) in one rat. Data originally published in Barry et al. (1974).

The strength-duration curve in figure 11b specifies the combinations of pulse duration and current intensity that produce a mean running speed approximately equal to 30. The experimental error associated with the estimates of current intensity is on the order of $\pm$ .05 log units, that is, approximately 10%. This estimate of experimental error follows from two considerations: (a) The data points on the output-vs.-input curves in figure 11a occur at 0.1 log unit intervals. (b) In general, the running-speed criterion of 30 lies outside the 95% confidence intervals associated with the data points above and below the point where the criterion intersects a curve. In other words, a current intensity approximately 0.05 log units below the abscissa of the intersection produces a running speed significantly less than 30, and a current intensity 0.05 log units beyond the intersection produces a running speed significantly greater than 30. Hence, the current intensity that produces a running speed of 30 lies within the 0.1 log unit interval between the upper and lower data points.

The indirect method of obtaining trade-off (equivalent-stimuli) functions from families of curves has two advantages: In cases where the experimental data are necessarily in the form of mean performance over several trials, the experimental error associated with the points in the trade-off function can be estimated by the method I have just sketched. This is otherwise a troublesome problem for which there are no clearly established statistical techniques. A second advantage of this approach is that one can determine the trade-off function for any level of output. If, as in the present data, the output-vs.-input curves are parallel when plotted against a logarithmic abscissa, then the trade-off function is independent of the output level. Or, to put it more accurately, trade-off functions for different levels will differ only by a multiplicative constant. In many determinations of trade-off functions a single output level (usually the threshold for an effect) is used. The question of what the trade-off function might look like at other output levels is left unanswered.

At the time of writing, we have determined strength-duration curves for both the priming effect and the reinforcing effect in only one rat. Obviously, the data presently available do not warrant extensive discussion; nonetheless, they are presented in figure 12 for two reasons: First, we replicated both of the determinations. In figure 12 the two determinations for the priming effect are plotted as solid lines with filled circles. The two determinations for the reinforcement effect (dashed line with open circles) yielded functions so nearly superimposable that they cannot be separately plotted on a graph scaled to the dimensions of figure 12. The close agreement between the original determinations and their respective replications confirms our conclusion that the experimental error associated with points on these functions is, in general, no greater than $\pm 10\%$ ($\simeq \pm 0.05$ log units). Second, at two points (1 msec. and 0.1 msec.) the curve for the priming effect diverges from the curve for the reinforcing effect by amounts that are appreciably greater than the margin of experimental error. This divergence tends to substantiate the conclusion drawn from the refractory-period experiments, namely, that the priming effect and the reinforcing effect derive from the direct stimulation of two distinct substrates.

The possible discontinuity (at 0.32 msec.) in the slope of the function for the priming effect suggests that the substrate for this effect may itself have two components. However, any such conclusion will have to await detailed exploration of this apparent discontinuity in a number of additional rats.

## Temporal Summation

*Early work.* Sherrington's work was largely devoted to deriving the properties of synaptic summation from a study of reflexes in the spinal cat. This work is too well known to require review. One point, however, should be made as a prelude to the studies that follow: The temporal summation of the excitatory effects of two electrical stimuli delivered more than 1-5 msec. apart is almost always achieved in the synaptic network "downstream" (or-thodromic) from the point of excitation, rather than at the point of initial electrical excitation. This is true for two reasons: First, electrically excitable membrane only sums current by virtue of its resistance-capacitance characteristic, and the time constant of this characteristic is usually on the order of a few tenths of a millisecond. Second, the production of a conducted spike wipes out the excitatory potential (depolarization) that precedes it, leaving the membrane temporarily refractory to further stimulation. Thus psychophysical studies on the effects of varying pulse spacing at intervals greater than 5 msec. yield data that probably reflect the time course of *synaptic* summation processes in the substrate for the behavior being studied.

*Self-stimulation.* Coons and his coworkers have studied the effect on lever pressing of varying the temporal pattern in the resulting train of pulses. Holding constant the number of pulses and the train duration, they studied the effect of moving every second pulse (designated the *T* pulse) closer to the preceding pulse (designated the *C* pulse). In other words, they manipulated the *intra*pair interval, just as in the refractory period studies. In their work, however, the *inter*pair interval (designated the *C-C* interval) was made as long as possible (60-400 msec.), so that they could study the effect of varying the *intra*pair interval (designated the *C-T* interval) over a wide range of values. (The maximum possible value occurs when the *C-T* interval equals half the *C-C* interval, i.e., when the pulses are evenly spaced.)

In the first study (Smith & Coons, 1970) both the C and the T pulses were delivered through the same electrode. Using an equivalent-stimuli paradigm, they found that moving the T pulse closer to the C pulse improved the efficacy of stimulation, that is, produced more effective overall temporal summation. However, at very short C-T intervals ($<$ 1.2 msec.) the refractory-period effect diminished the efficacy of the second pulse (the T pulse). The second study (Ungerleider & Coons, 1970) involved two changes in procedure: (a) They switched to an output-vs.-input paradigm, and (b) they delivered the C pulses through an electrode on one side of the brain and the T pulse through a similarly located electrode on the other side of the brain. Under these conditions, varying the C-T interval amounts to varying the phase relation between two trains of pulses being delivered to similar sites on opposite sides of the brain. They found that the more they brought the two trains into phase, the more effective the bilateral summation. As expected, there was no evidence of refractory period under these conditions (because the C and T pulses were not stimulating the same tissue). Bilateral summation was most effective when the trains were perfectly in phase and least effective when they were 180° out of phase.

The experiments just reviewed place some constraints on the synaptic summation processes in the substrate(s) for self-stimulation, but they have three drawbacks: First, the effects of patterning are not large (cf. Ungerleider & Coons, 1970; Halboth & Coons, 1973; German & Holloway, 1973). Second, the experimental design did not distinguish the priming effect from the reinforcing effect. Thus, one does not know whether the substrates for these two effects differ in their temporal summation characteristics, nor whether the data reflect the characteristics of one substrate, the other substrate, or the combined characteristics of both substrates. Third, the C-T technique (paired-pulse technique) is neither the simplest nor most powerful technique for studying the ability of a synaptic network to sum the excitatory effects of a train of pulses. That the synaptic network can sum fairly widely spaced excitatory volleys is evident from the fact that a train of several widely spaced pulses will sustain self-stimulation, whereas a train having only 1 or 2 pulses will not.

Edmonds, Stellar, and Gallistel (1974) reasoned that the simplest way to define psychophysically the course of temporal summation in the substrates for self-stimulation was to determine how much one had to increase other parameters of the stimulation in order to compensate for increases in the interval between evenly spaced pulses. We assumed that the synaptic network would behave as a leaky integrator: In response to each excitatory volley, synaptic processses would rise and then decay. As other volleys came along, their excitation would add to whatever excitation remained from the earlier ones. The longer the interval between volleys, the greater the decay of excitation; hence, the less effective the temporal summation. One could compensate for the diminished efficiency of temporal summation either by increasing the size of the individual volleys (increasing current intensity) or by adding more volleys (increasing the number of pulses in the train). The amount of compensation required would reflect the degree to which the increase in the interval between volleys had diminished the efficiency of synaptic summation. If synaptic processes decayed slowly, then an increase in the interval between pulses from, say, 10 msec. to 30 msec. would require only a small compensatory adjustment of current intensity or number of pulses. If, on the other hand, the decay were rapid, then a large compensatory adjustment of the other parameters would be required.

Put more formally, equivalent-stimuli data on the trade-off between interpulse interval and either current intensity or number of pulses should serve to define the impulse response of the leaky integrator, that is, the impulse response of the synaptic network that summates the excitation.

We thought it would be particularly interesting to characterize the impulse response of the substrate for the reinforcement effect in self-stimulation. As pointed out in the Introduction, the excitation of this substrate results in a quasi-permanent structural alteration. At some point the transient excitation in the substrate is converted to a permanent alteration of some kind, that is, to what might be called a memory. And the magnitude of this alteration — as gauged by its subsequent behavioral effects — is an increasing function of the summated excitation in the substrate. Thus, the characterization of this substrate may prove valuable in understanding the neurophysiological basis of learned alterations in the behavior of higher vertebrates.

In order to separate the reinforcement effect from the priming effect, we again used the runway and waiting box paradigm. The priming effect was held at a constant maximum, by giving a large

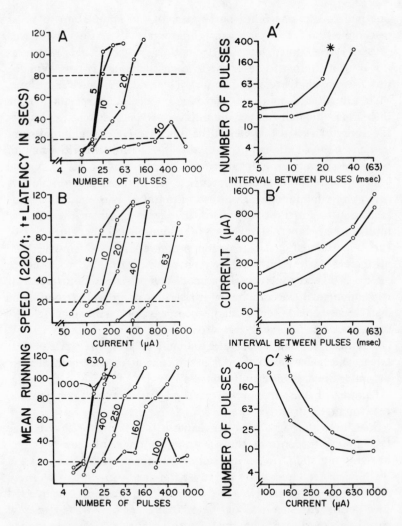

FIG. 13. A: Running speed as a function of number of pulses at different intervals between the pulses. The interpulse interval (in msec.) is indicated alongside each curve. A': The trade-off functions for number of pulses vs. interpulse interval. The upper curve was derived using an output level of 80, the lower curve using an output level of 20. B and B': The trade-off between current and interpulse interval, derived as in A and A'. C and C': The trade-off between number of pulses and current, derived as in A and A'. Data originally published in Edmonds et al. (1974).

amount of priming stimulation just before each trial. We varied the interval between pulses, the current intensity, and the number of pulses in the stimulation received for pressing the goal lever. As in the strength-duration experiments, these parameters of stimulation were varied in a way that generated families of output-vs.-input curves. Each curve in a given family showed mean running speed as a function of, say, current intensity, at some interval between pulses. From the family of curves we derived a trade-off function (current-vs.-interpulse-interval in the case of the example just mentioned).

Altogether, we determined three trade-off functions — current vs. interval, number vs. interval, and number vs. current — in each of five rats. The data from one rat, which are representative of the data from the other four rats, are presented in figure 13. The curve families are on the left (figure 13 a, b, c) and the derived trade-off (i.e., equivalent-stimuli functions) on the right (fig. 13 a', b', c').

At least in the number-vs.-current and the number-vs.-interval experiments, the curves within each family are not completely parallel. Therefore, we derived two trade-off functions from each family. One function (the lower one in each of the graphs a', b', and c') was derived with a low-output criterion (running speed = 20). The other one (upper functions in a', b', and c') was derived from a high-output criterion (running speed = 80).

The data in figure 13 confirm the assumption that the synaptic network in the substrate for the reinforcement effect has the qualitative properties of a leaky integrator. The longer the temporal interval over which the successive volleys must be summed, the less the sum. The sum can be restored to a reference level either by increasing the size of the volleys (fig. 13a') or by increasing the number of volleys (fig. 13b'). A reduction in the size of the volleys can be compensated by an increase in the number of volleys (fig. 13c').

The trade-off functions in figure 13a', and b', and c' place quantitative constraints on the processes underlying the temporal summation of excitation in the substrate for the reinforcement effect. This year, I am working with Duncan Luce to see whether the application of conjoint measurement techniques (Krantz, Luce, Suppes, & Tversky, 1971, chap. 6) to these data yields any relatively simple mathematical description of summation characteristics in this

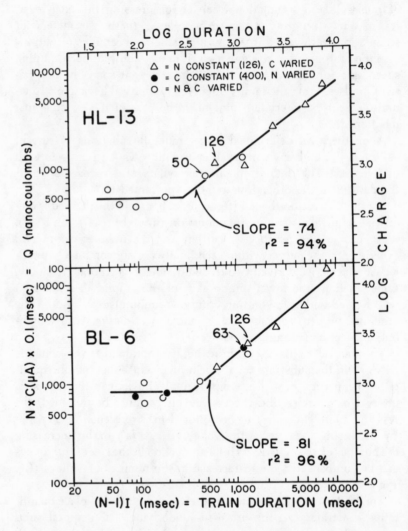

FIGS. 14 AND 15. A reanalysis of the data from Edmonds et al. (1974). The product of $N$ (the number of pulses in a train), $C$ (the current intensity), and 0.1 msec. (the pulse duration) is plotted as a function of train duration ($D$) on double logarithmic coordinates. By inspection the data seem to fall into two segments — a flat segment at short train durations and a linearly increasing segment at longer train durations. The line segments drawn on the graphs are the two-segment represen-

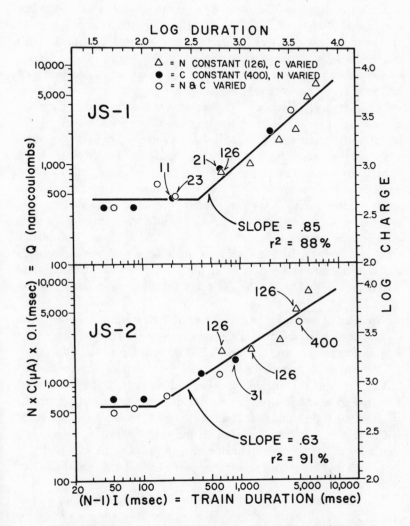

tations that minimize the sum of the residual variances. The square of the product-moment correlation coefficient, $r$, gives the percent of variance in log $Q$ accounted for by the least squares linear regression equation for log $Q$ as a function of log $D$, over the range where log $Q$ is increasing. Points of special interest (see text) have the value of $N$ indicated on the graph. From Gallistel (1974). Reproduced by permission of the American Psychological Association.

substrate. One result of this work was a reanalysis of the three trade-off experiments in figure 13 from the standpoint of the duration of the train of pulses (Gallistel, 1974). If one spreads a train of pulses out over a longer interval, i.e., lengthens the train duration, then the train is less effective at producing a reward. This diminished effectiveness is a consequence of the leaky integrator characteristic of the neural pathway that conveys the neural signal to that part of the system that converts the summated signal into a permanent effect (memory) of some kind. The effect of lengthening the train duration can be offset by increasing the number of pulses, by increasing the intensity of the pulses, or by increasing both the number and the intensity of the pulses. Each of the three trade-off experiments in figure 13 can be viewed as an experiment that used one of these three options in order to compensate for increases in train duration. Thus, one can present the data from all three experiments by plotting the product of $N$ and $C$ as a function of train duration. Since pulse duration (0.1 msec. in all cases) also affects stimulus efficacy, it is advisable to include this in the analysis as a scaling factor. The resulting plots of $N \cdot C$ $(\mu A) \cdot 0.1$ (msec.) $= Q$ (nanocoulumbs) as a function of train duration are shown in figures 14 and 15.

When analyzed from the standpoint of train duration, the temporal summation characteristics of the neural network carrying the signal for reinforcement can be simply summarized. Up to train durations on the order of 250 msec., train duration has no effect on the net efficacy of the stimulus pulses. Beyond 250 msec. the total input required to maintain a given level of efficacy increases as a power function of train duration. That the required values of $N$, or $C$, or $N \cdot C$, are a power function of train duration follows from the fact that they fall along a straight line on a double logarithmic plot (see figs. 14 & 15). The slope of this line gives the exponent of the power function.

The most remarkable feature of the data in figures 14 and 15 is that *it does not matter whether the increased input is achieved by increasing the number of pulses or by increasing current intensity; exactly the same increase in the product of N and C is required in either case.* The surprising equivalence between number of pulses and current intensity is highlighted in figures 14 and 15 by giving the value of $N$ for nearby points whenever these nearby points involved more than twofold differences in $N$ and $C$. The most extreme

example occurs at a train duration of about 600 msec. in the data
for Rat JS-1 (fig. 15). Note that one train had 21 pulses while the
other had 126 pulses. Since the product of $N$ and $C$ was almost the
same for both trains, it follows that the sixfold difference in number
of pulses was offset by an approximately sixfold difference in current intensity. And, in fact, the current intensity of the 21-pulse
train was $400\mu A$ while the current intensity of the 126-pulse train
was $63\mu A$. In other words, this analysis reveals a surprisingly linear
trade-off between $N$ and $C$.

The linear trade-off between $N$ and $C$ is most simply accounted
for by assuming that both parameters of the stimulation make nearly
linear contributions to the summated neural signal that is translated
into a memory (permanent effect) at some later point in the reinforcement system. Neurophysiologically speaking, the assumption
that the number of pulses contributes linearly to the summated
signal would mean that there was no appreciable facilitation or
accommodation in the neural network over the range of parametric
values covered by these trade-off experiments. Both facilitation
and accommodation are *by definition* phenomena in which the effects
of successive pulses are not additive. That is, the effect of a second
or third pulse is either greater than (facilitation) or less than (accommodation) the effect of the initial pulse or pulses.

The assumption that $C$ contributes linearly to the summated neural
signal amounts to assuming that the number of relevant neurons
fired by a stimulus pulse increases linearly with current intensity.
The single-unit work of Rolls (1971a) indicates that neurons fire
only once to a 0.1-msec. pulse in the range of current intensities
covered by the trade-off experiments. Thus, the only way current
intensity can contribute linearly to the summated signal is for the
number of neurons fired by a pulse (i.e., the number of suprathreshold neurons) to increase linearly with current intensity.
That such should be the case is at least plausible in the light of some
simple physical considerations.[6] If the electrode tip is located within
a bundle of more or less evenly distributed neurons, then the number
of neurons passing within some radius, $r$, of the electrode tip increases as the square of $r$. If the current spreads out approximately
evenly from the electrode tip, then the electrical flux per unit area
will obey an inverse square law. Hence, the radius within which

6. I am indebted to Robert Hawkins for pointing this out.

the membrane current per unit area exceeds some critical (threshold) value will increase as the square root of current intensity. With the radius of suprathreshold current, $r_k$, increasing as the square root of current intensity and the number of neurons within $r_k$ increasing as the square of $r_k$, the relation between number of neurons fired and current intensity will be a linear one.

The comments in the last several paragraphs on the implications of the data of Edmonds et al. (1974) vis-à-vis the neurophysiological properties of the substrate for reinforcement show how psychophysical data produce potentially testable hypotheses about the neurophysiological properties of the substrate. We have done some pilot work that uses similarly derived trade-off functions to characterize quantitatively temporal summation in the substrate for the priming effect. I am not sufficiently confident of the generality of our data to present them at this time. They do, however, suggest that synaptic processes in the substrate for priming decay more slowly than in the substrate for reinforcement. In fact, it appears as if this characteristic may differentiate between the substrates more strikingly than any other characteristic.

*Stimulation-elicited consummatory behavior.* Mogenson, Gentil, and Stevenson(1971) have published data suggesting that the substrates for stimulation-elicited eating and stimulation-elicited drinking have different temporal summation characteristics. In studying electrodes that elicited both eating and drinking in rats, they found that low-frequency stimulation favored eating while high-frequency stimulation favored drinking. If synaptic processes in the substrate for eating decayed more slowly than synaptic processes in the substrate for drinking, then the substrate for eating would sum widely spaced volleys more effectively than the substrate for drinking. Thus a substrate that is prepotent at high frequencies (e.g., drinking) may become subordinate to another substrate (e.g., eating) at low frequencies.

The inference that the excitation from a volley in the substrate for eating decays slowly is supported, albeit indirectly, by Halboth and Coons's (1973) findings. They report that patterning stimulation to the eating system via the C-T (paired-pulse) technique has no effect on the efficacy of summation, at least for C-T intervals ranging from 5 to 30 msec.

The data of Mogenson et al. (1971) do not *necessarily* conflict with Valenstein, Cox, and Kakolewski's (1970) contention that a single

lateral hypothalamic substrate is common to all the stimulation-elicited consummatory behaviors. As pointed out at the beginning
of the section on temporal summation, the temporal summation
of stimulus pulses spaced more than a few milliseconds apart probably occurs at synaptic junctions. The synaptic network mediating
this summation may be remote from the site of initial electrical
excitation, and/or it may be a complex network spread over a number
of brain loci. Thus, the eating and drinking effects may depend
on the stimulation of one and the same lateral hypothalamic substrate, a substrate that feeds into two distinct synaptic networks,
one mediating drinking, the other eating. The Mogenson et al. (1971)
data do, however, suggest that the two substrates "see" the volleys
of excitation produced by successive pulses early enough so that
the separate volleys have not been smoothed out and summed
together into a single rise and fall of excitation.


Psychophysical Approach to the Pharmacology of the Substrate

If the data in figures 14 and 15 portray synaptic summation in the
substrate for the reinforcement effect in self-stimulation, then the
procedure used to generate those data might also be used to determine the extent to which various drugs affect the synaptic processes.
A drug that blocked some of the receptor sites on the subsynaptic
membranes or one that diminished the supply of the relevant
synaptic transmitter substance should diminish the efficacy of synaptic summation. One could then compensate for this drug-induced
impairment of synaptic summation by increasing the number of
pulses or by increasing the current intensity

Before employing this approach, however, one needs to determine
whether or not a similar effect would be produced by drugs that
do not affect the substrate for reinforcement but do affect other
variables that influence our behavioral index. We know, for example,
that the rat's running speed, using brain stimulation as a reward,
is affected by the priming effect of pretrial stimulation. Could we
distinguish drug effects on the substrate for priming from drug
effects on the substrate for reinforcement? Considerable research
has already been devoted to determining the pharmacology of the
substrate for reward in self-stimulation. Most of this research has
not confronted the problem of distinguishing between drug effects

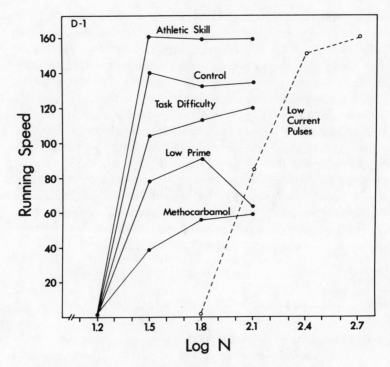

FIG. 16. The effect of a number of performance variables on the running-speed vs. number-of-pulses function, as contrasted with the effect of reducing the current intensity in the reward. All of the performance variables (including those not shown—curarization, extreme atropinization, and mortal pneumonia) lowered or raised asymptotic running speed but produced only small ($<$ 2. 5db) shifts in the locus of the function. From Edmonds & Gallistel (1974). Reproduced by permission of the American Psychological Association.

on the reward function and drug effects on the performance function. By reward function, I mean the processes that translate electrical stimulation into a summated excitation in the substrate for reinforcement. By performance function, I mean all of the other processes that affect the behavioral index of this excitation. Most commonly, the rate of pressing a lever for brain-stimulation reward is used as the behavioral index. Drug-induced reductions in the rate of pressing are assumed to indicate a drug-induced reduction of excitation in the substrate for reinforcement. The assumptions underlying such interpretations are open to question. Curare will reduce the rat's rate of pressing, yet few will argue that the neuromuscular junction is the substrate for reinforcement. The failure to distinguish drug effects on variables such as priming or general arousal from drug effects on reinforcement has already led to controversy in the literature (Antelman, Lippa, & Fisher, 1972; Roll, 1970; Stein & Wise, 1971; Wise & Stein, 1969).

Edmonds and Gallistel (1974) have recently investigated the effect of a variety of variables on the function relating mean running speed to the number of pulses in the train of reward stimulation. Most of these variables were assumed to be performance variables (priming, task difficulty, general health, amount of practice, debilitating drugs, etc.). For comparison we also manipulated a variable — current intensity — that we knew would affect the summated excitation in the substrate for reinforcement.

Our findings are summarized by figure 16. All of the performance variables raised or lowered the asymptotic running speed but had relatively minor effects on the location of the sharp rise in the function (solid lines in fig. 16). By contrast, reducing the intensity of the pulses in the reward had no effect on asymptotic running speed but shifted the function considerably to the right (dashed line in fig. 16). The magnitude of this shift to the right represents the increased number of pulses required to compensate for the reduction in current (cf. fig. 13a & c).

Our data suggest a method for distinguishing pharmacological effects on the substrate for reinforcement from pharmacological effects on other performance variables. Running speed as a function of the number of pulses in the reward may be used as the behavioral index. Decreases in the asymptote of this function indicate the magnitude of a drug's effect on performance variables. The amount by which the function shifts to the right indicates the magnitude of the drug's effect on the substrate for reinforcement. The ratio between these two drug effects (the decrease in asymptote and the shift to the right) can then serve as a measure of the degree to which a drug has a selective or specific effect on the substrate for reinforcement.

Edmonds is now employing this approach to evaluate the effect of $\alpha$-methyl-p-tyrosine. This drug produces a long-lasting inhibition of catecholamine synthesis, thereby depleting the brain's stores of the catecholamine neurotransmitters, norepinephrine and dopamine.

refractoriness at around 0.8–1.1 msecs. after an initial stimulus pulse. The substrate for the reinforcing effect recovers at around 0.5–0.6 msec. (Deutsch, 1964; Gallistel et al., 1969). Preliminary data further suggest that the two substrates have different strength-duration curves (Barry et al., 1974) and different synaptic summation characteristics. Thus, the limited psychophysical data presently available suggest that these two effects should be regarded as functionally distinct processes mediated by distinct substrates in the MFB. That the processes are functionally distinct is not surprising, since the behavioral responses to a sudden change in one or the other process differ strikingly (see the section Motivation and Reinforcement in Self-stimulation, in the Introduction). The essence of the functional difference between these two effects is that one is a time-dependent motivational variable, while the other is an event-dependent variable that produces a structural alteration of some kind.

Refractory-period data suggest, albeit very tentatively, that a third substrate (or family of substrates) mediates stimulation-elicited consummatory behavior (Beagley, 1973; Hu, 1973; Rolls, 1973). Although stimulation-elicited consummatory effects are certainly motivational in character, the suggestion that they might be functionally distinct from the motivational aftereffect in self-stimulation is consistent with other findings: Cox et al. (1969) found that the aftereffects of MFB stimulation actually inhibited eating in rats that ate during the stimulation. And Stellar and Gallistel (1975, in press) found that pretrial priming stimulation inhibited rats' running to a food reward. Whatever the nature of the appetitive motivational state that occurs as an aftereffect of MFB stimulation, it is not directed toward a food reward. On the other hand, the motivational state that arises *during* stimulation often is directed toward such a reward. Thus, the two states would appear to be functionally distinct.

Data on the effect of pulse spacing (Mogenson et al., 1971) suggest that stimulation-elicited eating and stimulation-elicited drinking have substrates whose synaptic networks, at least, are distinct. Other psychophysical analyses (e.g., strength-duration) should help to decide whether these substrates are distinct at the level of the lateral hypothalamus, that is, at the point where the electrical stimulation excites the neural tissue.

Refractory-period data on two other aftereffects of MFB stimulation — the analgesic aftereffect and the grooming aftereffect — are consistent with the hypothesis that these behavioral effects

Thus, Edmonds is testing the widely entertained hypothesis that one of these is the principal neurotransmitter in the substrate for reinforcement. So far, his data indicate that $\alpha$-methyl-p-tyrosine does, at least in some rats, have a specific effect on the substrate for reinforcement. Some rats have shown only a nonspecific effect, but these failures may reflect shortcoming in Edmond's pharmacological technique. The problem requires the use of a variety of pharmacological techniques in conjunction with an unambiguous behavioral index. Several pharmacological manipulations remain to be tried before one would wish to draw any but the most tentative conclusions. At present, I wish mainly to suggest that our behavioral index of pharmacological effects on reinforcement is less ambiguous than the behavioral indices most commonly employed.

CONCLUSIONS

The comparatively recent discovery that motivating and reinforcing processes may be activated by electrical stimulation of certain loci in the brain presents a unique opportunity for studying the neurophysiological bases of such processes. The adoption of the psychophysical methods employed by the neurophysiologists who worked before the advent of modern recording techniques should permit us to take maximum advantage of this opportunity. Using the general psychophysical technique of determining trade-off functions — the relations between parametric values that yield equivalent performance — we can construct *quantitative* characterizations of the substrates underlying the behavioral effects of the stimulation. These quantitative characterizations can, in turn, make an important contribution to two facets of brain-stimulation research — functional analysis and neurophysiological analysis.

Functional Analysis

The psychophysical data I have just reviewed suggest that the priming and reinforcing effects in electrical self-stimulation are mediated by distinct substrates, having different quantitative characteristics. The substrate for the priming effect recovers from are manifestations of the same transient appetitive motivational state that appears as the priming effect in self-stimulation. One currently tenable interpretation of these three aftereffects is that: (1) The priming effect reflects the motivational state's ability to potentiate certain behaviors. (2) The analgesic effect reflects the ability of this same motivational signal to inhibit competing behavior. (3) The grooming effect is a displacement activity, which occurs when the environment does not permit the execution of the goal-directed behavior(s) potentiated by the appetitive motivational signal.

The above conclusions about the functional relations between the various behavioral effects of electrical stimulation are sprinkled with hedging adjectives and adverbs, which were used advisedly. I am sure that many, perhaps all, of these conclusions will prove to have been overhasty. However, I believe that in the future the evidence for and against these and similar conclusions will come in good measure from psychophysical studies of the kind I have reviewed.

I have advanced these conclusions here primarily to show the import of psychophysical data on the functional analysis of the behavioral effects of brain stimulation. When psychophysical analysis of diverse behavioral effects suggest a common substrate, then one looks for a functional analysis that can explain those behavioral effects as manifestations of a single process or system. When psychophysical analysis suggests different substrates, then one assumes that the processes or systems underlying the effects are separable and one asks what relation holds among them.

The Introduction presents a hypothesis about the relation between motivational and reinforcement variables in self-stimulation. Motivational variables are assumed to be signals that wax and wane with time as a function of internal and external stimuli. These signals organize behavioral output by selectively potentiating certain functional units of sensorimotor coordination, while inhibiting competing units. The organization that a given motivational signal imposes on behavior is determined by the pattern of distribution of that signal within the sensorimotor hierarchy. The pattern of distribution is determined by the structure of the hierarchy. Reinforcement variables are event-dependent variables that restructure the sensorimotor hierarchy, thereby altering the pattern of distribution for one or more motivational signals.

The "Linkage" Problem

As a physiological psychologist I would like some day to be able to explain behavioral phenomena in terms of the neurophysiological events that I believe must underlie those phenomena. To be securely founded, any such account must, I believe, be based in part on a direct study of neurophysiological events by techniques such as single-unit recording and neurochemical analysis. Only such techniques can provide unequivocal evidence that a particular *neuro-physiologically defined* system does in fact exist. And only such techniques can determine why that neurophysiological system displays the properties peculiar to it.

However, a reductionist account of behavioral phenomena must also include the reasons for believing that a particular neurophysiologically defined system is in fact the system that underlies the behaviorally defined phenomena. In other words, one must be able to justify linking a neurophysiologically defined system to a set of behaviorally defined phenomena. Psychophysical data can, I believe, play a central role in the construction of such "linkage" hypotheses (Brindley, 1970, chap. 5). Psychophysical data place quantitative constraints on the processes that underlie a behavioral effect. The demonstration that a particular neurophysiological system satisfied these quantitative constraints then forms an important part of the justification for linking that system to the behavioral phenomenon.

The explicit use of such a strategy in the electrophysiological analysis of self-stimulation has just begun (Gallistel, Rolls, & Greene, 1969; Rolls, 1971b). However, this strategy was an important part of the electrophysiology of the peripheral nervous system, from Bernstein's early researches (see Introduction) until the 1950s, when the electrical basis of neural conduction was conclusively established by the work of Hodgkin and Huxley (1952) and a host of other modern neurophysiologists. This strategy is also an explicit part of modern sensory system electrophysiology, most notably in the work of DeValois (DeValois, Morgan, & Polson, 1974; DeValois & Jacobs, 1971). The discovery that motivation and reinforcement processes can be activated by electrical stimulation of the central nervous system makes it possible to employ this strategy in studying the neurophysiological basis of central organizing and reorganizing processes.

REFERENCES

Adler, N. T. The biopsychology of hormones and behavior. In D. Dewsbury (Ed.), Comparative psychology: A modern survey. New York: McGraw-Hill, 1973.

Adrian, E. D. The electrical reactions of muscles before and after nerve injury. Brain, 1916, 39, 1-33.

Adrian, E. D. The mechanism of nervous action, Philadelphia: University of Pennsylvania Press, 1932.

Adrian, E. D., & Olmstead, J.M.D. The refractory phase in a reflex arc. Journal of Physiology, 1922, 56, 426-443.

Antelman, S. M., Lippa, A. S., & Fisher, A. E. 6-Hydroxydopamine, noradrenergic reward, and schizophrenia. Science, 1972, 175, 919-920.

Ball, G. G. Electrical self-stimulation of the brain and sensory inhibition. Psychonomic Science, 1967, 8, 489-490.

Bard, P. The hypothalamus and sexual behavior. Association of Nervous and Mental Disease Research Publications, 1940, 20, 551-579.

Barry, F. E., Walters, M.S., & Gallistel, C. R. On the optimal pulse duration in electrical stimulation of the brain. Physiology and Behavior, 1974, 12, 749-754.

Bazett, H. C. Observations on the refractory period of the sartorius of the frog. Journal of Physiology, 1908, 36, 414-430.

Beagley, W. K. Grooming in the rat as an aftereffect of lateral hypothalamic stimulation. Unpublished Ph.D. dissertation, University of Pennsylvania, 1973.

Bernstein, J. Untersuchungen über den Erregungsvorgang im Nerven- und Muskelsysteme. Heidelberg: Winter, 1871.

Bernstein, J. Elektrobiologie. Braunschweig: Vieweg, 1912.

Brindley, G. S. Physiology of the retina and visual pathway. (2nd ed.) Baltimore: Williams and Wilkins, 1970.

Cox, V. C., Kakolewski, J. W., & Valenstein, E. S. Inhibition of eating and drinking following hypothalamic stimulation in the rat. Journal of Comparative and Physiological Psychology, 1969, 68, 530-535.

Davis, W. J., Siegler, M. V. S., & Mpitsos, G. J. Distributed neuronal oscillators and efference copy in the feeding system of pleurobranchae. Journal of Neurophysiology, 1973, 36, 258-274.

Dethier, V. G. Insects and the concept of motivation. In D. Levine (Ed.), Nebraska Symposium on Motivation, 1966. Lincoln: University of Nebraska Press, 1966. Pp. 105-136.

Dethier, V. G., & Bodenstein, D. Hunger in the blowfly. Zeitschrift für Tierpsychologie, 1958, 15, 129-140.

Deutsch, J. A. The structural basis of behavior. Chicago: University of Chicago Press, 1960.

Deutsch, J. A. Behavioral measurement of the neural refractory period and its application to intracranial self-stimulation. *Journal of Comparative Physiology and Psychology*, 1964, **58**, 1-9.

Deutsch, J. A., Adams, D. W., & Metzner, R. J. Choice of intracranial stimulation as a function of delay between stimulations and strength of competing drive. *Journal of Comparative and Physiological Psychology*, 1964, **57**, 241-243.

Deutsch, J. A., & Howarth, C. I. Some tests of a theory of intracranial self-stimulation. *Psychological Review*, 1963, **70**, 444-460.

DeValois, R. L. Analysis and coding of color vision in the primate visual system. *Cold Spring Harbor Symposia on Quantitative Biology*, 1965, **30**, 567-579.

DeValois, R. L., & Jacobs, G. H. Vision. In A. M. Schrier & F. Stollnitz (Eds.), *Behavior of nonhuman primates*. Vol. 3. New York: Academic Press, 1971

DeValois, R. L., Morgan, H. C., Polson, M. C., Mead, W. R., & Hull, E. M. Psychophysical studies of monkey vision — I. Macaque luminosity and color vision tests. *Vision Research*, 1974, **14**, 53-67.

DuBois Reymond, E. *Animal Electricity*. London: Churchill, 1852.

Edmonds, D. E., & Gallistel, C. R. Parametric analysis of brain stimulation reward: III. Effect of performance variables on the reward summation function. *Journal of Comparative and Physiological Psychology*, 1974, **87**, 876-883.

Edmonds, D. E., Stellar, J. R., & Gallistel, C. R. The parametric analysis of brain stimulation reward in the rat: II. Temporal summation in the reward system. *Journal of Comparative and Physiological Psychology*, 1974, **87**, 860-869.

Flynn, J. P. Patterning mechanisms, patterned reflexes, and attack behavior in cats. In J. K. Cole & D. D. Jensen (Eds.), *Nebraska Symposium on Motivation*, 1972. Lincoln, University of Nebraska Press, 1973. Pp. 125-153.

Fraenkel, G. S., & Gunn, D. L. *The orientation of animals*. New York: Dover, 1961.

Gallistel, C. R. Intracranial stimulation and natural rewards: Differential effects of trial spacing. *Psychonomic Science*, 1967, **9**, 167-168.

Gallistel, C. R. Comments on Panksepp et al. *Psychonomic Science*, 1969, **16**, 25-26. (a)

Gallistel, C. R. The incentive of brain stimulation reward. *Journal of Comparative and Physiological Psychology*, 1969, **69**, 713-721. (b)

Gallistel, C. R. Self-stimulation: The neurophysiology of reward and motivation. In J. A. Deutsch (Ed.), *The physiological basis of memory*. New York: Academic Press, 1973.

Gallistel, C. R. Note on temporal summation in the reward system. *Journal of Comparative and Physiological Psychology*, 1974, **87**, 870-875.

Gallistel, C. R., Rolls, E. T., & Greene, D. Neuron function inferred by behavioral and electrophysiological measurement of refractory period. *Science*, 1969, **166**, 1028-1030.

Gallistel, C. R., Stellar, J. R., & Bubis, E. The parametric analysis of brain stimulation reward in the rat: I. The transient process and the memory-containing process. *Journal of Comparative and Physiological Psychology*, 1974, **87**, 848-859.

German, D. C., & Holloway, F. A. Directionality of rewarding impulses within the medial forebrain bundle self-stimulation system of the rat. *Science,* 1973, **179**, 1345-1347.

Gotch, F., & Burch, G. J. The electrical response of nerve to two stimuli. *Journal of Physiology*, 1899, **24**, 410-426.

Grundfest, H. Bioelectric potentials. *Annual Review of Physiology*, 1940, **2**, 213-242.

Halboth, P. H., & Coons, E. E. Behavioral measurements of the neural poststimulation recovery cycle in the lateral hypothalamic eating system of the rat. *Journal of Comparative and Physiological Psychology*, 1973, **83**, 429-433.

Hart, B. L. Gonadal hormones and sexual reflexes in the female rat. *Hormones and Behavior*, 1969, **1**, 65-71.

Helmholtz, H. Messungen über den zeitlichen Verlauf der Zuckung animalischer Muskeln and die Fortpflanzungsgeschwindigkeit der Reizung in den Nerven. *Archiv für Anatomie, Physiologie, und wissenschaftliche Medizin*, 1850, 276-364.

Helmholtz, H. Messungen über Fortpflanzungsgeschwindigkeit der Reizung in den Nerven. *Archiv für Anatomie, Physiologie, und Wissenschaftliche Medizin*, 1852, 199-216.

Helmholtz, H. Über die Geschwindigkeit einiger Vorgänge in Muskeln und Nerven. *Bericht über die zur Bekanntmachung geeigneten Verhandlungen der Königl. Preuss. Akademie der Wissenshaften zu Berlin*, 1854, 328-332. (Forerunner of *Berichte d. Berlin. Akademie.*)

Hermann, L. *Handbuch der Physiologie*. Vol. 2. Pt. 1. Leipzig: Vogel, 1879.

Hess, W. R. *The Functional organization of the diencephalon*. New York: Grune and Stratton, 1957.

Hill, A. V. Excitation and accommodation in nerve. *Proceedings of the Royal Society of London*, Ser. B, 1936, **119**, 305-355.

Hodgkin, A. L., & Huxley, A. F. A quantitative description of membrane current and its application to conduction and excitation in nerve. *Journal of Physiology*, 1952, **117**, 500-544.

Holst, E. von. Die relative Koordination als Phänomen and als Methode zentralnervöser Funktionsanalyse. *Ergebnisse der Physiologie*, 1939, **42**, 228-306.

Holst, E. von, & St. Paul, U. von On the functional organization of drives. *Animal Behaviour*, 1963, **11**, 1-20.

Hoorweg, L. Über die elektrische Nervenerregung. *Pflügers Archiv für die gesamte Physiologie*, 1892, **52**, 87-108.

Howell, W. H. *A textbook of physiology for medical students and physicians*. Philadelphia: Saunders, 1905.

Hu, J. W. Refractory period of hypothalamic thirst pathways in the rat. *Journal of Comparative and Physiological Psychology*. 1973, **85**, 463-468.

Hull, C. L. *Principles of behavior*. New York: Appleton-Century-Crofts, 1943.

Kavanau, J. L. Behavior of captive white-footed mice. In E. R. Willems & H. L. Raush (Eds.), *Naturalistic viewpoints in psychology*. New York: Holt, Rinehart, and Winston, 1969.

Krantz, D. H., Luce, R. D., Suppes, P., & Tversky, A. *Foundations of Measurement*. Vol. 1. New York: Academic Press, 1971.

Lapicque, L. Recherches quantitatives sur l'excitation électrique des nerfs traitée comme une polarisation. *Journal de Physiologie et de Pathologie Générale*, 1907, **9**, 620-635.

Lapicque, L. *L'excitabilité en fonction du temps*. Paris: Presses Universitaire, 1926.

Lashley, K. S. The problem of serial order in behavior. In L. A. Jeffres (Ed.), *Cerebral Mechanisms in Behavior*. New York: Wiley, 1951.

Lisk, R. D. Diencephalic placement of estradiol and sexual receptivity in the female rat. *American Journal of Physiology*, 1962, **203**, 493-496.

Lucas, K. On the optimal electric stimuli of normal and curarized muscle. *Journal of Physiology*, 1906, **34**, 372-390.

Lucas, K. The analysis of complex excitable tissues by their response to electric currents of short duration. *Journal of Physiology*, 1906-1907, **35**, 310-331. (a)

Lucas, K. On the optimal electric stimuli of muscle and nerve. *Journal of Physiology*, 1906-1907, **35**, 103-115. (b)

Lucas, K. The excitable substances of amphibian muscle. *Journal of Physiology*, 1907-1908, **36**, 113-135.

Lucas, K. *The conduction of the nervous impulse*. London: Longmans, Green, 1917. (a)

Lucas, K. On summation of propagated disturbances in the claw of astacus, and on the double neuro-muscular system of the adductor. *Journal of Physiology*, 1917, **51**, 1-35. (b)

MacDonnell, M. F., & Flynn, J. P. Control of sensory fields by stimulation of the hypothalamus. *Science*, 1966, **152**, 1406-1408.

Mayer, D. J., Wolfe, T. L., Akil, H., Carder, B., & Liebeskind, J. C. Analgesia from electrical stimulation in the brainstem of the rat. *Science*, 1971, **174**, 1351-1354.

Menzel, E. W. Chimpanzee spatial memory organization. *Science*, 1973, **182**, 943-945.

Miller, N. E. Learning and performance motivated by direct stimulation of the brain. In D. E. Sheer (Ed.), *Electrical stimulation of the brain*. Austin: University of Texas Press, 1961.

Mogenson, G. J., Gentil, C. G., & Stevenson, J. A. F. Feeding and drinking elicited by low and high frequencies of hypothalamic stimulation. *Brain Research*, 1971, **33**, 127-137.

Olds, J., & Milner, P. Positive reinforcement produced by electrical stimulation of septal area and other regions of the rat brain. *Journal of Comparative and Physiological Psychology*, 1954, **47**, 419-427.

Panksepp, J., Gandelman, R., & Trowill, J. The effect of intertrial interval on running performance for ESB. *Psychonomic Science*, 1968, **13**, 135-136.

Ratliff, F. *Mach bands: Quantitative studies on neural networks in the retina*. San Francisco: Holden-Day, 1965.

Reid, L. D., Hunsicker, J. P., Kent, E. W., Lindsay, J. L., & Gallistel, C. R. Incidence and magnitude of the "priming effect" in self-stimulating rats. *Journal of Comparative and Physiological Psychology*, 1973, **82**, 286-293.

Reynolds, D. Surgery in the rat during electrical analgesia induced by focal brain stimulation. *Science*, 1969, **164**, 444-445.

Reynolds, D. Reduced response to aversive stimuli during focal brain stimulation: Electrical analgesia and electrical anesthesia. In D. Reynolds & A. Sjoberg (Eds.), *Neuroelectric research*. Springfield, Ill.: Thomas, 1971.

Roberts, W. W. Hypothalamic mechanisms for motivational and species-typical behavior. In R. E. Whalen, R. F. Thompson, M. Verzeano, & N. M. Weinberger (Eds.), *The neural control of behavior*. New York: Academic Press, 1970.

Roeder, K. D. *Nerve cells and insect behavior*. Cambridge: Harvard University Press, 1967.

Roll, S. K. Intracranial self-stimulation and wakefulness: Effect of manipulating ambient brain catecholamines. *Science*, 1970, **168**, 1370-1372.

Rolls, E. T. Absolute refractory period of neurons involved in MFB self-stimulation. *Physiology and Behavior*, 1971, **7**, 311-316. (a)

Rolls, E. T. Involvement of brainstem units in medial forebrain bundle self-stimulation. *Physiology and Behavior*, 1971, **7**, 297-310. (b)

Rolls, E. T. Refractory periods of neurons directly excited in stimulus-bound eating and drinking in the rat. *Journal of Comparative and Physiological Psychology*, 1973, **82**, 15-22.

Rolls, E. T., & Kelly, P. H. Neural basis of stimulus-bound locomotor activity in the rat. *Journal of Comparative and Physiological Psychology*, 1972, **81**, 173-182.

Rose, M. D. Pain reducing properties of rewarding electrical brain stimulation. Unpublished Ph.D. dissertation, University of Pennsylvania, 1972.

Rose, M. D. Pain reducing properties of rewarding electrical brain stimulation in the rat. *Journal of Comparative and Physiological Psychology*, 1974, **87**, 607-617.

Rushton, W. A. H. The normal presence of α and γ excitabilities in the nerve-muscle complex. *Journal of Physiology*, 1931, **72**, 265-287.

Sherrington, C. S. *The integrative action of the nervous system.* New Haven: Yale University Press, 1906. (Reprinted 1961.)

Sherrington, C. S., & Sowton, S. C. M. Observations of reflex responses to single break-shocks. *Journal of Physiology*, 1915, **49**, 331-348.

Skinner, B. F. *The behavior of organisms.* New York: Appleton-Century-Crofts, 1938.

Smith, N. W., & Coons, E. E. Temporal summation and refractoriness in hypothalamic reward neurons as measured by self-stimulation behavior. *Science*, 1970, **169**, 782-784.

Stein, L., & Wise, C. D. Possible etiology of schizophrenia: Progressive damage to the noradrenergic reward system by 6-hydroxydopamine. *Science*, 1971, **171**, 1032-1036.

Stellar, E. Drive and motivation. In J. Field, H. W. Magoun, & V. E. Hall (Eds.), *Handbook of Physiology. Section I: Neurophysiology*, vol. 3. Washington, D.C.: American Physiological Society, 1960.

Stellar, J. R., & Gallistel, C. R. Runway performance for brain-stimulation or food reward: Effects of hunger and priming. *Journal of Comparative and Physiological Psychology*, 1975, in press.

Stumpf, W. E. Estradiol-concentrating neurons: Topography in the hypothalamus by dry-mount autoradiography. *Science*, 1968, **162**, 1001-1003.

Szabo, I. Neural refractory periods in lateral hypothalamic reward structures: A reinterpretation. *Recent Developments of Neurobiology in Hungary*, 1973, **4**, 201-213. (a)

Szabo, I. Path neuron system of medial forebrain bundle as possible substrate for hypothalamic self-stimulation. *Physiology and Behavior*, 1973, **10**, 315-328. (b)

Teitelbaum, P., & Epstein, A. N. The lateral hypothalamic syndrome: Recovery of feeding and drinking after lateral hypothalamic lesions. *Psychological Review*, 1962, **69**, 74-90.

Tinbergen, N. *The study of instinct.* London: Oxford University Press, 1951.

Ungerleider, L. G., Coons, E. E. A behavioral measure of homosynaptic and heterosynaptic temporal summation in the self-stimulation system of rats. *Science*, 1970, **169**, 785-787.

Valenstein, E. S., Cox, V. C., & Kakolewski, J. W. Reexamination of the role of the hypothalamus in motivation. *Psychological Review*, 1970, **77**, 16-31.

Weiss, P. Self-differentiation of the basic patterns of coordination. *Comparative Psychology Monographs*, 1938, **17**, 1-96.

Wilson, D. M. Insect walking. *Annual Review of Entomology*, 1966, **11**, 103-122.

Wine, J. J., & Krasne, F. B. Organization of escape behavior in the crayfish. *Journal of Experimental Biology*, 1972, **56**, 1-18.

Wise, C. D., & Stein, L. Facilitation of brain self-stimulation by central administration of norepinephrine. *Science*, 1969, **163**, 299-301.

Yeomans, J. S. Behavioral measurement of neural temporal excitability changes including refractory periods: A re-evaluation. Unpublished Ph.D. dissertation, University of California, San Diego, 1974.

# Brain Stimulation and Behavior Control[1]

## Elliot S. Valenstein
*University of Michigan*

BRAIN STIMULATION AND
BEHAVIOR: THE SOCIAL
AND INTELLECTUAL CLIMATE

*A*lfred Binet is said to have commented to a young researcher about to embark on a project, "Tell me what you are looking for and I will tell you what you will find." It is safe to assume that Binet knew that it is possible to find things one is not looking for, but he obviously believed it important to recognize that the questions asked influence the methods used and the answers that are usually found. The importance of this influence is often very apparent when we look back at what appears to be the "tunnel vision" of earlier scientists. The observations that were counted and those that were discounted can be seen to have resulted from a selective filtering by the issues paramount at the time. This process is operating in the present period as well, even though it is difficult to achieve sufficient perspective to recognize it. In spite of the difficulty, it is important to try to understand how the social and intellectual climate influences present research. Because the interplay between recent brain stimulation studies of motivation and the contemporary social and intellectual climate has been particularly strong, it may be useful to review some of the major trends in this field of study.

In looking back over the brain stimulation studies in this country during the period from 1950 to the present, two major influences can be detected. One of these has been the pressure to accumulate evidence demonstrating that electrical stimulation of discrete brain areas evokes natural motivational states. The other influence, which

1. The author's research reported in this paper was supported by NIMH Research Grant 2 RO1 MH20811-03.

interestingly is primarily an American phenomenon, is the increasing preoccupation with brain stimulation as a means of controlling behavior. The importance of these two factors can be illustrated by taking a brief look at the historical context which influenced developments in this field. A more complete history has been presented elsewhere (Valenstein, 1973).

For psychologists interested in studying the process of learning, the early 1950s was a time of increasing rejection of theories based on changes in hypothetical drive states assumed to take place in the brain. (Indeed, this was a period when it was often maintained that the CNS, the common abbreviation for the central nervous system, in reality meant the "conceptual nervous system.") These drive-reduction learning theories, as they are called, emphasized that we learn only (or in the weaker versions of the theory, we learn best) those stimulus-response connections that are associated with changes in level of drive state. Although it was recognized that peripheral body factors may contribute to drive state, a number of experiments had made it evident that drives such as hunger and thirst did not depend upon intensity of stomach contractions, dryness of mouth, or other obvious bodily cues. Drive states, therefore, were presumed to be represented mainly by the level of activity in functionally specific neural systems within the brain. However, this conclusion was inferential, and therefore the properties of drive, the major variable in the theory, had to be inferred and could not be measured. The field was rapidly degenerating into unresolvable arguments of little interest to anyone not indoctrinated into this specialty.

Drive-reduction theorists desperately needed some new input into their system. Although the Swiss physiologist Walter Hess had received a Nobel prize by this time, the details of his German publications were not well known in the United States. Hess had been stimulating the diencephalon in cats, using a technique that permitted him to study the responses evoked in awake, relatively unrestrained animals. Most of his observations were directed toward understanding the regulation of so-called autonomic responses such as changes in pupil size, blood pressure, heart rate, respiration, and the like. When Hess was invited to speak at Harvard in 1952, a number of people became aware for the first time that some of his studies seemed to demonstrate that electrical stimulation of certain areas in the diencephalon could suddenly make peaceful cats aggressive or satiated cats hungry. These reports were seized upon, for they seemed to provide a means to manipulate drives and to measure them directly.

Neal Miller has recently reflected on his initial interest in brain stimulation studies and described it as follows:

If I could find an area of the brain where electrical stimulation has the other properties of normal hunger, would the sudden termination of this stimulation function as a reward? If I could find such an area, perhaps recording from it would provide a way of measuring hunger which would allow me to see the effects of a small nibble of food that is large enough to serve as a reward, but not large enough to produce complete satiation. Would such a nibble produce a prompt, appreciable reduction in hunger, as demanded by the drive-reduction hypothesis? [Miller, 1973, pp. 54-55]

This certainly does not reflect the sophistication of Miller's current thinking on the problem, but it does illustrate the earlier intellectual climate that produced a great need to find similarities between behaviors elicited by brain stimulation, such as eating, drinking, and aggression, and the same behaviors when motivated by natural internal states. Similarities were searched for and found. What was found was that eating, drinking, grooming, gnawing, aggression, foot thumping, copulation, carrying of young, and many other behaviors could be triggered by brain stimulation. What was claimed was that discrete brain centers were identified which, when stimulated electrically, would evoke specific and natural states such as hunger, thirst, sexual appetite, and maternal drives. Tests were designed to emphasize the naturalness of the evoked states and dissimilarities were disregarded or dismissed as experimental noise. A personal experience illustrates the influence of the prevailing bias. When I reported at a meeting that the same brain stimulus frequently evoked eating, drinking, and other behaviors, noting that these and other observations raised some serious questions about the belief that natural drive states were evoked, a colleague told me that he had made similar observations several years earlier. However, since they interfered with the planned experiments, the testing conditions were arranged so that the stimulated animals had no chance to express these "irrelevant" behaviors.

In addition to overlooking behavioral observations inconsistent with the assumption that natural drive states could be duplicated by stimulating single points in the brain, several other trends characterized the period from 1955 to 1970. There was a tendency to rush into print with every new observation of a different behavior that could be evoked by brain stimulation. The competition for priority of discovery and the need to demonstrate progress to the granting agencies often interfered with any serious attempt to understand the relation between brain stimulation and behavior change. One active researcher remarked to me that he would not be "scooped" again, after bemoaning the fact that someone had beat him into press with an article describing a new behavior that could be evoked by brain stimulation. The list of such behaviors kept growing. One other factor that had a major impact was the belief that each evoked behavior was triggered from different and discrete brain sites. In some cases, reports that encouraged the growth of this belief actually presented little or no anatomical information, but in spite of this deficiency, there was little hesitancy to use loosely defined anatomical terms (really pseudoanatomical) such as the "perifornical drinking area." Other reports presented very complete histological data, but where the authors emphasized the separateness of brain areas eliciting different behaviors, others with a different bias could just as readily see diffuse localization and considerable overlap. In total, the impression was created that a large number of natural motivational states could be reliably controlled by "tapping into" discrete brain sites.

As the reports of these experiments began to be generally disseminated, a number of other distortions were introduced. These accounts fed the growing fear that this new brain technology might be used to control human behavior. The emphasis on control, by numerous demonstrations of behavior being turned "on and off" and by selective and oversimplified descriptions of these demonstrations in the popular press, has had a predictable effect. The possibility of behavior control by various brain interventions has become a popular topic for novels, television shows, movies, magazines, feature articles in newspapers, and even essays purporting to describe life in the not too distant future. Michael Crichton's *The Terminal Man* is only one of many novels that have used this theme. It may be no exaggeration to say that this story may have a greater impact (because it is believed by more people) than Mary Shelley's *Frankenstein*. Taking a different tack, an article that appeared in *Esquire* magazine described a government of the future, an "electroligarchy," where everyone is controlled by electrodes (Rorvik, 1969). It is not necessary to insist that all of this material is believed by everyone, or even by most people, in order to recognize that the virtual bombardment from the media has had a profound effect.

Even the material meant only for our amusement, and not intended to be taken seriously, gradually begins to become a part of our serious thinking and influences our perception of interpersonal relations. A *New York Times* article dated September 12, 1971, described the scientists who

> have been learning to tinker with the brains of animals and men and to manipulate their thoughts and behavior. . . . Though their methods are still crude and not always predictable, there can remain little doubt that the next few years will bring a frightening array of refined techniques for making human beings act according to the will of the psychotechnologist.

With more drama and expressing less reservation, Perry London, a professional psychologist, has written:

> All the ancient dreams of mastery over man and all the tales of zombies, golems, and Frankensteins involved some magic formula, or ritual, or incantation that would magically yield the key to dominion. But no one could be sure, from the old Greeks down to Mrs. Shelley, either by speculation or vivisection, whether there was any door for which to find that key. . . . This has been changing gradually, as knowledge of the brain has grown and been compounded since the nineteenth century, until today a whole technology exists for physically penetrating and controlling the brain's own mechanisms of control. It is sometimes called "brain implantation," which means placing electrical or chemical stimulating devices in strategic brain tissues. . . . These methods have been used experimentally on myriad aspects of animal behavior, and clinically on a growing number of people. . . . The number of activities connected to specific places and processes in the brain and aroused, excited, augmented, inhibited, or suppressed at will by stimulation of the proper site is simply huge. Animals and men can be oriented toward each other with emotions ranging from stark terror or morbidity to passionate affection and sexual desire. . . . Eating, drinking, sleeping, moving of bowels or limbs or organs

of sensation gracefully or in spastic comedy, can all be managed
on electrical demand by puppeteers whose flawless strings are
pulled from miles away by the unseen call of radio and whose
puppets made of flesh and blood, look "like electronic toys,"
so little self-direction do they seem to have. [London, 1969,
p. 137]

It is little wonder that the feeling of being controlled by surrep-
titiously implanted brain devices has become an increasingly common delusion in paranoia.

While most people emphasize the potential misuse of these new
brain-manipulating techniques, there are some who have stressed
what they believe is their positive potential. They see in them a
possible cure not only for intractable psychiatric disorders, but
intractable social problems as well — particularly those related to
violent crimes and wars. This potential of brain intervention to
achieve desirable ends has been expressed by Kenneth Clark in
his Presidential Address to the 1971 convention of the American
Psychological Association. Clark suggested that: "we might be on
the threshold of that type of scientific biochemical intervention
which could stabilize and make dominant the moral and ethical
propensities of man and subordinate, if not eliminate, his negative
and primitive behavioral tendencies." Proposals of this type can
best be discussed after a more realistic foundation is prepared
for critically examining the capacity of physical techniques to modify
brain-behavior relationships.

A CRITICAL EXAMINATION OF THE EVIDENCE

It should be recognized from the outset that evidence not going
beyond the demonstration of inhibition of evocation of some behavior pattern can be very misleading. Such demonstrations convey the
impression that there is a very simple and predictable relationship
between specific brain sites and complex behavior patterns. Also,
the implication that only one behavior is influenced by the electrical
stimulation encourages the inference that the control is very precise
and selective.

It might not be inappropriate to begin the critical examination
with a demonstration that is familiar to most people, Delgado's
purported demonstration of brain stimulation inhibiting aggressive-

ness in a bull (Delgado, 1969). An article in the *New York Times* described the event as it is typically reported:

> Dr. Delgado implanted a radio-controlled electrode deep within the brain of a *brave* bull, a variety bred to respond with a raging charge when it sees any human being. But when Dr. Delgado pressed a button on a transmitter, sending a signal to a battery-powered receiver attached to the bull's horns, an impulse went into the bull's brain and the animal would cease his charge. After several stimulations, the bull's naturally aggressive behavior disappeared. It was as placid as Ferdinand. [*New York Times*, September 12, 1971]

Although this interpretation is commonly accepted, there is actually little evidence supporting the conclusion that the stimulation had a specific effect on the bull's aggressive tendencies. A viewing of the film record of this demonstration should make it apparent to all but the most uncritical observer that the stimulation forced the bull to turn in circles in a very stereotyped fashion. This should not surprise anyone familiar with the brain, as the stimulating electrode was located in the caudate nucleus, a structure known to play an important role in regulating bodily movements. It is true that the bull's aggressive charges were stopped for a short period, but there is no evidence that it was because aggression was inhibited. Rather, because it was forced to turn in circles every time it came close to its target, the confused bull eventually stopped charging. Patients receiving caudate nucleus stimulation also display various types of stereotyped motor responses. Sometimes all movement is stopped in an "arrest response," so that a person instructed to continue tapping a table with his hand may be immobilized in midair by the stimulation (Van Buren, 1966). Destruction of the caudate nucleus in cats and other animals has been reported to produce a syndrome called *obstinate progression*, a curious phenomenon characterized by persistent walking movements even when an animal's head may be wedged into a corner (Mettler & Mettler, 1942). In humans, movement disorders such as the spasticity and tremors seen in Parkinson's disease have frequently been linked to caudate nucleus pathology.[2]

2. Plotnik and Delgado (1970) have presented evidence that stimulation of the caudate nucleus, putamen, gyrus pyriformis, and the gyrus rectus may

Caudate stimulation has also been reported to cause confusion and to interfere with speech (Van Buren, 1963). There are several animal studies indicating that caudate stimulation interferes with the normal habituation of responses to novel stimuli when they are presented repeatedly (e.g., Deadwyler & Wyers, 1972), and Luria (1973) has suggested that in humans the caudate nucleus is important for focusing attention because of its filtering role in selectively inhibiting responses to irrelevant stimuli. Kirkby and Kimble (1968) reported that rats have difficulty inhibiting responses in passive avoidance tests following damage to the caudate nucleus, while Rosvold, Mishkin, and Szwarcbart (1958) have concluded that this structure is involved in delayed alternation and visual discrimination performance of monkeys.

Many more functions of the caudate nucleus are described in the scientific literature, but a cataloguing of them all is not necessary for our present purpose. It should be clear, though, that we will not advance very far in our attempt to analyze the contribution of the caudate nucleus to behavior if we restrict ourselves to listing the complex behaviors affected by electrical stimulation. What is needed is a testing program designed to characterize functional changes with increasing precision by dissecting out the elements common to behaviors appearing to be very different.

The fact that it is possible to inhibit or evoke different complex behaviors by electrical stimulation has led some people to conclude that specific behaviors might be modified by destroying the neural area around the tip of the stimulating electrode. Thus, using the electrode implanted in the bull's caudate nucleus to destroy a portion of this structure would be expected to have altered the aggressive temperament of that animal. Although the specific experiment has not been done, there is no reason to believe that this would be the case. Destruction of the caudate nucleus does not change the aggressive tendencies of other animals, but it may produce various movement deficits or impairments on tasks requiring a selective

---

inhibit the threatening grimaces of monkeys that normally followed delivery of tail shock. Although only a minimum amount of data were presented in this brief report, these changes in the monkeys' behavior did not seem to be accompanied by motor disturbances or general disorientation. While this report suggests that stimulation of some structures may inhibit the expression of aggressive displays at current intensities that do not produce gross motor disturbances, there is no reason to assume that the large number of other functions believed to be regulated by these brain areas were unaffected.

inhibition of sensory and motor processes and the connections between them.[3] Similarly, if one destroys the hypothalamic area under an electrode that evokes aggressive behavior in a cat or rat, no change in natural aggressiveness will be induced unless the area destroyed is so extensive that the animal is capable of little behavior at all. Even after surgical isolation of the entire hypothalamus, a cat is still capable of displaying integrated attack and rage responses when provoked, as Ellison and Flynn (1968) have demonstrated. Earlier, Hess described his disappointment at not being able to modify a behavior elicited by stimulation even after destroying the tissue around the electrode:

> This step, involving the use of the same electrodes, seemed to be most promising, inasmuch as we expected that a comparison of stimulation and destruction effects would provide us with a reciprocal confirmation in the sense of a plus or minus effect. In reality, however, the results were disappointing. Today we know why. Since our procedure aimed for the greatest possible precision, we often produced only corresponding small foci of coagulation. As is shown by the stimulation study, however, even the best demarcated "foci" are relatively diffuse. [Hess, 1957, p.43]

Luria has commented that localization of complex functions in specific regions of the brain is always misleading. What is needed, he says, is to "ascertain by careful analysis which groups of concertedly working zones of the brain are responsible for the performance of complex mental activity; what contribution is made by each of these zones to the complex functional system" (Luria, 1973, pp. 33-34). Luria also notes that while it is appropriate to speak of the secretion of bile as a function of the liver, insulin secretion as a function of certain cells in the pancreas, and the transduction of light by photosensitive elements in the retina, when we speak of such functions as digestion or perception, "it is abundantly clear that [they]

3. None of this evidence is meant to argue against the possibility that parts of the caudate nucleus may be more involved in one type of process than another. It has been shown that specific parts of the caudate nucleus receive input from the orbital frontal, the dorsolateral frontal, or the inferotemporal cortex and the deficits that follow selective destruction of portions of this complex structure differ accordingly (Divac, Rosvold, & Szwarcbart, 1967). The behavioral manifestations of these deficits, however, vary with the demands of the situation.

cannot be understood as a function of a particular tissue." Similarly, Luria quotes Pavlov on the question of a "respiratory center": "Whereas at the beginning we thought that this was something the size of a pinhead in the medulla...now it has proved to be extremely elusive, climbing up into the brain and down into the spinal cord, and at present nobody can draw its boundaries at all accurately" (Pavlov as quoted by Luria, 1973, p. 30).

The idea that the brain is organized into convenient discrete compartments whose function corresponds to our social needs is simply not in accord with reality. The brain does not work that way. A concept such as aggression is a man-made abstraction and it therefore should not be expected to exist as a separate entity in the nervous system. Many parts of the nervous system play roles in regulating what most of us would label aggressive behavior and each of these parts also plays a role in regulating other functions as well. A recent paper by Paxinos and Bindra (1972) illustrates this point quite well. These investigators destroyed a small amount of the hypothalamic tissue in a rat by means of a specially designed knife. The title of their paper is "Hypothalamic Knife Cuts: Effects on Eating, Drinking, Irritability, Aggression and Copulation in the Male Rat." Even though not all of these behaviors were affected equally, the possibility of modifying a large number of behaviors by destroying even a small amount of brain tissue is quite clear. In drawing conclusions from brain stimulation experiments, what is almost always overlooked is that just about *every area of the brain is involved in many different functions and all but the simplest functions have multiple representation in the brain.*

The eagerness to believe that discrete and natural motivational states such as hunger can be manipulated by brain stimulation has resulted in a selective perception of even some of the pioneering work in this field. For example, although Hess is consistently mentioned as having produced bulimia by hypothalamic stimulation, it sometimes seems that his classic papers are not read as often as they are cited. What Hess acually wrote is as follows: "Stimulation here produces bulimia. If the animal has previously taken neither milk nor meat, it now devours or drinks greedily. As a matter of fact, *that animal may even take into its mouth or gnaw on objects that are unsuitable as food, such as forceps, keys, or sticks*" (Hess, 1957, p. 25; italics added). It has to be recognized that most hungry cats are more discriminating than Hess's brain-stimulated animals.

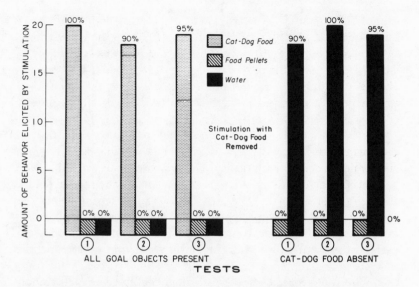

FIG. 1. Behavior evoked by brain stimulation in a choice-testing situation. During the initial 3 tests, the rats received brain stimulation in the presence of a commercial cat-dog food, their regular food pellets, and a water bottle. Stimulation evoked eating of the cat-dog food only. The cat-dog food was then removed. It was assumed that if stimulation evoked a hunger state the animals would readily switch to eating the food pellets. Instead, stimulation gradually started to evoke drinking with increasing regularity (see fig. 5). After stimulation was evoking drinking regularly, 3 additional tests were administered with food pellets and a water bottle available. The animal drank almost every time the stimulation was administered. Stimulus parameters were always the same. Each test consisted of 20 stimulations (20-sec. duration). The maximum score for any one behavior was 20, but animals could display more than one behavior during a single 20-second stimulation period. (Data from Valenstein, Cox, & Kakolewski, 1968b.)

In the studies from my own laboratory, it has been shown that the behavior evoked by brain stimulation is very different from behavior motivated by natural states. A stimulated animal may eat one type of food, but not the food it normally eats in its home cage (fig. 1), or it may not eat even the same food if it is changed in texture, as when food pellets are offered as a ground mash. Stimulated animals may drink water from a drinking tube, but not from an open dish (fig. 2), and the taste preferences of an animal drinking

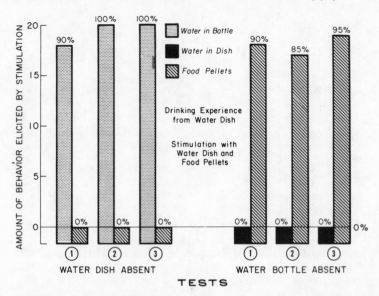

FIG. 2. Behavior evoked by brain stimulation in a choice-testing situation. During the initial 3 tests, the rat drank from the water almost every time the stimulation was administered, but did not drink water from a dish or eat the food pellets. Afterwards, the animal drank all its water from the dish for 3 days (this was natural drinking; no brain stimulation was administered), before periodic stimulation in the presence of the water dish and food pellets was initiated. It was assumed that if thirst had been induced by the stimulation during the initial tests, the rat would rapidly switch to drinking water from the dish when stimulated. Instead, stimulation gradually started to evoke eating of the food pellets. During 3 stimulation tests given with the water dish and food pellets available, the rat did not drink, but ate the food pellets during most of the stimulation trials. Stimulus parameters were always the same. Each test consisted of 20 stimulations (20-sec. duration). The maximum score for any one behavior was 20, but animals could display more than one behavior during a single 20-second stimulation period. (Data from Valenstein, Kakolewski, & Cox, 1968.)

in response to stimulation differ from those of a thirsty animal (fig. 3). Most important from the point of view of behavior control (or lack of it), the elicited behavior may change even in response to identical brain stimulation. A rat that only drinks in response to stimulation, for example, may start to eat when stimulated at a later time (figs. 4 and 5). Moreover, the brain sites from which eating and drinking may be evoked are much more widespread than usually implied. There is no anatomically discrete focus for

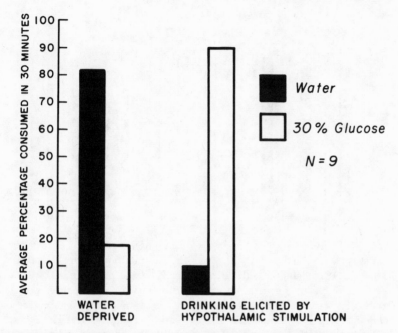

FIG. 3. Preference for water and glucose by rats receiving brain stimulation and when the same animals were deprived of water for 48 hours. All rats initially drank water when stimulated and did not eat food. In a two-bottle choice test, they preferred glucose when receiving brain stimulation, but water when they were thirsty. (Data from Valenstein, Kakolewski, & Cox, 1968.)

this phenomenon, although there are brain areas where the probability of evoking eating and drinking is very low (Cox & Valenstein, 1969). More recently, Reis, Doba, and Nathan (1973) reached a similar conclusion. These investigators found that they could evoke grooming, eating, and predatory behavior (depending on the intensity of the stimulating current) from almost all electrodes placed in the fastigial nucleus of the cat's cerebellum. Since the behaviors always appeared in the same order as the stimulus intensity was increased, regardless of the electrode placement within the fastigial nucleus, the investigators concluded:

Thus, it is the intensity of the stimulus and not the location of the electrode which is one of the determinants of the identity of the behavior. Second, the observation that the nature of the behavior evoked from a single electrode at a fixed stimulus intensity could be changed by altering the availability of goal

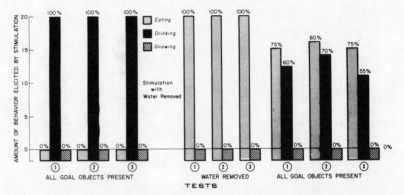

FIG. 4. Behavior evoked by brain stimulation in a choice situation. Initially, the animal only drank when the stimulation was presented (first 3 tests). After being stimulated periodically in the presence of food and a wooden block (for gnawing), but without the water bottle, the rat gradually began to eat the food pellets when stimulated. The next 3 tests demonstrated that stimulation evoked eating regularly. The last 3 tests demonstrated that even in testing with the water bottle present, stimulation elicited eating as well as drinking. Stimulus parameters were always the same. Each test consisted of 20 stimulations (20-sec. duration). The maximum score for any one behavior was 20, but animals could display more than one behavior during a single 20-second stimulation period. (Data from Valenstein, Kakolewski, & Cox, 1968a.)

objects (such as food or prey) is another demonstration that the locus of the electrode is not critical. Thus, our findings suggest that the behavioral responses from fastigial stimulation are probably not due to excitation of discretely organized neural pathways. [P. 847]

The conclusion to be drawn from these experiments is certainly not that stimulation at any brain site can evoke any behavior if the contingencies are arranged appropriately or that stimulation at different sites all evoke the same general state. These misinterpretations continue to appear in print although we made an effort to be clear on these points. For example: "We are not suggesting that any elicited response may substitute for any other, but rather that the states induced by hypothalamic stimulation are not sufficiently specified to exclude the possibility of response substitution" (Valenstein, Cox, & Kakolewski, 1970, p. 30). And similarly, "[It]

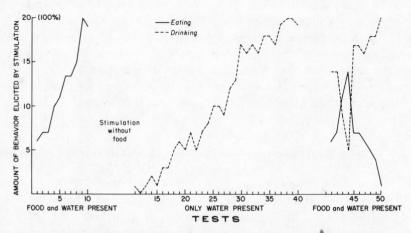

FIG. 5. The gradual development of behavior evoked by brain stimulation. The rat was tested shortly after the first demonstration of eating in response to stimulation. Over 10 successive tests, eating was evoked by brain stimulation with increasing regularity. Although water was available, stimulation never evoked drinking. The animal was then given periodic stimulation over a 1-week period until it started to drink in response to stimulation. Over 40 tests, the rat drank in response to stimulation with increasing regularity. During the last 10 tests, both food and water were present. During most of the tests the rat both ate and drank when stimulation was administered, although drinking gradually became the dominant evoked response. Stimulus parameters were always the same. Each test consisted of 20 stimulations (20-sec. duration). The maximum score for any one behavior was 20, but animals could display more than one behavior during a single 20-second stimulation period. (Data from Valenstein, 1971.)

is not meant to imply that it will not be possible to differentiate the effects of stimulation at different hypothalamic regions, but rather that the application of specific terms such as hunger, thirst and sex may not be justified" (Valenstein, 1969, p. 300).

It seems clear that some behaviors are more likely to be interchangeable than others. This probably reflects the role of the sensory, motor, and visceral changes induced by the stimulation in channeling behavior in certain directions. While these bodily changes do not duplicate natural motivational states, they play an important role in determining the types of behavior that will, or will not, be seen during stimulation.

To date, the direct effects of stimulation have been relatively neglected. While it is often stated that stimulation does not produce behavior changes unless the appropriate stimulus is available, such changes are actually often neglected even when the data suggest their importance. For example, the first description of drinking evoked by brain stimulation contained a strong suggestion that motor responses may have been more important in directing behavior than any presumed thirst state. In his report, Greer wrote:

> Stimulation of the animal began 24 hours after the electrodes were implanted. It was immediately apparent that the animal was under great compulsion to perform violent "licking" activity when a current was passed between the hypothalamic electrodes. In response to stimulation, it would stand on its hind legs and run vigorously around the glass enclosed circular cage, licking wildly at the glass wall. This behavior would cease immediately upon shutting off the current. If the voltage were slowly increased, licking would gradually become more vigorous.
> With stimulation continuing by timer control, the reaction of the animal changed during the first night. The water bottle containing 200 ml was found completely empty at 9 a.m. even though it had been filled at 6 p.m. the previous evening. It was now found that stimulation would result in violent drinking activity. The non-specific licking response had been lost. As soon as the current was turned on, the animal would jump for the water bottle and continue to drink avidly until the switch was turned off. If the water bottle was removed and the current then turned on, the rat would go back to its "licking" behavior of the previous day, but would immediately transfer it to drinking behavior when the water bottle was replaced. [Greer, 1955, pp. 60-61]

Visceral changes produced by the stimulation may also play a role in determining the behavior that will be evoked by brain stimulation. For example, Folkow and Rubinstein (1965) have contrasted the visceral changes produced by hypothalamic stimulation which evokes eating with those changes produced by electrodes evoking rage reactions. Among the prominent bodily changes produced by stimulation that caused rats to eat were a marked increase of intestinal motility and change in stomach volume plus mild increases in blood pressure and heart rate. The pattern was different when rage was evoked; intestinal and gastric motility were inhibited, and the blood pressure and blood distribution patterns differed from those present when electrodes evoked eating. Recently, Ball (1974) also stressed the importance of visceral changes for evoked eating. In rats displaying this response, Ball sectioned the vagus nerve at a point close to where it innervates the stomach. He reported that the stimulus threshold for elicitation of eating was raised significantly even after the animals recovered from surgery and were eating at least the normal amount of food in their home cage. Even though the thresholds increased, it was clear that the visceral changes controlled by this branch of the vagus nerve were not necesssary for the evoked behavior, as stimulation continued to evoke eating. Similarly, as noted earlier, Reis, Doba, and Nathan (1973) reported that electrical stimulation of the rostral fastigial nucleus of the cat's cerebellum elicited either grooming, feeding, or killing of a rat, depending on the intensity of stimulation used. The magnitude of the cardiovascular responses (heart rate and blood pressure) differed for each of the three behaviors evoked, but the behaviors were still displayed after these visceral responses were blocked by an injection of phentolamine. It is evident from the many important studies by Flynn and his colleagues (see review by Flynn, Edwards, and Bandler, 1971) that brain stimulation produces many different sensory and motor changes as well as visceral changes. Blocking one or two of these changes is unlikely to be very disruptive once an elicited behavior has become established.

In addition to producing sensory and motor changes, the positive or aversive motivational effects evoked by brain stimulation may also serve to channel behavior and determine which behaviors are interchangeable. Plotnik (1974) has summarized the motivational consequences of 174 brain stimulation sites in monkeys. He found that 117 were neutral, 22 were positive or rewarding, and 35 were aversive or negative. Of the 14 points that elicited aggressive behavior directed at other monkeys, all of them had previously been determined to have aversive motivational properties. In other words, all sites that elicited aggression were aversive, although the converse was not true. Plotnik views the aggression displayed as "secondary aggression" produced by reaction to an aversive stimulus. In such cases, it would be as misleading to conclude that there was a direct relation between natural aggression and the brain site stimulated

as there would be to conclude the same about the soles of the feet
when electric shock delivered to them produced fighting. The point
is well illustrated by Black and Vanderwolf (1969), who reported
that foot-thumping response could be evoked in the rabbit by
stimulation of sites in the hypothalamus, thalamus, central grey,
septum, reticular formation, and fornix-fimbria. Rather than
describing a complex "thumping circuit" in the rabbit brain, Black
and Vanderwolf noted that thumping could be elicited by foot shock
and they concluded that "thumping behavior in the rabbit is a fear
or pain response" (p. 448).

The significance of motivational properties of brain stimulation
is made clearer by distinguishing predatory from aggressive behaviors. In animals such as cats and rats, hypothalamic stimulation
has evoked both types of behaviors. In these animals, a predatory,
stalking behavior (called "quiet biting attack" in the rat), which
is well directed at an appropriate prey, has been distinguished from
a diffusely directed "affective rage attack" (Panksepp, 1971;
Wasman & Flynn, 1962). Stimulation at sites that evoke the predatory (or appetitive) behavior has been shown to also evoke positive
or rewarding effects (Panksepp, 1971), while stimulation at sites
evoking "affective attack" has been demonstrated to be aversive
(Adams & Flynn, 1966). In primates, the elicited aggression is in-
traspecific, resembling fighting rather than predatory behavior, and
is evoked primarily, if not exclusively, by stimulation having aversive motivational properties.[4] Although the evidence is inadequate,
aggression provoked by brain stimulation in humans also seems
to occur only in cases where the stimulation has aversive consequences (see Valenstein, 1973, for a review of this literature).
Considerations such as these, suggesting that certain behaviors are
compatible with aversive and others with positive states, may
determine which behaviors can be interchanged.

Although the somatic and motivational effects produced by brain
stimulation make it more likely that one group of behaviors will

4. Robinson, Alexander, and Browne (1969) reported one instance where
stimulation elicited aggressive attacks on another monkey and also supported
self-stimulation behavior. This suggests that brain stimulation that elicits
intraspecies aggression may be motivationally positive. However, as self-
stimulation was tested with brief (0.5-sec.) stimulus trains and aggression
was elicited by relatively long (10-40-sec.) stimulus trains, this exception may
be more apparent than real.

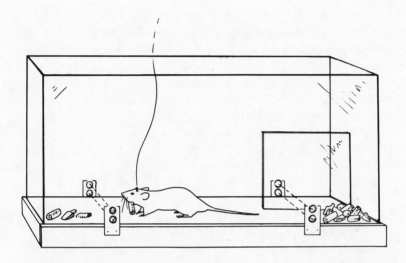

FIG. 6. Illustration of a rat carrying a wooden dowel stock from stimulation (right) to nonstimulation (left) side of test chamber. (In this variation of the basic experiment, animals were given a choice between receiving hypothalamic stimulation with or without the opportunity to carry objects; they chose the former.) (Data from Phillips et al., 1969. Figure reproduced from Valenstein, Cox, & Kakolewski, 1970; copyright 1970 by the American Psychological Association and reproduced by permission.)

be evoked than another, these factors are by no means sufficient to determine completely the specific behavior displayed or the motivational states induced. Environmental factors and individual or species characteristics can also be very important determinants. An experiment from my own laboratory demonstrates this point and also illustrates how easily one can be misled by first impressions in brain stimulation experiments.

Figure 6 illustrates a two-compartment chamber used to test the behavior of rats receiving rewarding hypothalamic stimulation (Phillips, Cox, Kakolewski, & Valenstein, 1969). The equipment has been arranged so that when the rat interrupts the photo cells on the right side of the chamber, brain stimulation is turned on, and it remains on until the animal interrupts the photo cell in the left compartment. In an amazingly short time, the rat learns to play the game, running to the right side and turning the stimulation on for a period, then running to the opposite side and turning the stimulation off. This behavior is repeated rapidly over and over again. The rat is stimulating its own brain and apparently enjoying it — at least it keeps on doing it.

At this point, we placed food pellets on the right, the stimulation side. After a brief delay, the rat started to pick up the pellets when stimulated and to carry them (as pictured in figure 6) to the opposite side of the chamber, where they were dropped as soon as the brain stimulation was turned off. We were fascinated by this unexpected turn of events, as it seemed possible that we had stumbled on a region of the rat's brain that regulated food-hoarding behavior. At least that is what we were thinking until we investigated a little further. When we substituted rubber erasers and pieces of dowel sticks, the rat carried them just as readily. If we mixed the edible and inedible objects together, the rat did not discriminate between them. It carried both. This was a very strange type of food-hoarding behavior! Next we placed some rat pups on the right side and found that these also were carried to the other side. It dawned on us that had we started with the rat pups and gone no further, we would have been convinced that we were activating the brain structures that controlled the pup-retrieval component of maternal behavior. Probably we would have found it difficult to resist speculating about the significance of the fact that males carried pups as readily as females.

Once the rats started carrying objects regularly, they would pick up and carry almost anything in response to the stimulation. The compulsion to carry things when the stimulation was on became so strong that when all the objects were removed, the rats carried parts of their own bodies. A rat might pick up its tail or a front leg with its mouth and carry it over to the other side where it was "deposited" as soon as the stimulation was turned off.

Finally, we found that if the very same stimulation was delivered to the rat's brain under different conditions, objects were no longer carried. We programmed the equipment to deliver the same temporal pattern of stimulation the rat had previously self-administered, controlled now by a clock rather than by the rat's position. This procedural change resulted in the possibility of the animal being stimulated anyplace in the test chamber instead of the stimulation being turned on and off consistently in different parts of the chamber. The outcome was that the identical electric stimulus, delivered to the same brain site, through the same electrode, no longer evoked the carrying of objects even if the animal was directly over several of the objects when the stimulation was turned on.

We believe that the answer to this puzzling phenomenon lies partly in the fact that rats tend to carry objects (food, pups, even shiny objects) from an open field, where the rat is vulnerable and therefore highly aroused, back to the relatively secure and calming environment of the nest site. When stimulation is delivered regularly in certain parts of the rat's life space and turned off regularly in other parts, it not only produces alternating arousal and calming states, but it links these states to specific parts of the environment. In addition, because rats prefer to turn off even rewarding brain stimuli after a period of time (Valenstein & Valenstein, 1964), they are forced to move back and forth in the test chamber. Taken all together, we may have inadvertently duplicated all the internal and external conditions that exist when a rat makes repeated forays from its nest site to the outside world.

Admittedly, this explanation is speculative. It is quite clear, however, that the behavior produced by stimulation is not determined in any simple fashion by the location of the electrode in the brain. (Actually, we achieved the same results with electrodes in very different rewarding sites.) The behavior produced by the stimulation can only be understood by considering the natural propensities of the rat in the environmental conditions in which it is tested.

If the response to brain stimulation is variable in inbred rats, it is certainly much more variable in the monkey and human. In monkeys, for example, brain stimulation may initiate drinking when the animal is confined to a restraining chair. However, when the stimulation is administered when the monkeys are in a cage and not restrained, they do not drink, even though they may be sitting within inches of the water dispenser when the stimulation is administered (Bowden, Galkin, & Rosvold, in press). In humans, brain stimulation may evoke general emotional states that are somewhat predictable in the sense that certain areas tend to produce unpleasant feelings while other areas tend to produce positive emotional states. Patients may report feeling tension, agitation, anxiety, fear, or anger, or they may describe their feelings as being very pleasant or relaxed. Different patients report different feelings from stimulation of what is presumed to be the same brain area, and the same person may have very different experiences from identical stimulation administered at different times (see Valenstein, 1973, for a review of this literature). The impression that brain stimulation can evoke the identical emotional state repeatedly in humans is simply a myth, perhaps perpetuated in part because of its dramatic impact. Janice Stevens and her colleagues have stressed this variability: "Subjective changes were elicitable in similar but not identical form repeatedly on the same day, *but often were altered when stimulation was carried out at the same point on different days*" (Stevens et. al., 1969, p. 164).

Many people have formed the impression that the results of brain stimulation are very predictable because of the reports that the same visual hallucinations and memories can be evoked repeatedly by brain stimulation. It is true that Wilder Penfield, who operated on the temporal lobes of patients suffering from intractable epilepsy, had emphasized that electrical stimulation of this brain region may repeatedly evoke the same memory. Considerable excitement was generated by reports that these evoked memories had the fidelity of tape recording playbacks of past, forgotten experiences. Indeed, on the basis of these reports, a few psychoanalysts began to speculate about the neural basis of repressed memories (Kubie, 1953). What was generally overlooked, however, was the fact that Penfield reported that the same response could be evoked within a minute or two, but if they waited a little longer and stimulated the same brain site, a different response was obtained (see Penfield and Perot, 1963). The similarity of this conclusion to that of Stevens, et al. (cited above) is apparent. Moreover, recent studies have made it clear that the occurrence of these evoked memories is rare and when they do occur it can usually be shown that they were determined by what was on the patient's mind or some other aspect of the situation when stimulation was administered (Mahl et al., 1964; Van Buren, 1961).

Even relatively simple motor and sensory responses to stimulation of specific areas of the cerebral cortex of primates may vary with time and between individuals. When Leyton and Sherrington (1917) reported their observations following cortical stimulation of the chimpanzee, orang-utan, and gorilla, they noted considerable evidence of "functional instability of cortical motor points." Not only did thresholds vary and stimulation of a particular brain site produce either extension or at other times flexion of the same joint, but the muscles involved might also change. Leyton and Sherrington reported that often a particular response became dominant and was elicited from a variety of cortical points that had previously elicited very different responses. They also observed that stimulation of the same cortical points produced different responses from different individuals and even from opposite hemispheres within the same individual. This is not to deny that there was general agreement on the parts of the frontal cortex most likely to produce movement of some kind in specific muscle groups, but Leyton and Sherrington emphasized that in regard to details the movements would not be the same if the experiment was repeated. Observations of this type have also been made following stimulation of the human cortex. Penfield and Boldrey (1937, p. 402) noted that stimulation at a point on the post-central gyrus which does not elicit a particular response may gain this capability if it is tested after stimulating a brain point that does evoke the response. Similar observations of variation of responses have been reported following electrical stimulation of sensory cortical areas in humans. Penfield and Welch (1949), for example, noted that if a brain site evoked sensation seeming to originate in the thumb, the same stimulation might later evoke sensations experienced as coming from the lips if the stimulation was preceeded by activation of another site that evoked lip sensations. These authors have called such variability "deviation of sensory response." Libet (1973) has discussed the variability in the response of humans to electrical stimulation in more detail.

It is totally unrealistic to believe that stimulation of a discrete point in the brain will invariably elicit the same memory, emotional state, or behavior. The changes produced by the stimulation depend upon what is going on in the rest of the brain and in the environment at the time. The understandable need in science to eliminate variability and to demonstrate control over phenomena may, when applied to the study of the brain, distort reality by concealing the very plasticity that is an essential aspect of adaptive behavior.

CONTROL OF HUMAN BEHAVIOR:
FACT AND FANTASY

No discussion of electrical brain stimulation and behavior control would be complete without considering the existence of rewarding brain stimulation. As everyone surely knows by now, Olds and Milner (1954) accidentally discovered about 20 years ago that electrical stimulation of certain brain structures can serve as an effective reward for rats. Subsequent studies of the behavior of rats and other animals indicated, in many different ways, that pleasurable sensations can be evoked by brain stimulation (see review by Olds, 1973). No other single discovery in the brain-behavior field has produced more theoretical speculation than the phenomenon that animals are highly motivated to stimulate their own brains. Arthur C. Clarke's reaction to this discovery is representative:

> Perhaps the most sensational results of this experimentation, which may be fraught with more social consequences than the early work of the nuclear physicists, is the discovery of the so-called pleasure or rewarding centers in the brain. Animals with electrodes implanted in these areas quickly learn to operate the switch controlling the immensely enjoyable electrical stimulus, and develop such an addiction that nothing else interests them. Monkeys have been known to press the reward button three times a second for eighteen hours on end, completely undistracted either by food or sex. There are also pain and punishment areas of the brain; an animal will work with equal singlemindedness to switch off any current fed into these.
>
> The possibilities here, for good and evil, are so obvious that there is no point in exaggerating or discounting them. Electronic possession of human robots controlled from a central broadcasting station is something that even George Orwell never thought of, but it may be technically possible long before 1984. [Clarke, 1964, pp. 200-201]

In part, because the pleasurable reactions have been produced by direct stimulation of the brain and involve electronic gadgetry, there is a tendency to conjure up images of "pure pleasure" that are completely irresistible. It should surprise no one that science fiction writers have seized this phenomenon as a theme for their stories. In Larry Niven's story "Death by Ecstasy," for example, the presumed omnipotence of rewarding brain stimulation is at the very center of the "perfect crime." The story takes place in the year 2123 and Owen Jennison's body has just been discovered under conditions that appear to indicate a suicide, but the death actually was the result of a carefully planned murder:

Owen Jennison sat grinning in a water stained silk dressing gown. . . . A month's growth of untended beard covered half his face . . . . A small black cylinder protruded from the top of his head. An electric cord trailed from the top of the cylinder and ran to a small wall socket.

The cylinder was a droud, a current addict's transformer. . . .

It was a standard surgical job. Owen could have had it done anywhere. A hole in his scalp, invisible under the hair, nearly impossible to find even if you knew what you were looking for. Even your best friends wouldn't know, unless they caught you and the droud plugged in. But the tiny hole marked a bigger plug set in the bone of the skull. I touched the ecstasy plug with my imaginary fingertips, then ran them down the hair-fine wire going deep into Owen's brain, down into the pleasure center.

He had starved to death sitting in that chair. . . . .

Consider the details of the hypothetical murder. Owen Jennison is drugged no doubt — an ecstasy plug is attached — He is tied up and allowed to waken. . . . The killer then plugs Mr. Jennison into a wall. A current trickles through his brain, and Owen Jennison knows pure pleasure for the first time in his life.

He is left tied up for, let us say, three hours. In the first few minutes he would be a hopeless addict. . . .

No more than three hours by our hypothesis. . . . They would cut the ropes and leave Owen Jennison to starve to death. In the space of a month the evidence of his drugging would vanish, as would any abrasions left by ropes, lumps on his head, mercy needle punctures, and like. A carefully detailed, well thought out plan, don't you agree? [Niven, 1970]

The readiness to believe that artificial stimulation of the brain can evoke such intense and irresistible pleasures reveals more about our desires than about our brain. Routtenberg and Lindy (1965) did demonstrate that some rats actually starved themselves to death because they continued to stimulate their brains rather than eat. However, one can be terribly misled by the popular accounts of this experiment. In the actual experiment, rats with electrodes implanted in rewarding brain structures were given only one hour a day to press a lever for food. It was necessary for them to eat during that hour in order to stay alive. After the rats were on this feeding schedule for a period, they were given a second lever that offered brain stimulation as a reward. Some of them spent enough time on this second lever so that they did not receive sufficient food to keep them alive until the next day's hourly session. This is quite different from the picture most people have in mind about what took place. In the special conditions of a brief test designed to emphasize the controlling power of brain stimulation, some of the rats were apparently not able to anticipate the consequences of choosing the brain stimulation lever. Under conditions providing rats with free access to brain stimulation and food, they never starve themselves. In fact, they eat their usual amount of food (Valenstein & Beer, 1964).

Rewarding brain stimulation is not equally compelling for all species. In humans, it does not seem capable of inducing an irresistible pleasure experience. Robert Heath, who is probably more experienced than anyone else with the types of pleasure reactions which brain stimulation can evoke in humans, has commented that it does not seem able to induce a euphoria equal to that produced by drugs (personal communication). This is not to deny the fact that patients have reported feeling considerable pleasure during brain stimulation or that they were willing to repeat the experience, particularly after receiving the impression that this was part of the therapeutic program. (See Valenstein, 1973, for a review of the reports of pleasure evoked by brain stimulation in humans.) Brain stimulation has evoked orgasms, but there is a tendency to attach too much significance to this fact. It is usually overlooked that, as with masturbation, brain stimulation that produces an orgasm does not continue to be as pleasurable afterwards.

The emotional state induced in humans by brain stimulation varies with the emotional and physical conditions of the patient. Heath has written:

When the same stimulus was repeated in the same patient, responses varied. The most intense pleasurable responses occurred in patients stimulated while they were suffering from intense pain, whether emotional and reflected by despair, anguish, intense fear or rage, or physical, such as that caused by carcinoma. The feelings induced by stimulation of pleasure sites obliterated these patients' awareness of physical pain. *Patients who felt well at the time of stimulation, on the other hand, experienced only slight pleasure.* [Heath, John, & Fontana, 1968, p. 186; italics added]

The existence of circuits in the brain that can induce both pleasure and arousal may be telling us something very important about neural mechanisms that have evolved to help focus attention, to increase involvement in a task, and to facilitate the consolidation of memories (see discussion in Valenstein, 1973, pp. 40-44). There are speculations that malfunctioning of these reward circuits is responsible for such psychiatric conditions as depression and schizophrenia (see Stein, 1971). Speculations about the functional significance of hypothesized "rewarding neural circuits" have very different consequences than suggestions of applications to the control of human behavior.

It would be difficult to fabricate a better example of the distortions that can result from a preoccupation with behavior control than that contained in a proposal, apparently seriously advanced, by Ingraham and Smith (1972). These two criminologists suggest that techniques are available for maintaining a surveillance on paroled prisoners and for controlling their behavior. They propose that implanted devices could be used to keep track of the location of the parolee and his physiological state while remotely operated brain stimulation could deliver either rewards or punishments or control behavior in other ways. For example, Ingraham and Smith suggest the following scenario:

> A parolee with a past record of burglaries is tracked to a downtown shopping district (in fact, is exactly placed in a store known to be locked up for the night) and the physiological data reveals an increased respiration rate, a tension in the musculature and an increased flow of adrenalin. It would be a safe guess, certainly, that he was up to no good. The computer in this case, *weighing the probabilities,* would come to a decision and alert the police or parole officer so that they could hasten to the scene; or, if the subject were equipped with an implanted radio-telemeter, it could transmit an electrical signal which could block further action by the subject by causing him to forget or abandon his project. [P. 42]

It is impossible to be certain, but it seems highly unlikely that a trial of such a scheme would be authorized. The more serious problem is the amount of creative energy diverted from the search for realistic solutions to important social problems by this type of thinking. It sometimes seems that difficulties in implementing necessary social changes encourage people to search for solutions in a world of fantasy.

Hopefully, it is clear by now that the responses that can be evoked from stimulating discrete brain areas are too variable and affect too many different functions to be useful in behavior-control schemes. The evoked behavior depends on what is going on elsewhere in the brain, as well as individual and species characteristics, and is very much influenced by situational factors. Those who prefer to think only in terms of control may be very disappointed to learn this. Those who think that the basic concern of science is understanding may find it useful to be reminded of the complex relationship between brain and behavior.

The subject of violence control has generated the most speculation that biological solutions are, or soon will be, available. These speculations, and some actual proposals, have taken very different forms. In his address to the American Psychological Association mentioned earlier, Kenneth Clark stated:

> Given the urgency of the immediate survival problem, the psychological and social sciences must enable us to control the animalistic, barbaric and primitive propensities in man and subordinate these negatives to the uniquely human moral and ethical characteristics of love, kindness and empathy. . . . We can no longer afford to rely solely on the traditional prescientific attempts to contain human cruelty and destructiveness.
>
> Given these contemporary facts, it would seem that a requirement imposed on all power-controlling leaders — and those who aspire to such leadership — would be that they accept and use the earliest perfected form of psycho-technological, biochemical intervention which would assure their positive use of power and reduce or block the possibility of using power destructively. It would assure that there would be no absurd or barbaric use of power. It would provide the masses of human beings with the security that their leaders would not sacrifice them on the altars of their personal ego. [K. B. Clark, Presidential Address, American Psychological Association, 1971]

Undoubtedly, Kenneth Clark is seriously concerned about possible misuse of the enormous capabilities for destruction that exist. His suggested solution makes it apparent that he has been greatly influenced by the brain experiments which seem to be revealing innate neural circuits that regulate aggression. Stripped to its essentials, his proposal appears as a modern variant of phrenology — a belief that the brain is organized into convenient functional systems that conform to our value-laden categories of behavior. Clark seems to believe that we need only to exorcise those critical regions of the brain that are responsible for undesirable behavior, or to suppress them biochemically, and goodness will dominate — mankind will be saved by a "goodness pill." The great impact of the many distorted perceptions of the power of brain-control techniques becomes especially evident when even social scientists accept the questionable hypotheses that wars are mainly caused by man's animallike aggressive tendencies and that biological interventions offers a practical way to prevent them. Clark has not suggested any specific biological intervention, so it is not possible to discuss his proposal in any detail. The situation is different with the proposal advanced by Vernon Mark and Frank Ervin.

In their book *Violence and the Brain*, Mark and Ervin (1970) stress the magnitude of the problem of violence in the United States and the belief that a biological approach can make a significant contribution toward finding a solution. The following are typical of a number of statements in the book: "Violence is, without question, both prominent and prevalent in American life. In 1968 more Americans were the victims of murder and aggravated assault in the United States than were killed and wounded in seven-and-one-half years of the Vietnam War; and altogether almost half a million of us were the victims of homicide, rape, and assault" (p. 3). They introduce their book with the statement that "we have written this book to stimulate a new and biologically oriented approach to the problem of human violence" (Preface). While in the foreword to the book, William Sweet, a neurosurgeon affiliated with Harvard University and the Massachusetts General Hospital and a frequent collaborator of Mark and Ervin, has expressed "the hope that knowledge gained about emotional brain function in violent persons with brain disease can be applied to combat the violence-triggering mechanisms in the brains of the non-diseased." Clearly a biological solution to the problem of violence is sought.

Mark and Ervin suggest that abnormal brain foci in the amygdala are responsible for a significant number of violent crimes. They believe that these abnormal foci often respond to internal and external stimuli by triggering violent behavior. Mark and Ervin have implanted stimulating electrodes in patients that display a history of episodic violence and claim to be able to locate the "brain triggers" by determining the area from which violent behavior can be evoked. The treatment consists of destroying the area believed to be responsible for the abnormal behavior.

The relevance of temporal lobe structures for aggressive behavior can be traced back to the seminal studies of Heinrich Klüver and Paul Bucy (1939), although there were several earlier reports that contained similar observations (for example, Brown & Schäfer, 1888; Goltz, 1892). Most investigators now believe that the temporal lobes and particularly the amygdala nuclei play an important, although complex, role in the expression of aggression, but Klüver and Bucy and all subsequent investigators have emphasized the very many different behavioral changes that follow destruction of this brain region in animals (see Valenstein, 1973, pp. 131-143).

In addition to a "taming" of monkeys (and other animals) after temporal lobe ablation, hypersexuality, increased orality, and a so-called psychic blindness[5] have also been observed. Others have emphasized the emotional "flatness" of the amygdalectomized animal (e.g., Schwartzbaum, 1960). The behavior changes may take very different forms — even diametrically opposite expression — under different circumstances. Amygdalectomized monkeys may become less aggressive toward man, but as Rosvold, Mirsky, and Pribram (1954) reported a number of years ago, the changes in dominance patterns between animals may be more dependent on the history of their social interactions than on the particular brain area destroyed.

Arthur Kling and his colleagues have recently reported even more striking evidence of the fallacy of describing complex change in response tendencies by such shorthand expressions as "increased tameness" (Kling, Lancaster, & Benitone, 1970; Kling, 1972). Kling captured and amygdalectomized wild monkeys in Africa and on Caijo Santiago. Control monkeys that were captured and released rejoined their troupe although some initial fighting was necessary. Before they were released, the amygdalectomized monkeys seemed tamer when approached by the experimenters, but when released

5. "Psychic blindness" refers to a loss of higher integrative visual functions rather than a loss in visual acuity.

into their own troupe they were completely unable to cope with the complexities of monkey social life. The behavior of the amygdalectomized monkeys was often inappropriate. Sometimes they displayed aggression toward dominant animals, a trait never exhibited before. In not too long a period, *all* the amygdalectomized monkeys either were driven from or retreated out of the troupe and eventually either died from starvation or were killed by predators. These observations demonstrate the multiplicity of behavioral changes that usually occur following brain lesions and the dependency of these on environmental conditions. It is interesting, for example, that the compulsive sexual mounting commonly observed in amygdalectomized monkeys housed in the laboratory was never seen under natural conditions.

The results of amygdalectomy in humans have been less systematically studied. These operations have been performed on patients exhibiting aggressive, hyperkinetic, and destructive behavior, usually (but not always) accompanied by temporal lobe epilepsy. While hypersexuality and orality have been observed to occur postoperatively in humans, most neurosurgeons claim these symptoms are rare and when they occur they subside after several months (see Valenstein, 1973, pp. 209-233, for a review of the clinical literature). Although "psychic blindness" has not been reported, there exist few serious studies of intellectual changes following amygdalectomy in humans. In one study, Ruth Andersen (1972) tested 15 patients after amygdalectomy, and even though 13 of them had undergone only unilateral operations, she reported evidence of a loss of ability to shift attention and respond emotionally. She concluded:

> Typically the patient tends to become more inert, and shows less zest and intensity of emotions. His spontaneous activity tends to be reduced and he becomes less capable of creative productivity. . . .
> With these changes in initiative and control of behavior, our patients resemble those with frontal lesions. It must be pointed out, however, that the changes are very discrete and there is no evidence of serious disturbance in the establishment and execution of their major plans of action. . . .
> Presumably he will [function best] in well-structured situations of a somewhat monotonous and simple character. [P. 182]

Typically, amygdalectomy in humans involves destruction of an appreciable proportion of this structure. For example, both Heimburger et al. (1966) and Balasubramaniam et al. (1970) estimate that they destroy over 50 percent of the amygdala on each side. In view of the animal literature and Ruth Andersen's observations, one might suspect that had adequate postoperative testing been generally used, intellectual and emotional deficits would have been detected more often. In *Violence and the Brain*, Mark and Ervin imply that their lesions need not be large because of the use of stimulating electrodes to locate the discrete focus that is triggering the violence. They argue that postoperative deficits would be minimized by the smaller, more selective stereotaxic lesions their technique makes possible. For example:

> ... tiny electrodes are implanted in the brain and used to destroy a very small number of cells in a precisely determined area. As a surgical technique, it has three great advantages over lobectomy: it requires much less of an opening in the surfaces of the brain than lobectomy does; it destroys less than one-tenth as much brain tissue; and once the electrodes have been inserted in the brain, they can be left without harm to the patient until the surgeon is sure which brain cells are firing abnormally and causing the symptoms of seizures and violence. [Mark & Ervin, 1970, p. 70]

It is important, therefore, to examine critically the validity of the claim that electrical stimulation is a reliable means of locating a "brain trigger of violence."

A few years ago, while studying the elicitation of behavior by hypothalamic electrodes, we noticed an interesting trend (Cox & Valenstein, 1969). In each of the rats we had implanted two electrodes, one on each side of the midline, but they were usually not placed symmetrically. It was observed that in a number of animals the same response was evoked from very different placements, while in other animals either different, or no specific, behavior was elicited from electrodes that often seemed to be in the same locations (fig. 7). We concluded that within certain anatomical limits, a "prepotent response" tendency of the animal (Valenstein, 1969) appeared to be a more important determinant of the behavior evoked than the exact location of the electrode in the brain.

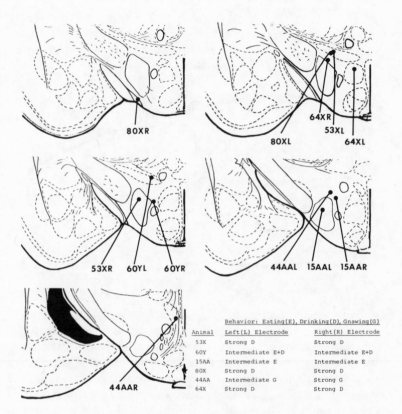

FIG. 7. Illustration of different anatomical locations of two electrodes that evoked the same behavior in a given animal. (Data from Valenstein, Cox, & Kakolewski, 1970. Brain diagrams from König & Klippel, 1963).

Many people were skeptical of our conclusion and cited examples from the literature, or from their own laboratory experience, that demonstrated that two electrodes could evoke different behaviors in the same animal. We had never denied this, but had argued that many electrodes evoke states that are sufficiently similar, yet not specifically identifiable, that the stimulated animal's behavioral characteristics become a major determinant of the effects produced by stimulation. Subsequently, additional information has accumulated supporting our impression. In a recent study using monkeys as experimental animals, it was noted that in some monkeys drinking was elicited initially by only a few electrodes, but over time an

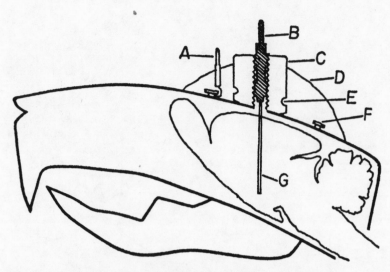

FIG. 8. Illustration of an electrode assembly that can be raised and lowered in the animal's brain. (See Wise, 1971, for details.)

increasing number of electrodes located at different brain sites gained the capacity to evoke drinking. Stimulation at an equally varied distribution of sites in other monkeys did not evoke any drinking. Some monkeys seem to respond to brain stimulation at many different sites by engaging in drinking behavior, while others do not (Bowden, Galkin, & Rosvold, in press). A similar conclusion may be drawn from an earlier study by Wise (1971) in which rats were implanted with electrodes capable of being moved up and down within the brain (fig. 8). It was found that in some rats, as the electrode was advanced over a large dorsoventral extent of the hypothalamus, eating and drinking were continuously evoked, but in other rats, these behaviors were not observed in response to stimulation at any site (fig. 9).

Panksepp (1971) has also provided information that supports our "prepotency hypothesis." He has studied the elicitation of mouse-killing responses in rats and has concluded that the ability to elicit mouse killing by stimulating the brain of a rat "interacted with the behavioral typology of individual animals. . . . animals normally inclined to kill mice were more likely to kill during hypothalamic stimulation than nonkillers. Thus, the electrically elicited response

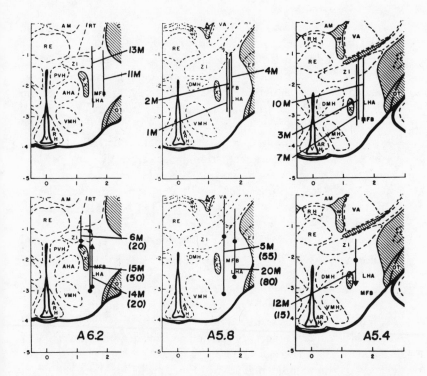

FIG. 9. Path of electrodes used to explore brain for regions evoking eating and drinking. Electrodes were advanced in 0.5-mm. steps descending along the path of the tract. Upper sections show the paths of electrode penetrations which did not evoke eating or drinking. In lower sections, eating and drinking were both evoked from all positions between upper and lower circles. Each electrode was placed in a different animal. (See Wise, 1971, for more details.)

was probably not determined by specific functions of the tissue under the electrode but by the personality of the rat" (p. 327).

In regard to the human, Kim and Umbach (1973) recently reported the effects of stimulating the amygdala of aggressive and nonaggressive patients. They concluded that during amygdala stimulation of aggressive patients "aggressiveness increased, whereas no aggressive reaction was observed in non-violent cases. Thus the amygdaloid complex seems not to be specific for anxiety alone or for aggression alone, and shows no specificity of the subnuclei for these emotional states" (p. 184).

There is little reason, therefore, to believe that brain stimulation is a reliable technique for locating discrete foci that trigger violence even if such foci exist. In the violence-prone patients that are studied by Mark and Ervin, violence can be triggered by a great number of brain stimulation sites and probably also by a pinch on the skin. The ability of stimulation techniques to ferret out a "critical focus" is far from what it has been touted. Indeed, the fact that Mark and Ervin found it necessary to make bilateral lesions to produce any significant effect strongly suggests that no "critical focus" was found. Also supporting this interpretation is the fact that the bilateral lesions are usually made progressively larger until the desired behavior change is believed to have been achieved. Although Mark and Ervin have presented their approach very seductively by implying that they can locate and eliminate small and discrete "brain triggers of violence," in actual practice, they seem to be performing "standard" bilateral amygdalectomies.

There is little doubt that there are well-documented cases where the onset of assaultive behavior can be traced to temporal lobe damage. There is also little doubt that there are cases where, by all reasonable standards, surgery has led to considerable improvement in behavior (Gloor, 1967). There has, however, been a gross exaggeration of the amount of violence that can be attributed to brain pathology. The evidence presented by Mark and Ervin has been extremely weak. It consists mainly of a recitation of parallel statistics on the numbers of murders, rapes, assaultive acts, automobile accidents, and assassinations, on one hand, and the number of cases of epilepsy, cerebral palsy, mental retardation, and other indications of brain damage, on the other hand. Not only are no causal connections established, but the statistical evidence does not support the conclusion that the correlation of brain damage and violence is high.[6] Mark and Ervin have also bolstered their general argument

6. The older neurological and psychiatric literature often contained statements that epileptics, particularly temporal lobe epileptics, are very much prone to violence. Most neurologists today refute the earlier figures. Current estimates of the incidence of violence among epileptics ranges between 1 and 4 percent and if corrections are made for age (onset of temporal epilepsy is later than for other epilepsies) the relationship is no higher for the temporal

by presenting several dramatic and violent incidents such as the Charles Whitman shooting from the University of Texas tower and implying that brain pathology was responsible.[7] Totally neglected in their description was Whitman's personal history which could readily have provided an explanation for his violence without any brain pathology. Nor was there any mention of the fact that Whitman's carefully laid plans did not conform to the pattern of sudden, unprovoked, episodic violence that Mark and Ervin describe as characteristic of those with abnormal brain foci. It may be relevant to point out that according to the newspapers, Whitman's brother was shot to death in a barroom dispute not too long ago. Is it likely that a temporal lobe tumor was the cause here, too?

There is a danger that the frustration produced by the inability to effectively reverse the accelerating rate of violence will cause those whose minds run towards simplified behavior-control schemes to accept the delusion that biological solutions are available for what are primarily social problems. The varying amounts of violence prevalent at different times and in different societies make it clear that violence is primarily a social phenomenon. If drug-related crimes are excluded, most of the present upsurge in violence can be related to the rejection of previously accepted social roles, the large numbers of people who do not believe they have a vested interest in the stability of our society, and the increasing belief that our institutions cannot — or will not — initiate the changes that are needed. These are not easy problems to remedy, but we will surely be in serious trouble if a number of influential people become convinced that violence is mainly a product of a diseased brain rather than a diseased society.

---

lobe subgroup. Recently, Rodin (1973) induced seizure in 150 epileptic patients using the EEG-activating drug bemigride. He reported that there was no incident of aggressive behavior during or after the psychomotor automatisms that occurred in 57 of the patients. Rodin argues that the often reported relationship between aggression and psychomotor epilepsy has been exaggerated.

7. It has frequently been stated that the cancerous tumor (glioblastoma multiforme) was located in the amygdala. Actually, because of the mishandling of the brain at the time of autopsy, the location of the tumor was never clearly established (Frank Ervin, personal communication.).

REFERENCES


Adams, D., & Flynn, J. P. Transfer of an escape response from tail shock to brain stimulated attack behavior. *Journal of the Experimental Analysis of Behavior*, 1966, **9**, 401-408.

Andersen, R. Differences in the course of learning as measured by various memory tasks after amygdalectomy in man. In E. Hitchcock, L. Laitinen, & K. Vaernet (Eds.), *Psychosurgery*. Springfield, Ill.: Charles C. Thomas, 1972. Pp. 177-183.

Balasubramaniam, V., Kanaka, T. S., & Ramamurthi, B. Surgical treatment of hyperkinetic and behavior disorders. *International Surgery*, 1970, **54**, 18-23.

Ball, G. G. Vagotomy: Effect on electrically elicited eating and self-stimulation in the lateral hypothalamus. *Science*, 1974, **184**, 484-485.

Black, S. L., & Vanderwolf, C. H. Thumping behavior in the rabbit. *Physiology and Behavior*, 1969, **4**, 445-449.

Bowden, D. M., Galkin, T., & Rosvold, H. E. Plasticity of the drinking system as defined by electrical stimulation of the brain (ESB) in monkeys. *Physiology and Behavior*, in press.

Brown, S., & Schäfer, E. A. An investigation into the functions of the occipital and temporal lobes of the monkey's brain. *Philosophical Transactions of the Royal Society of London*, 1888, **179B**, 303-327.

Clarke, A. C. *Profiles of the future*. New York: Bantam, 1964.

Cox, V. C., & Valenstein, E. S. Distribution of hypothalamic sites yielding stimulus-bound behavior. *Brain, Behavior, and Evolution*, 1969, **2**, 359-376.

Crichton, M. *The terminal man*. New York: Alfred Knopf, 1972.

Deadwyler, S. A., & Wyers, E. J. Description of habituation by caudate nuclear stimulation in the rat. *Behavioral Biology*, 1972, **7**, 55-64.

Delgado, J.M.R. *Physical control of the mind*. New York: Harper & Row, 1969.

Divac, I., Rosvold, H. E., & Szwarcbart, M. K. Behavioral effects of selective ablation of the caudate nucleus. *Journal of Comparative and Physiological Psychology*, 1967, **63**, 184-190.

Ellison, G. D., & Flynn, J. P. Organized aggressive behavior in cats after surgical isolation of the hypothalamus. *Archives Italiennes de Biologie*, 1968, **106**, 1-20.

Flynn, J. P., Edwards, S. B., & Bandler, R. J., Jr. Changes in sensory and motor systems during centrally elicited attack. *Behavioral Science*, 1971, **16**, 1-19.

Folkow, B., & Rubinstein, E. H. Behavioural and autonomic patterns evoked by stimulation of the lateral hypothalamic area in the cat. *Acta Physiologica Scandinavica*, 1965, **65**, 292-299.

Gloor, P. Discussion. In C. D. Clemente & D. B. Lindsley (Eds.), *Aggression and defense, neural mechanisms and social patterns.* Los Angeles: University of California Press, 1967. Pp. 116-124.

Goltz, F. Der Hund ohne Grosshirn. *Pflüger's Archiv für die Gesamte Physiologie*, 1892, **51**, 570-614.

Greer, M. A. Suggestive evidence of a primary "drinking center" in the hypothalamus of the rat. *Proceedings of the Society for Experimental Biology and Medicine*, 1955, **89**, 59-62.

Heath, R. G., John, S. B., & Fontana, C. J. The pleasure response: Studies by stereotaxic technique in patients. In N. Kline & E. Laska (Eds.), *Computers and electronic devices in psychiatry.* New York: Grune & Stratton, 1968. Pp. 178-189.

Heimburger, R. F., Whitlock, C. C., & Kalsbeck, J. E. Stereotaxic amygdalectomy for epilepsy with aggressive behavior. *Journal of the American Medical Association*, 1966, **198**, 741-745.

Hess, W. R. *The functional organization of the diencephalon.* New York: Grune & Stratton, 1957.

Ingraham, B. L., & Smith, G. W. The use of electronics in the observation and control of human behavior and its possible use in rehabilitation and parole. *Issues in Criminology*, 1972, **7**, 35-53.

Kim, Y. K., & Umbach, W. Combined stereotaxic lesions for treatment of behaviour disorders and severe pain. In L. V. Laitinen & K. E. Livingston (Eds.), *Surgical approaches in psychiatry.* Baltimore, Md.: University Park Press, 1973. Pp. 182-188.

Kirkby, R. J., & Kimble, D. P. Avoidance and escape behavior following striatal lesions in the rat. *Experimental Neurology*, 1968, **20**, 215-227.

Kling, A. Effects of amygdalectomy on social-affective behavior in nonhuman primates. In B. E. Eleftheriou (Ed.), *The neurobiology of the amygdala.* New York: Plenum Press, 1972. Pp. 511-536.

Kling, A., Lancaster, J., & Benitone, J. Amygdalectomy in the free ranging vervet (Cercopithecus althiops). *Journal of Psychiatric Research*, 1970, **7**, 191-199.

Klüver, H., & Bucy, P. C. Preliminary analysis of functions of the temporal lobe in monkeys. *Archives of Neurology and Psychiatry*, (Chicago), 1939, **42**, 979-1000.

König, J.F.R., & Klippel, R. A. *The rat brain: A stereotaxic atlas of the forebrain and lower parts of the brain stem.* Baltimore, Md.: William & Wilkins, 1963.

Kubie, L. S. Some implications for psychoanalysis of modern concepts of the organization of the brain. *Psychoanalytical Quarterly*, 1953, **22**, 21-52.

Leyton, A.S.F., & Sherrington, C. S. Observations on the excitable cortex of the chimpanzee, orang-utan, and gorilla. *Quarterly Journal of Experimental Physiology*, 1917, **11**, 135-222.

Libet, B. Electrical stimulation of cortex in human subjects and conscious sensory aspects. In A. Iggo (Ed.), *Handbook of sensory physiology.* Vol. 2. *Somatosensory system.* Berlin: Springer-Verlag, 1973. Pp. 743-790.

London, P. *Behavior control.* New York: Harper & Row, 1969.

Luria, A. R. *The working brain.* London: Penguin, 1973.

Mahl, G. F., Rothenberg, A., Delgado, J.M.R., & Hamlin, H. Psychological responses in the human to intracerebral electric stimulation. *Psychosomatic Medicine,* 1964, **26**, 337-368.

Mark, V. H., & Ervin, F. R. *Violence and the brain.* New York: Harper & Row, 1970.

Mettler, F. A., & Mettler, C. The effects of striatal injury. *Brain,* 1942, **65**, 242-255.

Miller, N. E. Commentary. In E. S. Valenstein (Ed.), *Brain stimulation and motivation.* Glenview, Ill.: Scott, Foresman, 1973. Pp. 53-68.

Niven, L. Death by ecstasy. In D. A. Wolheim & T. Carr (Eds.), *World's best science fiction.* New York: Ace, 1970.

Olds, J. Commentary. In E. S. Valenstein (Ed.), *Brain stimulation and motivation.* Glenview, Ill.: Scott, Foresman, 1973. Pp. 81-99.

Olds, J., & Milner, P. Positive reinforcement produced by electrical stimulation of septal area and other regions of the rat brain. *Journal of Comparative and Physiological Psychology,* 1954, **47**, 419-427.

Panksepp, J. Aggression elicited by electrical stimulation of the hypothalamus in albino rats. *Physiology and Behavior,* 1971, 6, 321-329.

Paxinos, G., & Bindra, D. Hypothalamic knife cuts: Effects on eating, drinking, irritability, aggression and copulation in the male rat. *Journal of Comparative and Physiological Psychology,* 1972, **79**, 219-229.

Penfield, W., & Boldrey, E. Somatic motor and sensory representation in the cerebral cortex of man as studied by electrical stimulation. *Brain,* 1937, **60**, 389-443.

Penfield, W., & Perot, P. The brain's record of auditory and visual experience: A final summary and discussion. *Brain,* 1963, **86**, 595-696.

Penfield, W., & Rasmussen, T. *The cerebral cortex of man.* New York: Macmillan, 1950.

Penfield, W., & Welch, K. Instability of response to stimulation of the sensori-motor cortex of man. *Journal of Physiology* (London), 1949, **109**, 358-365.

Phillips, A. G., Cox, V. C., Kakolewski, J. W., & Valenstein, E. S. Object-carrying by rats: An approach to the behavior produced by brain stimulation. *Science,* 1969, **166**, 903-905.

Plotnik, R. Brain stimulation and aggression: Monkeys, apes, and humans. In R. L. Holloway (Ed.), *Primate aggression, territoriality and xenophobia: A comparative approach.* New York: Academic Press, 1974. Pp. 138-149.

Plotnik, R., & Delgado, J.M.R. Emotional responses in monkeys inhibited with electrical stimulation. *Psychonomic Science*, 1970, **18**, 129-130.

Reis, D. J., Doba, N., & Nathan, M. A. Predatory attack, grooming, and consummatory behaviors evoked by electrical stimulation of cat cerebellar nuclei. *Science*, 1973, **182**, 845-847.

Robinson, B. W., Alexander, M., & Browne, G. Dominance reversal resulting from aggressive responses evoked by brain telestimulation. *Physiology and Behavior*, 1969, **4**, 749-752.

Rodin, E. A. Psychomotor epilepsy and aggressive behavior. *Archives of General Psychiatry*, 1973, **28**, 210-213.

Rorvik, D. Someone to watch over you (for less than 2 cents a day). *Esquire*, 1969, **72**, 164.

Rosvold, H. E., Mirsky, A. F., & Pribram, K. H. Influence of amygdalectomy on social behavior in monkeys. *Journal of Comparative and Physiological Psychology*, 1957, **47**, 173-178.

Rosvold, H. E., Mishkin, M., & Szwarcbart, M. K. Effects of subcortical lesions in monkeys on visual-discrimination and single-alternation performance. *Journal of Comparative and Physiological Psychology*, 1958, **51**, 437-444.

Routtenberg, A., & Lindy, J. Effects of the availability of rewarding septal and hypothalamic stimulation on bar-pressing for food under conditions of deprivation. *Journal of Comparative and Physiological Psychology*, 1965, **60**, 158-161.

Schwartzbaum, J. Changes in reinforcing properties of stimuli following ablation of the amygdaloid complex in monkeys. *Journal of Comparative and Physiological Psychology*, 1960, **53**, 388-395.

Stein, L. Neurochemistry of reward and punishment: Some implications for the etiology of schizophrenia. *Journal of Psychiatric Research*, 1971, **8**, 345-361.

Stevens, J. R., Mark, V. H., Ervin, F., Pacheco, P., & Suematsu, K. Deep temporal stimulation in man: Long latency, long lasting psychological changes. *Archives of Neurology* (Chicago), 1969, **21**, 157-169.

Valenstein, E. S. Behavior elicited by hypothalamic stimulation. A prepotency hypothesis. *Brain, Behavior and Evolution*, 1969, **2**, 295-316.

Valenstein, E. S. Channeling of responses elicited by hypothalamic stimulation. *Journal of Psychiatric Research*, 1971, **8**, 335-344.

Valenstein, E. S. *Brain control: A critical examination of brain stimulation and psychosurgery*. New York: John Wiley, 1973.

Valenstein, E. S., & Beer, B. Continuous opportunity for reinforcing brain stimulation. *Journal of the Experimental Analysis of Behavior*, 1964, **7**, 183-184.

Valenstein, E. S., Cox, V. C., & Kakolewski, J. W. Modification of motivated behavior elicited by electrical stimulation of the hypothalamus. *Science*, 1968, **159**, 1119-1121. (a)

Valenstein, E. S., Cox, V. C., & Kakolewski, J. W. The motivation underlying eating elicited by lateral hypothalamic stimulation. *Physiology and Behavior*, 1968, **3**, 969-971. (b)

Valenstein, E. S., Cox, V. C., & Kakolewski, J. W. Reexamination of the role of the hypothalamus in motivation. *Psychological Review*, 1970, **77**, 16-31.

Valenstein, E. S., Kakolewski, J. W., & Cox, V. C. A comparison of stimulus-bound drinking and drinking induced by water deprivation. *Communications in Behavioral Biology* (Part A), 1968, **2**, 227-233.

Valenstein, E. S., & Valenstein, T. Interaction of positive and negative reinforcing neural systems. *Science*, 1964, **145**, 1456-1458.

Van Buren, J. M. Sensory motor and autonomic effects of mesial temporal stimulation in man. *Journal of Neurosurgery*, 1961, **18**, 273-288.

Van Buren, J. M. Confusion and disturbance of speech from stimulation in the vicinity of the head of the caudate nucleus. *Journal of Neurosurgery*, 1963, **20**, 148-157.

Van Buren, J. M. Evidence regarding a more precise localization of the posterior frontal-caudate arrest response in man. *Journal of Neurosurgery*, 1966, **24**, 416-417.

Wasman, M., & Flynn, J. P. Directed attack elicited from hypothalamus. *Archives of Neurology*, 1962, **6**, 220-227.

Wise, R. A. Individual differences in effects of hypothalamic stimulation: The role of stimulation locus. *Physiology and Behavior*, 1971, **6**, 569-572.

# Subject Index

# Author Index